PRAISE FOR

PLAYING TO THE GODS

"Riveting."

—Bustle

"The best sort of dual biography, deftly intertwining the lives of two fascinating people. Rader masterfully plays these powerful women off each other. This is the book for all of us who binge-watched *Feud*."

—Daniel de Visé, author of *Andy & Don: The Making of a Friendship and a Classic American TV Show*

"*Playing to the Gods* argues that the Duse-Bernhardt rivalry, dragging on for years, was more than just personal, it was crucial to the art of modern acting. . . . [Rader] has done his research and he clearly has sympathy for his leading ladies."

—*The Wall Street Journal*

"Theater buffs will love the way Rader captures a global moment in theater—Ibsen, Chekhov, and Shaw all make appearances. A fascinating and thoroughly enjoyable book."

—*Booklist*

"Palpably sensuous. Rader brings surging back to life two nineteenth-century theatrical titans and the world they inhabited. Bravo!"

—Scott Eyman, bestselling author of *Hank & Jim: The Fifty-Year Friendship of Henry Fonda and James Stuart*

"Writing in a style both humorous and romantic, and throwing in juicy tidbits (catty notes, cheating lovers) all along . . . this entertaining chronicle illustrates how both women captivated audiences and made a lasting impact on the theater."

—*Publishers Weekly*

"Delightfully readable and informative, Rader's book examines a rivalry that defined modern theater while also exploring the origins of modern celebrity culture."

—*Kirkus Reviews*

"Entertaining and insightful. Rader has taken two legendary figures from theater's past and put flesh on their bones—bringing them to life, charting their amazing careers, and illuminating their impact on the modern stage."

—Richard Zoglin, author of
Hope: Entertainer of the Century

"Any complete biography ends in grief, but Rader tells us we missed so much, that so much went out of the world when these lionesses fell. Closing the book, one finds the loss suddenly unbearable."

—*The New York Times*

ALSO BY PETER RADER

Mike Wallace: A Life

PLAYING to the GODS

Sarah Bernhardt, Eleonora Duse,
and the Rivalry That
Changed Acting Forever

PETER RADER

Simon & Schuster Paperbacks

NEW YORK   LONDON   TORONTO   SYDNEY   NEW DELHI

Simon & Schuster Paperbacks
An Imprint of Simon & Schuster, Inc.
1230 Avenue of the Americas
New York, NY 10020

First Simon & Schuster paperback edition August 2019

SIMON & SCHUSTER PAPERBACKS and colophon are
registered trademarks of Simon & Schuster, Inc.

For information about special discounts for bulk purchases, please contact
Simon & Schuster Special Sales at 1-866-506-1949
or business@simonandschuster.com.

The Simon & Schuster Speakers Bureau can bring authors to your
live event. For more information or to book an event, contact the
Simon & Schuster Speakers Bureau at 1-866-248-3049
or visit our website at www.simonspeakers.com.

Interior design by Paul Dippolito

Manufactured in the United States of America

1   3   5   7   9   10   8   6   4   2

Library of Congress Cataloging-in-Publication Data is available.

ISBN 978-1-4767-3837-6
ISBN 978-1-4767-3838-3 (pbk)
ISBN 978-1-4767-3839-0 (ebook)

For Paola,
whose soul
helps me touch secrets.

Contents

PROLOGUE

César Ritz checked his pocket watch as the lavish carriage rolled into the roundabout. It was June 14, 1894—a quarter past ten in the evening. Right on schedule, thought Ritz, snapping his fingers at the footmen and adjusting his waistcoat in anticipation of the celebrity guest. She was a personal favorite of his, the Grande Dame of the theater, the greatest actress the world had ever known.

The hotelier forgave her many eccentricities, such as her penchant for traveling with a pet alligator—one that enjoyed champagne, no less. As the general manager of the Savoy, London's premier hotel, it was Ritz's job to cater to the whims of his customers, particularly the artists. When Claude Monet insisted on room 618 with its perfect view of Waterloo Bridge, it became the subject of a dozen canvases.

Artists had their desires; the hotelier accommodated them. What happened behind closed doors remained private. Ritz instructed his staff with the maxim: *See all without looking; hear all without listening; be attentive without being servile.*

Earlier that week, Ritz had quietly escorted the Prince of Wales and a "companion" to the honeymoon suite. Five floors up, the young Oscar Wilde was smoking opium-laced Egyptian cigarettes, sipping absinthe, and carrying on in ways that would soon put him on trial for committing "homosexual acts of gross indecency."

Everyone had his or her secrets, and the actress arriving that evening at the canopied roundabout of the Savoy was no exception. She flaunted her private affairs, in fact, to fuel her fame, which had been unsurpassed until now. As a footman opened the carriage door, Ritz inclined in a respectful bow to the dazzling figure that emerged, draped in jewels: the Divine Sarah Bernhardt.

The hotelier kissed her hand, taking pains not to seem obsequious but conscious that the aging actress might require a little extra attention this evening. Sarah had just returned from a performance at the Drury Lane, where she'd witnessed, for the first time, the spellbinding acting of her archrival: Eleonora Duse, who was leading a quiet revolution on the stage.

To showcase her radically new style of acting, the Italian Duse had chosen a very old play: Dumas's *La Dame aux camélias*, written in 1848 as a novel first, then adapted by the author for the theater. The play was popular around the world, quite risqué in its time—a poignant melodrama about a sickly courtesan in love with a client who leaves her to die alone. It was the signature role of Sarah Bernhardt, who had made a career of playing the part in capitals across the world. Now, Eleonora Duse was taking Bernhardt's play to those same capitals, forcing critics to make a choice between the old and the new. Sarah felt the affront, no doubt; how could she not? But the rivalry was not personal for Eleonora—not yet, at least. In fact, Sarah had been her idol.

A generation younger, Eleonora had risen to international stardom from a penniless family of itinerant troubadours. For the last decade, she'd been disrupting the Western theater world with a singular style that was both subtle and provocative, rooted in her body, yet profoundly mystical. Like a temple priestess performing an incantation, her power lay in the silence between the words—the realm of thought and intention—where she invited the audience to meet her as cocreators. By ignoring the crowd completely, she provoked people to sit forward in their chairs and read her mind. And by disappearing into the world of the play, she became the antithesis of Sarah Bernhardt, which is perhaps why Duse has largely been forgotten.

Sarah never disappeared. No one sobbed as well as Bernhardt, no one despaired, no one died. When people paid to see the great "Sarah Bernhardt," the actress gave them a show they would never forget. She relished her star power and the profound impact it had on her audiences; her roles were riveting and indelible. By the sheer enormity of her stage presence, Bernhardt had transformed the theater world, lifting acting from the disrepute into which it had fallen and raising it to its original stature as a true art.

Before Bernhardt's time, popular theater had been more vaudeville than opera, a largely social experience. Opera glasses panned the crowd as much as the performance. Actors were outcasts, actresses were courtesans—and when they died, they were buried, by law, in the local potter's field. The rising bourgeoisie who paid to see actors on the boards wouldn't have them in their cemeteries.

It cost pennies to buy a theater ticket, a pittance, and no one got rich as an actress—until Sarah. Her talent was such that she had earned the attention of the royals who had avoided "popular" theater. They had preferred Puccini to Pirandello. And why shouldn't they?

The actor's craft was a highly stylized affair, delivered in shrill voices within tableau-like blocking. Actors did not pretend to portray multidimensional, flesh-and-blood human beings; they were archetypes—the Empress, the Lover, the Evil Authority Figure, the Beloved—reenacting the human passion play for our entertainment.

Acting was a paint-by-numbers enterprise. There were manuals that showed you how to do it—a book of "poses" that represented the entire gamut of emotions, from devastation to rage. If a certain line called for "curiosity," for example, one need look no further than page nineteen of the *Handbook of Theatrical Poses* by Alamanno Morelli (*Prontuario delle pose sceniche*, published in 1854 and widely read). Any literate actor could assume the "curiosity" posture as prescribed:

> Listen with maximum interest, torso bent at the waist; head forward, somewhat turned; mouth open; right hand partially opened near the face . . . right foot forward, leg bent at the knee; left heel back.

It was absurdly specific. Yet talented actors were masters of these poses, reproducing them time and again in perfect detail, like championship athletes. They became known for their technical virtuosity in certain signature roles, often repeating the most popular speeches two or three times in spontaneous encores within a scene; this brought the drama to a standstill but delighted the adoring crowd. It was maddening to modernists like Duse and others who wanted theater to mirror real life. Norwegian playwright Henrik Ibsen noted dryly that actresses in Norway "always swooned on the left of the stage and always with a handkerchief in their left hand."

The writing was equally rote. Tragic plots invariably ended in death or suicide; comedies, in marriage. Attending the theater became a passive, predictable experience. Many in the audience might have already seen the play, often several times—so it was hardly necessary to pay close attention.

Then writers began creating more original plays. And certain actors were attempting to elevate the craft by performing the poses with such artistry that the theatrical tableaus became like living poetry. The undisputed master of this was Sarah Bernhardt, who continued to dazzle, even in her fifties, the average life expectancy for a Victorian woman.

Sarah seemed immortal; she continued to perform the plays that launched her—and no one played the coquette quite like her. But it was in tragedy that she truly shone, facing her doom with such pathos that it left her audience in tears. "By her extraordinary power of swooning," commented Jean Cocteau, "she filled the arms of the world."

Sarah's success was unparalleled. In her numerous tours of America, she occupied seven train cars, steaming from town to town on the "Bernhardt Special" as if she were on a presidential whistle-stop. As writer Henry James remarked: "She is too American not to succeed in America." She understood, like no one else, that a star's image could—and should—be manufactured; the more outsized, the better. In the words of critic Jules Lemaître:

> Sarah Bernhardt . . . is eminently a Russian princess, unless
> she is a Byzantine empress or a begum of Muscat, feline and
> impassioned . . . eccentric, enigmatic, woman-abyss, woman
> I know not what. . . . She could enter a convent, discover the
> North Pole, have herself inoculated with rabies, assassinate an
> emperor, or marry a Negro king without astonishing me.

Sarah invented the culture of the exotic, eccentric celebrity. There
would be no Lady Gaga without Bernhardt—no Madonna, Cher,
Liberace, Bowie, or countless others. As the world's first superstar, Sarah originated the notion of merchandising herself through
product endorsements, from aperitifs to beef bouillon. She commissioned a series of striking posters by Art Nouveau master
Alphonse Mucha, which fans on every continent could collect.
There were also souvenir postcards ("cabinet cards," as they were
known) of Sarah in every conceivable role and situation, including asleep in her signature coffin—a practice rumored to feed her
understanding of death and dying, which was her theatrical spe-
cialty. Sarah Bernhardt was known by millions, and she remains
so to this day. At the height of her career, not a day went by without her name appearing somewhere in print. This was by design.
It was a strategy.

As much as Sarah adored the spotlight, Eleonora Duse shied
away from it. While deeply private about her offstage life, she
would bare it all in the footlights—an actress who felt her roles with
such intensity that they exhausted her. Despite being fourteen years
Sarah's junior, Eleonora did not have nearly the stamina of Bernhardt, who booked twice as many shows during her endless tours,
lasting two years or more. Yet Duse's work was revolutionary—and
now Bernhardt had witnessed it for herself.

César Ritz could tell that the experience had unnerved the diva.
But he also knew that Sarah was damned if she'd let it show to the
dowagers scrutinizing her from the Savoy lobby.

"Did you order the bananas for Darwin?" Sarah asked Ritz

as he escorted her through the grand entryway. Darwin was her chimpanzee.

"But of course, Madame," responded Ritz, who is credited with coining the phrase "the customer is always right."

Before Ritz could whisk Sarah into his newly installed Otis elevator, they were accosted by a reporter who asked the question of the hour: "What do you think of Eleonora Duse?"

Sarah had a quick answer, rehearsed and ready: *She's of the vine* [meaning: a peasant], *not an actress.*

Delivered in French, the line produced the expected amusement. *Elle n'est pas une actrice, elle est de vigne.* It was a play on Sarah's own trademark descriptor: divine.

The house at the Drury Lane Theatre had been packed that night. One hour after curtain, the buzzing audience was finally gone, save a solitary figure perched up in "The Gods," the cheapest section of the house—so high up as to be in the realm of Mount Olympus. It was the only ticket Tebaldo Checchi could afford; he was fortunate to have obtained a last-row seat at all. Everyone in London was clamoring to catch a glimpse of the Italian sensation. Tebaldo, a Neapolitan, had traveled all the way from Uruguay for the experience. He'd seen Duse before, of course, countless times. He had even shared the stage with her. But this was different. Tonight her performance had been transcendent.

Tebaldo had been surrounded by students and impoverished artists, all eager to witness the artistry of La Duse, as she was known. None of them could afford opera glasses, which made it difficult to perceive the action on the distant stage. A world-class actress like Bernhardt knew to tilt her head backward to allow her voice to rise and reach those "popular" seats, with poses and gestures broad enough to be read by the back of the house.

Not so with Duse. She did just the opposite, turning upstage, having a private moment at the coat rack or mirror, speaking sotto voce. And yet all of this somehow carried to the uppermost balcony as an invisible *pulse of energy*. It had astonished Tebaldo.

At times, Duse had sat in silence—simply *thinking* onstage while the audience watched, either intrigued or utterly confused. It was scandalous in certain quarters, which held that the ticket-buying public paid to hear grand speeches, not these curious pauses best left to rehearsals. Why would an audience want the burden of having to guess what the actress might be thinking?

Attempting to read the mind of Eleonora Duse had been a central preoccupation of Tebaldo Checchi: they had been husband and wife. But even in their four years together, he had never been able to get inside her head. Checchi was a journeyman actor from Naples; Duse, a theatrical prophet. Her thoughts ran at a different frequency, which is why their relationship never really stood a chance. The wedding had been impulsive. Eleonora had been suicidal at the time; he swooped in, savior and protector. She needed his kindness and quiet support, and was grateful for it. But that was all in the past.

The last time Tebaldo had seen Eleonora was ten years prior, when they were on tour together in South America, several winters into their unsteady marriage. It was during that tour that she and Tebaldo had decided to separate. He stayed in Uruguay. But they had a child together—a girl, whom Tebaldo missed terribly. That's why he had traveled from South America to England in 1894: he had planned to demand visitation rights. But Tebaldo made the mistake of first seeing Eleonora perform.

That moment when Eleonora, as the ill-fated courtesan Camille, had allowed her eyes to flicker through a series of emotions, from indignation to shame, then a flash of embarrassment punctuated by a sudden blush . . . it was astonishing. Eleonora had developed such uncanny control of her instrument that she was able to blush at will—which is why she walked the stage without makeup. It made her, by all accounts, even more beautiful. But it was the beauty of her performance that had stunned Tebaldo.

Critics had remarked that Duse didn't have a technique. She acted from intuition—a sense that took her places where no other living actor dared to tread. One choice in act 3 had caused the crowd to let out a collective gasp, for Eleonora had broken the three most elementary rules of stagecraft:

1. Never turn your back on the audience.
2. Never deliver lines while in motion. Any trained actor would know to face the crowd squarely and assume the traditional posture required for that particular speech.
3. Declaim your lines with authority, not sotto voce, as she had done, so that her words were barely audible.

And yet Eleonora's choices seemed natural. It hardly mattered that the line was inaudible. This was one of theater's best-known plays. The English crowd was perfectly capable of following along, whether the play was performed in the original French, or, in this case, in Italian. Indeed, since the text was well known, there was a certain genius to Eleonora's choice of going for something subdued—to make her choices small and intimate.

Not only did Duse ignore the audience, she seemed entirely unaware of it. This was radical. As Goethe had stated unequivocally in his 1803 *Rules for Actors*: "the player must always divide his attention between two objects . . . between the person to whom he is speaking and his audience." Now, nearly a century later, Eleonora was shunning the audience altogether.

Tebaldo found it electrifying, this voyeuristic thrill of observing someone who seemed completely unaware of being "seen," a person at her most vulnerable. From his perch in the balcony, he felt like he had been watching the actors muddling their way through the very drama of the human condition.

Do you know how theater originated? Eleonora had once asked him after a performance, her dark eyes lighting up as they inevitably did when she talked about mysticism. Though completely unschooled, Eleonora had read voraciously her entire life, particularly books on spirituality.

Theater began as an offshoot of religion, she explained, with the singular purpose of helping us to understand what it means to be human—in all its poignancy, humor, and devastation. As our ancestors gazed up at the stars, trying to fathom our purpose, the high priest(ess) of the tribe—the shaman—would recount the stories of the past, enacting the different roles (the Hero, the Beloved, the Antagonist), allowing his body temporarily to become "possessed" and letting the spirit archetypes channel through him. This was the original acting, Eleonora whispered. It meant dissolving the ego.

"I call it 'The Grace,'" she said, admitting that the presence didn't "visit" her every performance. But in those moments when The Grace flowed through her, Eleonora felt connected to the entire universe.

Tebaldo heard the words but could not quite fathom their meaning ten years earlier. Now he had seen The Grace with his own eyes. He wanted to weep.

It hadn't always been a rivalry. A generation older, Sarah had been something of a mentor to the young Italian, and certainly had paved the way for her success. In Eleonora's youth, Sarah was already an icon—summoned to royal courts, a visiting artiste on the same level as Mozart. "It would be hard to imagine a more brilliant embodiment of feminine success," said Henry James, one of Sarah's most loyal fans.

In her twenties, she had famously walked away from the prestigious Comédie-Française to form her own company, a bold but brilliant move that had inspired Eleonora Duse to do likewise. But success had come much more slowly for Duse.

Odd as it may seem today, it was considered frivolous at the time, even harmful, for an actress to "feel" the part she was playing. As critic and philosopher Denis Diderot had written in

The Paradox of Acting (published in 1830): "Extreme sensitiveness makes poor actors; while absolute lack of sensitiveness is a quality of the highest acting." His bizarre argument went as follows:

> If the actor were full, really full, of feeling, how could he play the same part twice running with the same spirit and success? Full of fire at the first performance, he would be worn out and cold as a marble at the third.

For Diderot, acting was more akin to an athletic performance than an art—it required physical discipline. The ideal actor should feel nothing and be a master of physical mimicry. This antiemotional acting by imitation, or "indication," was known as Symbolism or the Symbolic style. It's what audiences had come to expect. If actors attempted to act more naturally, they were often booed from the stage. Michel Baron, the favorite pupil of French playwright Molière, attempted "to speak and not declaim," and he was hissed at by the seventeenth-century Parisian public.

The "struggle" between emotionalism and antiemotionalism—represented perfectly in the rivalry between Duse and Bernhardt—went back to Roman times and the very origins of the theater. William Archer, in his famous 1888 essay, *Masks or Faces?*, cited a first-century Roman rhetorician:

> Quintilian . . . is very explicit on the subject of stage tears. . . . "The great secret . . . for moving the passions is to be moved ourselves; for the imitation of grief, anger, indignation, will often be ridiculous, if our words and countenance alone conform to the emotion, not our heart."

To mimic the feeling from the outside in, as Sarah would do, was useless trickery, a disservice to the audience. Quintilian's counsel to actors: "Let our speech proceed from the very state of mind which we wish to induce in the judge."

But Quintilian was in the minority. Summoning an emotion on command was devilishly difficult, especially in colossal amphitheaters that seated tens of thousands. It was far easier to employ a language of gestures and masks, systematized by actors and accepted by the public as shorthand symbols. These millennia-old conventions—the tricks of the trade—were now woven into the very fabric of the theater. The idealized poses had become the hallmarks of great acting.

When the unschooled Eleonora began her career in the 1860s, she had certainly not been exposed to the writings of Diderot or Quintilian. Without any formal training, she simply began acting from the inside out—allowing her feelings to guide her on the stage. Those who recognized Duse's genius were floored by it. Russian actor-director Konstantin Stanislavski would one day codify Duse's craft into what would become the basis of method acting in America. But the Duse method, known as *verismo* ("realism"), was an abomination to Sarah Bernhardt and many others, who felt it made theater pedestrian. A tragic drama like *La Dame aux camélias* needed to be performed with grandeur. Sarah felt that Eleonora's work was returning the art to the ignominy from which she had lifted it.

By the following year, in the summer of 1895, the Duse-Bernhardt rivalry would reach its apogee in an extraordinary theatrical event: both actresses were booked to perform across the street from each other in London—in the *very same play*.

After years of competition, onstage and in their private lives, the two stars would finally be performing head-to-head in the decisive showcase of their radically different styles. Both actresses had their ardent proponents, and it was by no means clear which would prevail.

Ultimately they would each have an extraordinary impact: one would leave an enduring mark on the theater, the other would live in our imaginations forever. The path to this legacy, however, would be marked by high drama and low blows.

CHAPTER ONE

The legend is that Duse's birth took place on a moving train in the year 1858, as the locomotive steamed into Vigevano in northern Italy. Though this story, retold by several early biographers, is factually incorrect,* it is true in spirit, given Eleonora's restless nature and lifelong resistance to putting down roots.

Duse was born into a family of troubadours who moved from town to town, performing for pennies in the public square. It was a turbulent time in Italy—not yet a country, unsure of its future. The peninsula remained an amalgamation of fiefdoms, city-states with conflicting outlooks and cultures: the Austrian-controlled Republic of Venice, the Kingdom of the Two Sicilies, the Papal States of Rome, and the Kingdom of Sardinia, ruled by the progressive King Vittorio Emanuele II.

For centuries, Italian writers and scholars had urged unification. In the fourteenth century, humanist Francesco Petrarca (Petrarch) had rediscovered Cicero's letters—epistles filled with celebrations of classical civilization. Realizing with great sadness that Italy's warring tribes had lost touch with the beauty and propriety of a bygone era, Petrarch initiated the idea of a historical "Dark Ages." His eloquent canzone *Italia Mia* cried out for peace across the Italian peninsula.

By the nineteenth century Petrarch's plea had become a rallying

* *Time* magazine (July 30, 1923) reported the mythology of her origin even more erroneously: "Born in a wagon among the musty properties of a band of strolling players on the outskirts of Venice, she grew to womanhood behind the flickering footlights of mean country stages."

cry for Italian statehood. In 1859, one year after Eleonora's birth, unification forces would seize Lombardy from the Austrians and declare Vittorio Emanuele king of Italy, though it took another decade or two before the kingdom spanned the entire peninsula. This ongoing Italian revolution affected the Duse family personally when accusations of treason ended the career of Eleonora's grandfather, the highly gifted Luigi Duse, one of the most celebrated actors of his day.

Luigi had entered the profession against the wishes of his family, prosperous merchants who shipped goods up and down the Adriatic. In an era when sons were expected to enter the family trade, particularly when that trade was thriving and offered opportunities for upward mobility, it was unthinkable for the boy to pursue a "hobby" such as acting. But that is precisely what willful Luigi did.

He had been born in 1792, the year French revolutionaries imprisoned Marie Antoinette and composed "La Marseillaise." With recent advances in textiles and manufacturing, the Industrial Revolution had given birth to a newly prosperous merchant class in which the Duse family, importers of goods from foreign lands, was ensconced. They plied their trade in Chioggia, perched on the southern lip of the Venetian lagoon. Though not nearly as glamorous as its sister city to the north, Chioggia offered ample Venetian charm in its waterways, stone bridges, and secluded alleyways. Young Luigi, with his good looks and romantic ideas, would gaze for hours at the blue waters of the Adriatic, dreaming of touring the world.

In a vain attempt to rid him of his artistic delusions, Luigi was dispatched inland by his father to apprentice with his uncle, who worked as a clerk in the city of Padua. But the young Luigi quickly abandoned his post to join a company of touring actors. Both talented and ambitious, he soon launched his own company, founding the Teatro Duse in Padua in 1834. Though he shone at first in tragic roles, Luigi discovered that his true passion lay in comedic characterizations, which were extremely popular in the Veneto region.

At the time, Italian comedy took its inspiration from commedia dell'arte, which had originated in the sixteenth century. Playing on makeshift stages to largely illiterate and unsophisticated crowds, actors specialized in a specific *maschera* (a masked "type") or stock character whose antics were easy to follow. These archetypes included Pantalone (literally, "Trousers"), the patron or master—miserly and invariably cuckold, the butt of many jokes—and his servant, Arlecchino (Harlequin), perhaps the most famous, with his catlike mask, costume of multicolored triangles, and the stick with which he slapped the other actors around (the origin of the word *slapstick*). Other archetypes in the commedia pantheon were Il Capitano (The Captain)—bold, swaggering, but ultimately a trembling coward—and Il Dottore (The Doctor), a caricature of the learned professional, both a fraud and a pompous ass. The common theme, of course, was antiauthoritarianism, which is what made these comedies so popular with the masses as they cheered on the heroes: Gli Innamorati (the star-crossed Lovers), who must battle against society to fulfill their destiny. But these standardized vignettes were stifling for a talented thespian like Luigi Duse. The plots were contrived and hackneyed; all the actors wore masks, concealing their facial expressions and forcing them to perform with exaggerated gestures. Luigi felt it was time to take off the masks. But instead of overturning the commedia dell'arte tradition, Luigi rebelled within the system, by creating a new archetype—his own signature *maschera*, one *without* a mask, however.

With a long black ponytail, chevron hat, turquoise jacket, and floral waistcoat, Luigi turned himself into Giacometto, a bumbling fellow, always short of money, but jolly nonetheless. Giacometto became a staple of the Veneto region and established Luigi as a major Italian actor. French novelist George Sand ranked his talent above that of the finest French comics. A populist beloved by all,

"Gigi" allowed students to attend his performances by bartering salami, flowers, or even a bag of onions for admission. Theatergoers began calling him Amico (our friend) Duse; they trusted him implicitly. But even quicker than his ascent was his fall.

Gigi had become known for improvising asides, comical indictments of the establishment whispered conspiratorially to the delighted crowd. He once mocked Italian patriot and Populist Daniele Manin, who had been agitating to seize control of Venice from the Austrians—an extremely popular cause. Nothing was off-limits for the playful Gigi, especially when he walked the boards as Giacometto. This time he went too far, however. Luigi had rivals in the Veneto theater—other actors, jealous of his popularity and fame, who exploited the Manin incident to spread rumors that Duse was unpatriotic. It worked.

The rejection was sudden and absolute; Luigi's once-adoring audience abandoned him. In a few years, his namesake theater in Padua, the Teatro Duse, would be renamed Teatro Garibaldi, after the revolutionary leader of the "red shirts," the militia largely responsible for the unification of Italy. Luigi died, bitter and impoverished, in 1854, leaving four sons, all actors.

Like his father before him, Luigi had insisted that his children enter the new family business—though they would likely have done far better in other fields, for they shared neither Luigi's talent nor his enthusiasm for the stage. Eleonora's father, third-born Alessandro, had wanted to be a painter—but he, like his brothers, lacked the will to defy his father.

In one performance early in his undistinguished career, Alessandro bungled the final lines of a play and the curtain closed to tepid applause. His father witnessed the gaffe from the balcony and—moody and bitter after his forced retirement—shouted out: *"Asino!"* (Jackass!) The crowd turned to the box in which Luigi was seated and recognized the aging actor, whom they had once loved. Unable to resist their applause, the elder statesman made his way to the stage for a bow, overshadowing the curtain call of his own son, who stood in silent humiliation. Though Luigi was too old for a comeback, it certainly felt like a vindication.

The Compagnia Duse became a third-rate troupe—four brothers, their wives, and a handful of others related by blood or marriage. There were no fixed engagements, no security—it was busking, really, passing around a tin cup. They would pile their threadbare sets and rickety stage onto a donkey cart and walk from sunrise to sunset to reach the next town. Their inventory was rudimentary: a wall flat with a doorway, a multipurpose wooden bench. It did the job.

One day Eleonora's father found himself navigating a narrow alleyway in the medieval town of Vicenza, some thirty miles west of Venice, when a clump of dirt and leaves fell upon him. He glanced up to a second-story window to see an enchanting girl tending to a flower box where she was growing geraniums. A smitten Alessandro made certain to stroll down the same alley each day during the run in Vicenza. After a few more encounters with this dark-haired beauty, he mustered the courage to face the patriarch of the Cappelletto household, which was when it burst out of him: a spontaneous proposal of marriage. The courtship had consisted of a few furtive glances and shared smiles, but Alessandro had convinced himself the girl was heaven-sent. When he learned her name, it felt like a vindication: Angelica.

Angelica's father gave the nuptials his blessings. Angelica was the last in a sprawling family of twenty-one girls. Desperate for some peace and quiet, Signor Cappelletto dispatched his final offspring to join the Duse troubadours, where she became, by necessity rather than avocation, *prima donna*. She was beautiful, the brothers decided—talent came second.

Angelica was pregnant almost overnight, but lost this first child, a boy, in childbirth. She soon became pregnant again; the company did not slow down. They were traveling from Venice to Vigevano when Angelica came to term in late 1858.

Desperate not to lose another baby, Alessandro did what he

could to provide a suitable venue for the child's delivery. Scrounging together the coins in the kitty, he found an innkeeper willing to believe his lie that Angelica was "a woman of means"—it was the only way to secure the room. Alessandro repeated his fabrication on Eleonora's birth certificate, attempting perhaps to elevate his daughter's status. The child came into the world at 2:00 a.m. on October 3, 1858, and was baptized two days later. Her uncle Enrico was the godfather, and they listed Vigevano as their place of residence—"home," to a traveling actor, was an elusive matter. Born in a hotel room, Eleonora would tour her entire life and end up dying in one, too.

The Duses hardly had time to celebrate their baby's birth before they were, again, on the road. Eleonora was soon trudging along with the rest of them, holding the hem of her mother's dress. No home, no future, just the night's performance, and the hope that it might yield enough to buy some food.

Eleonora was thrust upon the stage at age four. "She did not choose to be an actress," said Eva Le Gallienne, a fellow actor who knew her: "She was forced to be one."

Eleonora's first play, fittingly, was *Les Misérables*—an Italian adaptation of Victor Hugo's novel of societal injustice, in whose preface he wrote:

> So long as the three problems of the age—the degradation of man by poverty, the ruin of women by starvation, and the dwarfing of childhood by physical and spiritual night—are not solved . . . books like this cannot be useless.

Eleonora certainly knew poverty, hunger, and spiritual darkness—it would seem more than appropriate to debut as Cosette, a penniless abandoned waif. So poor was the Duse troupe that they sent Eleonora out on the streets as a beggar; and that act of begging became a powerful acting coach—a girl who can read faces and summon tears at will is bound to get an extra lira or two.

Though she had no training as an actress, Eleonora exhibited a preternatural ability to imagine scenarios in her mind. Lacking any real friends—her cousins were older—she would talk to furniture.

Inanimate objects "in their silence, contained great enchantment," Eleonora once wrote.

Her mother recognized early on that Eleonora had the artist's gift of great sensitivity; she helped nurture her talents, allowing Eleonora time to play imaginary games. While Eleonora and Angelica felt strongly connected, her father looked at the child in more practical terms. Certain plays in their repertoire called for children, the other kids in the troupe were older—why not make use of Eleonora?

In Eleonora's very first performance as Cosette, a stage manager in the wings whacked her on the legs with a switch before pushing her onto the stage—she needed to cry in the scene, and couldn't possibly be expected to do so on her own. As biographer William Weaver noted: "She learned, early and without metaphor, that in order to entertain the public, the actor had to suffer."

And suffer she did. The company was constantly on the move, arriving in a new town when the streets were busy on a market day or after a fair. Traveling on foot sometimes for miles through the night, they took care to avoid the ongoing revolt against Austria. Theaters would be closed in battle areas and that meant going hungry.

Duse grew up desperately lonely: no home, no community. After learning to read, she buried her head in books—the few that they could afford, mainly scripts of new plays. She would read them again and again, trying to fathom the playwright's intention. Even at this young age, Duse had an instinct that there was more to acting than the rote recitation she observed in her company. But no one else saw it as she did, which only increased Eleonora's feeling of isolation.

One time in a village outside of Turin, Eleonora observed a

group of girls around her age who were playing merry-go-round. "Disheveled, giggling and shouting, unrestrained in the wind," is how she described them in an autobiography she began many years later but never finished. She was "dazzled by the hum, by that rotating fly wheel," sighing, "Ah! To enter there!"

Mustering her resolve, Eleonora joined the play, but the girls stopped suddenly and ogled the interloper; she ran back to her mother in tears.

Another day in another town, Eleonora again spotted a girl her age—by herself, this time, sitting near a fountain. Eleonora could sense that she, too, was lonely and approached. For a moment they stood side by side in silence, then Eleonora reached out boldly and took her hand. The apparently homeless girl stayed with the actors for several days as they played the town.

Duse told the story to an acquaintance some forty years later and still remembered the girl's name: Déjanira. "She was my first friend—my *only* childhood friend," Eleonora wrote. "I loved her."

Then she saw her first corpse; Eleonora was twelve, living in Tuscany. The river near their cottage overran its banks during a flood, and a little girl drowned. It was Eleonora, in fact, who discovered the dead body while crossing a bridge.

Keenly observant with a photographic memory for detail, Duse would record every aspect of the girl's appearance decades later in her unfinished autobiography, from the bare and swollen feet to the extreme pallor of her face. She took inventory of her clothing: "a ticking petticoat, a triangular handkerchief embroidered with little colored flowers knotted on her breast."

A crowd soon converged; Eleonora saw the girl's hysterical mother claw her way through the gawkers, crying out to the girl "with all the names of the heart."

The woman wailed, picked up her daughter—but she barely had the strength to carry her off. Eleonora's mother, Angelica, watched in horror alongside her neighbors. There was little they could say or do.

But Angelica stepped forward suddenly and invited the distraught woman into the cottage where they lived. Working together, the two mothers laid the lifeless girl upon Eleonora's little bed, and tried to remove her mud-soaked clothes; they could not bury her without first cleaning her. Eleonora was horrified and fascinated; the incident would remain etched in her mind.

With a naked corpse laid out upon her bed, Angelica grabbed an item from Eleonora's wardrobe—the only dress she owned—and offered it to the bereaved mother for the burial. The gift was profound. It forced Eleonora to think about her own mortality—like a spectator at her own funeral. She imagined the girl animate and gay one moment, then inert the next.

Where did her spirit go?

Whether Angelica had intended it as such, it became Eleonora's first awakening. She felt outside herself, almost as if she were watching a scene unfolding in a play.

Two years later, Duse experienced a second epiphany after traveling to Verona in 1873 to play in *Romeo and Juliet.* Eleonora had been poring over the role of Juliet for months. It was a mainstay of their repertoire—albeit a streamlined, simplified adaptation of Shakespeare's original. But the themes were all there; and Eleonora was intrigued by them.

Is there a love that can conquer death?

She dove headlong into the role; and Juliet transformed her. This was the story she repeated to close friends and lovers—authors, two of them, who would one day write about it. The events have undoubtedly been mythologized, especially by Eleonora herself—but it hardly matters. What happened in Verona changed Duse profoundly; of this there is no doubt.

As she entered the city's ancient gates, fourteen-year-old Eleonora clutched her script to her bosom, obsessed with the coincidence that Verona was Juliet's birthplace and Juliet was, herself, fourteen at the time of her death. Duse later described the feeling to lover Gabriele d'Annunzio, who made it a pivotal scene of his novel about their affair: "The gossip of the Nurse buzzed in my ears," says Foscarina, the fictionalized version of Eleonora: "Little by little my destiny seemed to be getting mixed up with the destiny of the Veronese maiden."

It was Duse's first visit to the bustling city, whose two-thousand-year history was apparent everywhere she looked. Eleonora saw coffins and imagined the body of Juliet inside them. She began to feel her own identity slip away, convinced she was a reincarnation of Shakespeare's heroine.

The performance was to take place in the vast Amfiteatro, a Coliseum-like outdoor arena that seated twenty-five thousand spectators and dated back to Roman times. The Duse troupe would not draw those kinds of numbers—they'd be lucky to have twenty-five. Municipalities like Verona built little wooden platforms in the corners of their amphitheaters to accommodate the strolling players that performed outdoors. Only a handful of larger, established acting companies in Italy could command an indoor stage and upper-class patrons.

Eleonora was happy to be outdoors that evening, for it was a sunset like no other. There was magic to that golden stage in the ruins of the ancient theater. It put the young actress into a heightened state. "At intervals," says the heroine of d'Annunzio's book, "my eyes would travel to the long grasses growing at the summit of the walls and there seemed to come to me from them I-know-not-what encouragement to what I was saying and doing."

Primordial muses hidden among those weeds seemed to beckon to her. Eleonora surrendered to them, and her "words flowed with strange facility, almost involuntarily, as if in a delirium." She was not, herself, speaking the lines; they were being spoken "through" her.

Eleonora felt she had become a channel, whether to the spirit of the Capulet maiden or something else. As d'Annunzio's heroine continues: "Every word before leaving my lips seemed to have passed through all the warmth of my blood. There was not a fiber in me that did not contribute to the harmony. Oh, Grace, it was a state of Grace!

"When I heard Romeo saying: 'O, she doth teach the torches to burn bright,' truly my whole being kindled. I became a flame."

By the final act, the sun had faded; it was dark when Juliet awakened in the Capulet crypt to find Romeo dead. She felt herself plunging into the bleakest of emotions: "My eyes sought the glimmer of light at the top of the wall. It had gone out." She felt the crowd impatient for the finale; some had been deeply moved, others deeply disturbed by her performance. There was the sense of a sacrificial rite as "Juliet" unsheathed her dagger. The arena hushed—they wanted her blood. Suddenly, Eleonora stabbed herself in a manner that seemed so real it shocked the crowd, "which let out such a great roar that I was terrified."

"Juliet" lost consciousness. The next thing she remembered was hearing the pealing of church bells and smelling roses she had used as a prop and the sooty torches, whose burning pitch irritated her nostrils.

After the show, Eleonora walked for hours through the streets of Verona, trying to make sense of what had transpired. Her mother followed at a respectful distance. Angelica knew something unique had happened to her daughter onstage that night, though she'd be hard-pressed to put it into words. Others in the blue-collar crowd had been electrified, too. Eleonora's fellow actors hadn't noticed anything particularly different. The boy playing Romeo likely shrugged it off to one of her many moods.

But something happened that night which she could not deny: the play became real. Eleonora was scared—and fascinated. She needed to walk, and think.

"We crossed a bridge, walked along the Adige," remembered Eleonora, "then crossed another bridge, entered a small street, lost ourselves in the dark alleys, found a square with a church. . . . My mother asked me now and then: 'Where are we going?'" Eleonora wasn't sure. She hoped to find a Franciscan convent, housing the hidden tomb of Juliet. She searched all night, but such a place, she realized, did not exist.

The following morning when it came time to move, Eleonora found herself riding in the back of the cart, gazing wistfully at shrinking spires and praying silently to this new force she now called The Grace.

"She had received her revelation," Count Giuseppe Primoli, one of Duse's numerous admirers, wrote many years later in writings that were never published. Acting was no longer simply the family business. For Duse, it had become Art.

CHAPTER TWO

Not quite a generation earlier, Sarah Bernhardt had entered the world with three strikes against her: she was the illegitimate daughter of a courtesan (well meaning, but largely absent), she had an unknown father, and she was Jewish.

This was Paris, 1844. Sarah's mother, Youle Bernard (Sarah would later change the spelling of her surname), was a runaway from Amsterdam. She had left Holland as a young teen in the early 1840s after her own mother died—fleeing to Germany with her younger sister, Rosine. The idea of two barely pubescent girls setting off on their own across Europe makes one wonder about conditions at home. Their father, Maurice, an oculist, had remarried; whether the girls escaped their father or new stepmother remains unclear. But run they did, supporting themselves by any means necessary, including sex. Youle soon found herself pregnant with twins by an unknown father, two girls who died within a week of their birth. Pregnant again a year later, she moved at age sixteen to Paris—where she gave birth to Sarah.

It was an exhilarating time to be in this vibrant metropolis. On the bridges and quays, one could marvel at acrobats, sit for a haircut, consult fortune-tellers, or dictate a letter to a sidewalk scribe. Napoleon III would soon be named president of France—the first elected by popular vote. But he would discard the constitution and seize power as emperor when parliament denied him a second term. The self-proclaimed sovereign (nephew of the original Bonaparte) had a grand vision for his reign. He began his makeover of France with a grand reconstruction of Paris, carving modern boulevards through the hive of narrow streets, adding monuments and gas streetlights that illuminated, among other things, the women of the night. And just beyond these brightly lit boulevards, in the dark and crooked alleyways, was another Paris, one where the poor lived in shacks in the shadows of grand palaces. Even the Louvre had its nearby shantytown of clapboard homes with raw sewage and rodents in the alleys.

Sarah's mother found employment as a seamstress. But it wasn't long before Youle, with her street smarts, took a good look at the class divide. There was high society, the *haut monde*, with its corsets, top hats, and paisley shawls; there were the have-nots living in misery; and there was the rising middle class, at once rebelling against the aristocracy and aspiring to be like it. Youle, with a newborn and younger sister in tow, knew they could not remain in the gutter.

The *petit bourgeois* way of doing this would be to marry the right man, which is the path Youle's eldest sister had taken in Martinique. But Youle chose a different path. She and Rosine, one year younger, were pretty, with auburn hair and petite figures. They played piano and knew how to entertain—both in the salon and in the bedroom.

It was a line of work not entirely frowned upon. Unlike in Italy, Catholic morality in France had lost much of its sway. Parisian society was far more permissive than the palazzos of Rome, with the pope so near. Many even admired the nocturnal ladies of the demimonde who threw the best soirees, wore the latest fashions, discussed the arts, and dazzled in bed. These were the "kept" women who dined at elegant cafés, attended the opera, mingled with counts. Some of these courtesans—such as the four who became known as *Les Grandes Horizontales*—attained almost legendary status. As the writer Maxime Du Camp expressed it: "One does not know today whether honest women are dressing like prostitutes, or prostitutes are dressed like honest women."

Youle had no shame about her profession, which is why she

would have few qualms about encouraging her own daughters to follow in her footsteps. It's a testament to her guile and formidable willpower that Youle, in a few short years, managed not only to raise a child, but also to build up a respectable salon with some distinguished patrons, including composer Gioachino Rossini, author Alexandre Dumas *père*, the Duc de Morny, and Baron Hippolyte Larrey, the personal physician of Napoleon III. Many of them would one day assist Sarah in her career.

As Sarah began her memoir: "My mother was fond of traveling: she would go from Spain to England, from London to Paris, from Paris to Berlin, and from there to Christiania [Oslo]; then she would come back, embrace me, and set out again." These passages from *My Double Life*, published in 1907 when she was in her sixties, have a languid, almost carefree tone—belying the likelihood that Sarah felt abandoned. A kept woman was expected to travel about Europe on the whims of her patrons; the baby was a nuisance. So Sarah was dispatched to the care of a wet nurse in Brittany, a peasant woman who nicknamed the child "Milk Blossom" due to her fair complexion. The nurse was "a good, kind woman," Sarah wrote, who, "as her own child had died, had only me to love. But she loved after the manner of poor people, when she had time."

One morning, the nurse went off to work in the fields, leaving baby Sarah in a high chair under the supervision of her invalid husband, who was bedridden. Sarah managed to escape her chair and found herself entranced by a nearby fireplace with its mesmerizing flames. Within moments, her clothing had caught fire. The husband, unable to move, croaked out to summon help, but his wife was too far away in the potato field. Neighbors, luckily, heard the child's shrieks.

"I was thrown, all smoking, into a large pail of fresh milk," recounted Sarah, almost proud of the incident:

For the next four days that quiet part of the country was ploughed by stage-coaches that arrived in rapid succession. My aunts came from all parts of the world, and my mother, in the greatest alarm, hastened from Brussels.

Youle was accompanied by patron-du-jour Baron Larrey, the royal physician. (Larrey's father had invented field ambulances and codified triage as battlefield surgeon to the first Napoleon.) A colleague accompanied Larrey on the country jaunt, so little Sarah, while her burns were minor, was attended by two of the finest doctors in France. The esteemed medics, in their top hats and English tweed, deferred to country wisdom, consenting with chuckles to the Breton peasant remedy for Sarah's burns: pigs' bladders stuffed with fresh butter and applied every two hours as a poultice.

Sarah was delighted to be the center of attention, a position she would come to expect in her adult life. She now had the luxury to observe her beloved mother up close. Sarah idolized the beautiful, often-absent woman, whom she likened to "a Madonna" (in appearance if not in virtue)—"her golden hair and her eyes fringed with such long lashes that they made a shadow on her cheeks when she looked down."

As she wrote her memoirs in later years, Sarah remained certain her mother "would have given her golden hair, her slender white fingers, her tiny feet, her life itself, in order to save her child to whom she had not given a moment's thought the week before."

The drama of Sarah's childhood continued when Youle moved Sarah and her country foster-parents to a pied-à-terre in Paris, where they would be more accessible should another crisis occur. But Youle never visited; she was forever leaving Paris on the arms of her numerous admirers. Sarah, not yet six, felt frustrated and lonely, and she acted out. As described by Madame Pierre Berton, a close acquaintance and early biographer:

One afternoon the janitor's wife returned from an errand and heard screams coming from the loge. Hastening there she discovered the butcher's son, aged six, stripped to the waist, and the diminutive Sarah laying on to him with a strap. "I am playing at being a Spaniard," she said in explanation, Spaniards having then a great reputation in France for cruelty.

Sarah, like Eleonora, playacted with great fervor. Duse did it with furniture, Bernhardt with boys—sometimes as their tormentor, if Madame Berton's 1923 memoir is to be believed. The story is certainly plausible, given who Sarah was, and what Berton describes as "her single-minded will to conquer." Most interesting, perhaps, is Madame Berton's conclusion: "I have never doubted that a streak of the primitive existed in Sarah."

The sickly foster father died; with little sentimentality, the peasant widow then married a concierge who lived in a better part of town. But while the neighborhood may have been a step up, their accommodations were not; Sarah was forced to sleep in a cramped, windowless room. The poor girl missed the open skies and fresh air of Brittany. Tuberculosis, which both Sarah and Eleonora would suffer from their entire lives, began to take root in her lungs.

Youle, traveling in ornate carriages across Europe, was unaware of her daughter's new address. Then came a turn of events described by biographer Robert Gottlieb as straight out of *Les Misérables*. As told by Sarah:

One day I was playing . . . when I saw my nurse's husband walking across the courtyard with two ladies, one of whom was most fashionably attired. I could only see their backs, but the voice of the fashionably attired lady caused my heart to stop beating.

"Do any of the windows look onto the courtyard?" she asked.

"Yes, Madame, those four," he replied, pointing to four open ones on the first floor.

The lady turned to look at them, and I uttered a cry of joy. "Aunt Rosine! Aunt Rosine!"

By uncanny coincidence, Aunt Rosine, the sister with whom Youle had fled Amsterdam, was apartment hunting in the very building where Sarah's new foster father served as concierge! The girl dashed into the courtyard. "I buried my face in her furs, stamping, sobbing, laughing, and tearing her wide lace sleeves in my frenzy of delight," gushed Sarah in her melodramatic memoir, which now delivers its denouement.

Sarah begged to be taken back to her mother. Aunt Rosine, embarrassed, promised to come back the following day and emptied her purse into the hands of the befuddled nurse, who whisked the little girl back into their apartment. But Sarah, apparently, jumped from the second-story window to catch the departing carriage, breaking her arm, shattering her kneecap, and passing out.

Like many stories in *My Double Life*, this one has the feeling of being embellished. Yet even if the events are contrived, they remain vivid windows into Sarah's emotional life: in this case, a child crying out for her mother's love. Whether she truly jumped from the window, her dramatics produced the desired result—another reunion between Sarah and Youle. And, of course, more heartbreak.

"I will pass over these two years of my life, which have left me only a vague memory of being petted and of a chronic state of torpor," says Sarah in her memoir. She was seven at the time, still fatherless, unschooled, unable to read, write, or even count. The solution: boarding school.

When Youle, who was pregnant again, delivered the news of

another prolonged separation to her temperamental daughter, everyone expected a tantrum. But Sarah, who used tantrums now only when they served her, appeared jubilant instead. Perhaps it was the beautiful blue velvet dress she was given to mark the occasion, or the promise of being able to play with girls her own age. Sarah, like Eleonora, had not one friend—a shared solitude that made them develop active imaginations and fierce independence.

Sarah's departure for school was a grand affair, with two splendid carriages, one for the ladies and a second for their gentlemen escorts—on this occasion, a general, a painter, and a banker. The carriages belonged to Aunt Rosine, even more successful as a courtesan than her sister. When it came little Sarah's turn to climb aboard the sumptuous vehicle, the seven-year-old "gave herself airs," she would later write, "because the concierge and some shopkeepers were staring." As the carriages rolled, Sarah felt hopeful, even eager, for what was to come—"my face pressed against the window and my eyes wide open."

In the hopes of it taming her unruly daughter, Youle had chosen Madame Fressard's School for Girls just outside of Auteuil, an upscale suburb to the west of Paris, which would one day be incorporated into the capital as its elegant 16th arrondissement. Auteuil had been home to Molière and Victor Hugo, and was the birthplace of Marcel Proust—writers who would all feature in Bernhardt's career decades hence. Sarah gazed up at the tall and ancient trees that lined the meandering lane. Officially, the tuition would be covered by Sarah's "father," but it was actually one of Youle's regulars who ended up footing the bill. Sarah was a handful, a newborn was on the way, they wanted her gone. This time, Sarah was ready to oblige them.

Head of school Madame Fressard, a plump woman with a slight mustache, greeted the new arrival with a warm embrace. Youle delivered a series of instructions to the matron: Sarah's unruly hair was to be brushed thoroughly as to be knot-free before any attempt was made to comb it. She handed over twelve pots of jam and six pounds of chocolate, to be given alternately as special treats every afternoon. And there was the cold cream—a special formula made by Youle herself—to be applied nightly to Sarah's delicate skin. The goods handed over, the courtesans and their escorts headed off to a trendy cabaret, where, as Sarah chose to remember it, "these gentlemen were to make arrangements for a little dinner . . . to console mamma for her great trouble in being separated from me."

Sarah was left to settle into her new life. "Reading, writing, and reckoning," is what they taught her. Complementing the basic academics were lessons in singing and embroidery, the talents of a dutiful wife. This was what the courtesans may have hoped for Sarah. But Sarah had her own plans—and ambition like her mother.

The girls at Sarah's boarding school could hardly contain their excitement. Madame Fressard had told them that Mademoiselle Colas, an ingénue from the Comédie-Française, was coming to perform for them. Stella Colas had a younger sister enrolled in Madame Fressard's school, so Sarah and the other girls felt a special connection to this up-and-coming starlet. Mesmerized by her performance, Sarah wrote: "I would thrill in every fiber when this frail, blonde, pale girl tackled the dream of Athalie."

"*Tremble! fille digne de moi,*" the actress wailed.

Athalie, written in 1691 and the final tragedy of Jean Racine, was viewed by many as a masterpiece. Voltaire considered the play the greatest triumph of the human mind. Whether Stella Colas's delivery on that particular morning did justice to the flowing, poetic text cannot be known; it's more than likely that she followed the Comédie-Française style of the time, which was melodramatic, overemotive, and pushed, meaning the emotions were forced rather than felt. Nevertheless, young Sarah was enchanted.

"*Tremble . . . trem . . . ble . . . trem-em-em-eble,*" the child recited later that night from her cot, drawing out the syllables, allowing herself to be swept up in a fantasy of fame and stardom. Then, upon hearing cackles from the nearby bunks, she lashed out right and left with kicks and slaps, starting a catfight in the dormitory—a fairly regular affair, one would imagine, with increasing consequences. With her Jewish roots and wild hair—African in texture and bright red—Sarah would never quite fit in, nor did she care to. Bourgeois life was boring. Sarah imagined a far loftier trajectory.

When she landed a key role some months later in the school play, Sarah felt vindicated. She had been cast in *Clotilde*, a popular fantasy for children, which had had a successful run at the Comédie-Française, starring her idol, Stella Colas.

Sarah was to play the Fairy Queen, a smaller but important role; the eight-year-old strutted through rehearsals with purpose, immensely proud of her fairy wings.

"My part," she explained to an early biographer, "involved some pretty realistic acting in the second act, when the Queen of the Fairies dies of mortification on hearing Clotilde affirm that the fairies do not really exist." This was to be her first big death scene.

But the Fairy Queen's fatal mortification was nothing compared to that which Bernhardt herself was about to endure. On the night of the play's debut, she glanced at the audience to see "six beautifully gowned ladies and two gentlemen": her mother, aunt, and several other courtesans, along with their gentlemen escorts. Sarah was stunned. While Sarah still craved Youle's attention, she was by now well aware of the nature of her mother's profession—and she was embarrassed by it. Would the other girls recognize them as courtesans? Would it make Sarah even more of an outcast? She froze up in mounting panic.

Sarah caught a stern look from Madame Fressard, urging her to deliver her line, but the poor girl remained immobilized. She stammered for a few seconds, then, unable to continue, ran sobbing from the stage.

Sarah was discovered later in the dormitories, her "head in the bedclothes, like an ostrich . . . weeping violently." Youle shook her head in bitter disappointment. "And to think," she said icily, "that this is a child of mine."

When Sarah turned nine, it was decided that Madame Fressard's little *école* had outlived its usefulness; Sarah would be sent to a convent instead. But as the courtesans appeared in Aunt Rosine's carriages to pick up the child, Sarah balked. She had paid her dues at Madame Fressard's; she was finding her place there, no longer feeling like a pariah.

"The idea that my wishes and mode of life were once again being violated without my consent threw me into an unspeakable rage," remembered Sarah. "I rolled on the floor, shrieked, and hurled reproaches against Mama, my aunts, and Madame Fressard." But after two hours of struggling—escaping into the trees and diving into the mud—she gave in.

Whether Sarah was truly this melodramatic as a young child or these myths were embellished as she aged, the underlying truth remains: Sarah was desperate to gain control of her own life. But how?

The convent school in Versailles looked grim from the exterior, like a prison. Yet when Mother Sainte-Sophie emerged to greet them with a beatific smile, Sarah felt strangely at home—for the first time in her life. The Reverend Mother radiated the unconditional love that Sarah so craved, with "the most gentle and smiling face possible. Big blue childlike eyes . . . a full smiling mouth, fine strong white teeth. Her air of kindness, strength, and gaiety made me throw myself at once into [her] arms."

Thus began Sarah's tenure at the Couvent de Grand-Champs. As a nun-in-training, Sarah would be receiving an annual salary of exactly one sou, symbolic of their poverty vow. Every child was given her own garden to tend, along with lessons in botany and other studies, none of which were of much interest to Sarah. Yet during her free time, she roamed the nearby woods, with its swings and hammocks. It was here that Sarah first developed a passion for animals, collecting insects and reptiles: adders, spiders, lizards, and crickets, which she kept in little boxes that she carried everywhere—both appalling and oddly appealing to the other girls.

Though still a renegade, Sarah was less of an outcast here. While the girls at Madame Fressard's were strictly bourgeois, the Couvent's more diverse population included a pair of twins from Jamaica—"both as dusky as two young moles," Sarah described them in her memoir.

She continued to get into trouble at the Couvent and even throw the occasional tantrum, which the sisters met with rapid signs of the cross and a nervous sprinkling of holy water to exorcise the evil spirits that had apparently taken possession of Sarah's little body. Whether the remedy worked or not is unknown, but Sarah would spend six happy years, all told, at the Couvent.

The most important event in these years was a visit by a person of fame, not an actress this time but a cleric. Monseigneur Sibour, the archbishop of Paris, was to be entertained by the girls, who would perform a play written by the Reverend Mother herself. When she cast the six speaking roles, however, Mother Sainte-Sophie passed over Sarah—offering the most coveted role, the Archangel Raphael, to her newfound "favorite playmate," Louise Buguet, instead.

"We certainly thought about you, dear," Mother Superior told Sarah, gently stroking her cheek, "but you are always so timid when you are asked anything." Sarah fumed. Her so-called timidity was limited to the classroom, particularly history and math.

Although crushed, Sarah learned Louise's lines alongside her friend. And so, when Louise faced a debilitating attack of stage fright on the day of the performance, Sarah stepped in as an understudy. While the memoir does not specify what caused Louise's opening night jitters, one wonders if Sarah had anything to do with it.

Despite her abysmal debut at Madame Fressard's or perhaps because of it, Sarah remained taken by the idea of being an actress. Bernhardt would battle stage fright—quite common among actors—her entire career. She was haunted by the image of her mother's cold, judging eyes, ogling her from the third row. But Sarah, with her formidable willpower, intended to conquer that demon. What better way to subjugate it than in the role of an archangel?

Ignoring her mother entirely this time, Sarah performed magnificently, according to her account of the evening. She adored the Catholic Church's rituals and pageantry, and acted her part with gusto, culminating in an ecstatic finale in which Sarah ascended to heaven in an "apotheosis." So impressed was Monseigneur Sibour that he agreed to officiate at Sarah's baptism. It was the monseigneur's idea to baptize the Jewess; Youle leaped at it. She even arranged to have Sarah's sisters baptized at the same time. They would be Jews no longer. Youle actually cried at the ceremony; Sarah saw it and was secretly elated. She dreamed, in fact, of becoming a nun.

After Sarah's impulsive conversion to Christianity, Youle decided it was time to plan for her daughter's future. So she convened a family council consisting of her courtesan sister along with some of their influential patrons, including the Duc de Morny, the illegitimate half brother of Emperor Napoleon III.

It was 1859. Sarah had just turned fifteen, the legal age for marriage—and that possibility was much discussed. It was why she had been sent to the convent to begin with. But despite her baptism and recent refinements, there were significant impediments to bourgeois matchmaking. Sarah remained the illegitimate daughter of a Jewish courtesan; the obvious choice for Sarah was to enter the family business.

While Youle may have secretly preferred a respectable betrothal for her daughter, there are rumors from several sources that she sold Sarah and her sisters to patrons as early as age thirteen. The most explicit of these accounts came from Sarah's former friend Marie Colombier. The two began together as young actresses, but Sarah's rise would leave the less talented Marie resentful. Twenty-five years on, as Sarah gained worldwide acclaim, Colombier would publish a mean-spirited unauthorized biography entitled *Les Mémoires de Sarah Barnum*, a mocking parody of her former friend's surname. Colombier's bias is obvious, but she remains one of the few eyewitnesses to this period of Sarah's young life.

When both girls were sixteen, Marie spent time in Youle's lively apartment, where courtesans mingled with clients amid drink and debauchery. Colombier recounts one night in 1860 when Youle (whom she renamed Esther in the book) forced her daughter to kiss the girl's elderly "godfather," Monsieur Régis, and allow him to caress her as she sat on his lap. Her illegitimate sisters each had their own "godfathers"—whether this is code for biological father or patron is unclear.

But Sarah wanted to distance herself at all costs from her mother's salon, which is why she announced one day that she had found herself a reliable husband—a man who would never abandon her. The courtesans glanced with sudden curiosity. The teenager told them she planned to wed the Lord Savior—she wanted to be a nun. This elicited titters of amusement.

The nunnery was not a good match for spirited Sarah, and finding a spouse would be a challenge, too. So the Duc de Morny proposed a third option: "Why not send the child to the Conservatoire?" It was an instinct, something he saw in her. (Morny may have been present the night Sarah performed as Raphael for the archbishop of Paris.)

Founded in 1795, the Conservatoire de Paris was a well-regarded college of music and drama. The courtesans thought Morny's idea was not so far-fetched, so they decided to persuade Sarah by taking her to her first performance at an actual theater. The teenager was delighted because, as she later explained, "it was now felt necessary to pamper and spoil me to get my consent.

I could no longer be forced to do what others wanted. My consent had to be sought. I felt so joyful and proud . . . that I almost inclined to give it. But, I said to myself, I would make them beg for it all the same."

Not much begging was needed. Sarah was whisked into a private box belonging to another patron of Youle's salon: Dumas *père*, author of *The Count of Monte Cristo*. "When the curtain slowly rose," Sarah would write in her memoir, "I thought I was going to faint. It was, in fact, the curtain of my life that was rising. Those columns . . . would be my palace. That backdrop would be my sky."

Tears rolled down the young girl's cheeks.

Bernhardt was infamous from the moment she entered the Conservatoire. She had had the temerity to recite a common folk fable at her audition, something that should have dashed her chances immediately. But the Duc de Morny pulled strings and a spot was hers.

Turbulent, always late, she did not win many friends. Indeed, her fellow students quickly grew to resent her. Their lessons included deportment, enunciation, vocal technique, and rote recitation of classical scenes. Certain instructors would demonstrate precisely how a particular speech was meant to be delivered, and the students were expected to mimic every inflection and every pose. Sarah tried things her own way—speaking tenderly on a line that was meant to be violent, for example. The behavior was met with disapproval, though some in the faculty noticed that Sarah was simply trying to make a more interesting choice. After two semesters of study, Bernhardt hoped to graduate at the top of her class, but the coveted prizes went to others.

"Well, you have completely failed," said her godfather Monsieur Régis, a bourgeois businessman and salon regular. "Why are you so set on acting? You are thin . . . your face is ugly at a distance, and your voice doesn't carry."

Defiant, Sarah vowed to become famous one day simply to spite him. Her motto, which she repeated like a mantra and would one day engrave on her dinner plates, was *Quand même* (meaning "in spite of it all"). But later, in the privacy of her room, she felt nothing but shame. Sarah had her heart set on joining the national theater company, the Comédie-Française. Now that felt unattainable.

Later that evening came a note. Morny had intervened again: Sarah's position at the Comédie-Française had been arranged.

It did not matter to Sarah that this was the oldest and most renowned acting company in the world; the rebel would push back at will. She recalls how she was lectured like a marionette on "the positions that I should take up, the moves we should make." She was told never to turn her back on the audience, but she tried it anyway. Like Eleonora, she chafed at the established rules. But instead of overturning them, Sarah stretched and bent them to her whims. If Sarah Bernhardt was going to use poses, they would be Sarah Bernhardt poses—things of beauty and grace . . . and power, not those ridiculous marionette gestures in the manuals. Sarah would one day take her signature poses to ecstatic heights. No one did them better.

But Sarah's first few outings on the boards showed little of that promise. In her 1862 Comédie debut, she was overcome by stage fright that left her frozen in the footlights. Fancisque Sarcey, the most influential critic in Paris, summed it up as follows: "Mlle. Bernhardt is tall and pretty and enunciates well, which is all that can be said for the moment."

"No stage presence," wrote another. "Sarah Bernhardt has no personality; she possesses only a voice," wrote a third. With notices like that, the Comédie-Française had little choice: they benched her. *Quand même.*

Far from being discouraged by this inauspicious start, Sarah remained determined "to become the best, most famous, and most envied of actresses." She counted off the qualities she would need: grace, charm, distinction, beauty, mystery, piquancy. "Oh everything! . . . I had them all," she wrote in her memoir, mocking her own youthful narcissism. But whether she possessed all the requisite qualities or not, she would advance no further at the Comédie-Française.

It didn't take long for Sarah to engineer the perfect out. The occasion: the birthday of playwright Molière on January 15, 1863, when the entire company honored the memory of its founder by forming a solemn procession to lay palm fronds before his bust. Sarah had taken her younger sister Régine to the ceremony and they found themselves behind "the very fat and very solemn Madame Nathalie," the terror of the company. When Régine accidently stepped on the train of her ostentatious dress, the woman pushed the child to the ground. "Nasty bitch!" shouted Sarah, and proceeded to slap the aging diva across her plump cheeks. Twice.

Whether the episode was planned, impulsive, or entirely fabricated, the message was clear: no one messes with a Bernhardt. But the slaps caused a scandal. Madame Nathalie was a *Sociétaire*, meaning she had tenure as a senior member of the company. Shocked by Sarah's insolence, the dowager fainted, followed by "tumult, brouhaha, indignation," wrote Sarah in her memoir. Her own feelings were "suppressed laughter" and "a sense of satisfied vengeance."

As expected, the Comédie-Française terminated Sarah's contract. In ten years they'd be begging for her return.

Chapter Three

It was ironic and, frankly, depressing—the only way for twenty-two-year-old Sarah to move out from under her mother's roof was to enter the family business. This was a price for independence she was willing to pay. And Sarah did nothing in half measures.

Before long, the consummate actress had attracted a group of regular patrons who were prominent, wealthy, and well connected. She slept with an occasional *amant de coeur* as well, such as her first true love, a handsome young hussar and nobleman, Le Comte de Kératry.

Then there was a broken heart and a pregnancy. Sarah, foolishly, had allowed herself to develop feelings for an aristocratic client: Prince de Ligne from Belgium. Worldly and charming, he had wooed Sarah with whispers of running away from his family and eloping with her. She had believed him. But when she became pregnant, the prince cruelly severed ties with Sarah and refused to recognize the child. The boy, Maurice, was born in 1864.

Quand même, thought Sarah—I was raised a bastard and managed to hold my head up high. I shall raise a bastard, too.

And she did so with zeal, doting on the child as her own mother never had on her. Years later, when twentysomething Maurice announced his engagement to a Polish princess, his estranged father hinted that he might be willing to recognize Maurice as his heir. But, with Sarah world-famous by then, Maurice told the Prince de Ligne he preferred to remain a "Bernhardt."

— — —

Some years after being fired from the Comédie-Française, Sarah began performing with the rival Théâtre Odéon—she got the job herself this time, not through her mother's patrons. The Odéon was a more popular theater intended for the masses. It was here, in 1869, that Sarah had her first big success—but not as a *prima donna*. She landed the part of Zanetto in *Le Passant* by François Coppée, the first of many men she would play onstage. It was a tradition that went back centuries: women putting on pants to portray youthful men. These so-called trouser roles culminated for Sarah in 1899 with the most famous male role of all: Hamlet.

Le Passant was simple by comparison: a one-act play set during the Renaissance in the Tuscan countryside, about an encounter between Sylvia, an aging courtesan, and Zanetto, a wandering minstrel. These plays are known, in theater parlance, as "two-handers," meaning Sarah would share the stage with only one other actor.

Le Passant's playwright, François Coppée, had limited expectations: "My little work had already given me great pleasure in creating it," he wrote in his journal. "I awaited its public presentation without illusions and without impatience." But when the curtain rose, he became intrigued.

Bernhardt had never before performed a male role, and she acted the part with gusto. The playwright was effusive, declaring, "What profound emotion, what intoxication, what joy, what madness of youth in my Zanetto!" He was captivated by Bernhardt's passion and charisma.

The passion was genuine; Sarah loved the part. "It's not that I prefer male roles," she later told a journalist, "it's that I prefer male minds." Bernhardt liked being direct, not coy.

"It was in this role that the poetic talent of M'lle Bernhardt was first made manifest," wrote Edgar L. Wakeman, an American author and journalist on a European tour, who published his observations in a syndicated column entitled "Wakeman's Wanderings."

What impressed Wakeman most about Sarah was "the witching music of her 'voice of gold.'"

He was not alone. Critics and theatergoers alike would soon become enamored of Sarah's melodic voice—she had worked tirelessly at it. Bernhardt seemed to weave music out of written words—especially so here, for Coppée's play had been composed in verse, and gentle music underscored the major speeches. Over time, many of Sarah's more elaborate productions would involve a style the French dubbed "*mélodrame*," drama enhanced by a melodic orchestral accompaniment that gave the audience added emotional cues. Even in modest plays, Sarah had a way of turning the most mundane lines into poetry. From her turn in *Le Passant*, it became clear that Sarah was destined for stardom. Wrote Wakeman: "The piece and its interpreters were lauded to the skies."

As a "man," Sarah became the most-talked-about actress in Paris. She'd play the part 140 times, culminating in a command performance at the Tuileries Palace for the emperor himself. Through her mother's circles, Sarah had already met Napoleon III, who likely did not remember their first encounter, but he was quite taken with her onstage. They are rumored, at some point, to have met in the bedroom.

Like other loyal subjects in the Second Empire, Sarah was a Bonapartist through and through, which is why she stood solidly by her emperor when he declared war, in 1870, on Prussia, a military powerhouse. It wasn't long before the Prussian artillery had Paris surrounded. The Prussian cannons, cast in steel, not bronze, could deliver larger projectiles over a far greater range.

But the Prussians were not the only enemy. The French were also fighting among themselves in a de facto civil war—on the one side, the followers of the Bonaparte emperor, on the other, the Republicans, Victor Hugo among them, who called for an end to the monarchy and restoration of the short-lived liberties that had been gained in the revolution.

On September 2, 1870, when Napoleon III was taken prisoner in the Battle of Sedan, the Republicans seized Paris to form a "Government of National Defense." But the new leaders could do nothing to halt the Prussians.

Ahead of the imminent siege of the French capital, Sarah secured safe passage for her mother, sisters, baby son, and aunt, and dispatched the family to Holland. But she wouldn't hear of joining them herself. The new darling of Paris was about to take on her most dramatic role. As the rockets soared overhead, Sarah did something that would forever endear her to the French public—with the blessing of its owners, she turned the Théâtre Odéon into a field hospital.

Caring for wounded soldiers was not an act; it took tremendous energy, perseverance, and courage. Although not a trained nurse, Sarah tended with great attention to the men, who poured in by the cartload. One miserable fellow she remembered vividly. "I raised my lantern to look at his face," she wrote in her memoir, "and found that his ear and a part of his jaw had been blown off . . . a wild look in his eyes." Sarah gave him brandy through a straw. There was little else she could do. They saw men like this every hour.

Fortunately, she was not alone, for Bernhardt had used her notoriety to attract numerous volunteers to the cause. As the prototype celebrity do-gooder, "[Sarah] set every woman and child of her acquaintance to work, making bandages and folding lint," recalled Madame Pierre Berton, who visited with her mother during the siege and who would one day write a biography of Bernhardt. The experience left quite an impression on the wide-eyed child. "How I loved Sarah Bernhardt in those days!" she remembered later as Sarah's friend and confidante. "She seemed to me to be glory personified."

In a time of rationing and shortages, Sarah did all she could to secure the requisite supplies, using her celebrity wherever possible, including the time she paid a personal visit to the prefect of police—he turned out to be none other than the Comte de Kératry, her first love. They had had a brief but passionate affair eight years prior, when Sarah was eighteen.

"I never thought I was coming to see *you!*" she exclaimed. "I am delighted, for you will let me have everything I ask for."

The comte laughed good-naturedly as Sarah pulled out her shopping list and demanded bread, milk, meat, vegetables, sugar, wine, brandy, potatoes, eggs, and coffee. Not only would her former lover accommodate all of Sarah's requests, she also walked away with his personal overcoat. That winter was so cold, people burned their furniture to stay warm.

Bernhardt had been a Bonapartist, but the demise of the Second Empire did little to hurt her career prospects. Sarah's wartime heroics had earned her the nation's esteem, and she would soon join forces, both onstage and in bed, with another national hero—the bearlike Victor Hugo, France's poet emeritus returning from exile, his beard now white. Despite an almost forty-three-year difference in age, it was a natural partnership: "The Goddess and The Genius" was how they became known. She stood in awe of him, the first man perhaps to affect her so. He recognized the raw talent in her and a stage presence like no other. It was the meeting of icons—one aging, one in the making.

Anticipation mounted as the public prepared for their 1879 revival of *Ruy Blas*, a controversial play by Hugo about a commoner who falls in love with a royal—it had been banned, along with many others, under Bonaparte for its reformist themes.

Madame Pierre Berton set the opening night scene: "Every seat had been taken days in advance, and hundreds crowded in to the space behind the back rows and stood up throughout the entire performance." The giddy Republican audience had not seen anything by Hugo for nearly two decades. Sarah took the stage with a vengeance. By the final curtain they were enthralled, summoning her to twenty curtain calls.

"She often told me," continued Berton, "that never again in her long career did she act so well as she did that night." Sarah was using poses, to be sure, but in her singular interpretations of them, she invoked the archetype—a queen like no other. Sarah had connected deeply to the play's ancient themes.

Afterward, Hugo rushed to meet Sarah backstage, dropped to his knee, and kissed her hand saying, "Thank you! Thank you!" Even the critics were giddy. As Francisque Sarcey wrote: "No role was ever better adapted to Mlle. Sarah Bernhardt's talents than that of this melancholy queen."

At age thirty-five, Sarah was now the queen of the Parisian stage. The public had fallen in love with her. It was time to take the world.

Later that year, Sarah traveled to London as a reinstated member of the Comédie-Française; the company had entreated her return. Sarah insisted on receiving *Sociétaire* status, meaning tenured for life. Though Madame Nathalie and other senior members of the company balked, they had no choice. Sarah was the one the British impresarios wanted—without Sarah there was no tour.

British papers had been covering Bernhardt's exploits since her career-launching turn as Zanetto ten years prior, and London critics, who often reviewed Parisian plays, had lauded Sarah's recent collaboration with Victor Hugo. So the public had been primed for her arrival.

"A sight I shall never forget was our landing at Folkestone," recalled Sarah. "There were thousands of people there, and it was the first time I had ever heard the cry of '*Vive Sarah Bernhardt!*'" Among the throng of admirers was the young Oscar Wilde, who would one day write *Salomé* with Sarah in mind. "Hip, hip, hurrah!" he shouted. "A cheer for Sarah Bernhardt!"

The highlight of the London engagement was to be *Phèdre*, the classic French tragedy by Racine, written in the seventeenth century and considered, in stature, akin to *Hamlet*. It had previously been performed in London by France's iconic Rachel, an international star of the prior generation, who, like Sarah, was Jewish and had had a tryst with Napoleon III. Comparisons between the two would be inevitable.

Rachel's 1843 version of the play had been stripped down to its essentials—spartan sets, an economy of gestures—that helped it to achieve a feeling of authenticity. According to the French writer and critic Théophile Gautier, when Sarah's predecessor performed the part, "she was not Mademoiselle Rachel, but Phèdre, herself, the illusion lasting every minute."

Theatergoers across Europe had been seduced by Rachel, one of a select group of nineteenth-century actors who had attempted, like Duse, to act more naturally onstage. But Rachel's impact was cut short by her premature death at age thirty-six of tuberculosis. Nonetheless, Sarah was feeling the pressure to match the star's success in her first performance before a foreign audience.

"Don't force your voice," counseled François Regnier, the company's administrator. "Push the role toward suffering and not towards fury; that will be better for everyone, even Racine." Sarah would be speaking French, of course. London theatergoers were accustomed to watching plays in foreign languages; a scene-by-scene synopsis was often part of the playbill.

As she waited in the wings for her entrance, Sarah began to sense the telltale gnawing in her belly: stage fright, after all these years—but a specific sort, "not the kind that paralyzes, but the kind that drives one wild." It was turmoil that could be harnessed in service of her character—perfect, in fact, for the tortured Phèdre in her forbidden lust for her stepson, Hippolyte, played by Jean Mounet-Sully, a senior member of the Comédie-Française.

Something happened to Sarah that night—similar, perhaps, to Duse's epiphany in Verona. "The gods were with me," Sarah would later recall. She had transmuted her fear into the fuel that carried her performance; the experience left her spent. "When the curtain fell, Mounet carried my inert body to my dressing room."

Oscar Wilde was so moved, he composed a sonnet for Sarah, which begins:

How vain and dull this common world must seem /
To such a One as thou.

Wilde would later jokingly declare that Bernhardt was one of three women he would actually consider marrying (the other two being actress Lillie Langtry and Her Majesty Queen Victoria).

Sarah had gone to England as a celebrity; she returned to France a legend. She would soon quit the Comédie-Française to form her own touring company and travel across Europe and America, taking her son with her to every stop. Though not the first to do so—Rachel had toured overseas, as well as Italy's Adelaide Ristori, and others—Bernhardt raised international stardom to another order of magnitude. Rachel and Ristori were names known to sophisticated theatergoers, but Bernhardt was a name known to everyone. She had moved from the theater pages to the front page.

The terms for Sarah's first American tour in 1880 were unprecedented—$1,000 per show, plus 50 percent of all receipts over $4,000. This tour—the first of nine she would do in America—increased Sarah's net worth by 900,000 francs, equivalent to $5 million in today's dollars. She was not yet forty.

CHAPTER FOUR

Five months after her epiphany as Juliet, Duse, still fourteen, found herself back in Verona—though this occasion was not so jubilant. Instead of playing Juliet, she was performing in one of the many third-rate melodramas that dominated the Duse Company's repertoire—variations of the same basic plots and crude translations, often, of popular French plays. There were too many to count. The company rotated plays nightly in hopes of attracting repeat customers.

Learning a new piece was not difficult for Eleonora, since they had a prompter on the stage with them, as did most Italian companies at the time. The public had grown accustomed to hearing the prompter's disembodied voice, often louder than the actors themselves, feeding lines so the cast rarely had to be off book. Actors needed only to assume the posture and wait for the line.

Eleonora had been promoted recently to *prima donna*, but under unfortunate circumstances: her mother, who had suffered from tuberculosis for some years, had been hospitalized in Ancona, on the Adriatic coast. As the lead actress in the company, Duse was now expected to learn quickly the roles of Pia de Tolommei, La trovatella di Santa Maria, Gaspara Stampa, and countless other women. Though barely an adolescent, she was playing full-grown adults.

Her young voice was now a problem, "still feeble when I forced it in big speeches," she later recalled, sometimes so much so that "someone behind the scenes hissed at me that I should speak louder, still louder." Her limited life lessons raised issues, too. "There were so many things that my young, inexperienced soul did not know or understand," she later confessed "and I do not know what woeful instinct led me to find the proper accent and shrieks that were needed to shake the miserable crowd from which we expected our daily bread."

Eleonora prayed that her mother might return to the company. Then came the telegram, dated September 15, 1873, and delivered backstage to Eleonora between acts on the rickety platform in Verona. It read simply:

MAMMA MORTA.

Eleonora was devastated. She kept her distance from her fellow actors at her mother's funeral, many of whom did not know quite what to make of the broody girl gazing numbly at the coffin. Unable to afford a mourning dress, she had sewn a fold of black crepe onto the bodice of the one dress she owned, which brought frowns from other actresses in the troupe. "Why don't you cry," asked one. "Why don't you dress yourself in mourning," demanded another. "If my mother died, I would sell myself to dress in proper mourning clothes."

If Duse's understatement of emotion had a beginning, it was here—at the burial of her mother. Others trumpeted their grief; Duse contained it.

The company fell apart after the loss of Angelica. Eleonora sank into a depression, as did her father. They called it *la smara*, a Venetian malaise that descends on you like a black fog; Eleonora would struggle with it for life. While others went their separate ways, father and daughter stuck together, joining a series of touring companies. She was the bigger draw, although demoted to *seconda donna*. Her father became *promiscuo* (utility player) or *generico primario* (general, background actor). They changed companies practically every season between 1875 and 1878.

No one was overly impressed by Eleonora's talent. Luigi Pezzana, a popular, older actor who had performed with the famed tragedienne Adelaide Ristori, is reported to have yelled during a rehearsal, "What makes you think you're an actress?" Her silent pauses and natural delivery were driving him mad. Pezzana was not alone in his disdain for her style; several colleagues even told her to quit. The public, too, didn't understand Eleonora's style; she was sometimes booed offstage. How jarring it must have been to have one actress attempting a subtle performance while others were still gesticulating.

Duse would rehearse alone, mostly mental preparations, as well as a thorough analysis of the play and the playwright's intentions. She believed deeply that her style of acting could bring the themes into high relief. But it could never work if her fellow actors did not play along. In fact, by insisting on her own style, Duse would actually be undermining a play's coherence. So, more often than not, she simply gave up—and did it their way. She posed.

It's a story as old as theater itself: the star actress gets sick, and the eager understudy is suddenly thrust upon the stage. That's exactly what happened to Eleonora in 1878, when Eleonora and her father traveled for an extended stay in Naples as part of the respected Ciotti-Belli-Blanes Company. With half a million residents, Naples was the largest city in Italy at the time—a passionate and colorful seaport, ripe with the smell of broiled shrimp on every corner. Within five years, a cholera epidemic from contaminated seafood would claim half the population. For now, the merriment continued.

One night, Giulia Gritti, *prima attrice* of the Ciotti-Belli-Blanes Company fell ill. *Seconda donna* Eleonora, age twenty, was called upon to replace her in an Italian translation of Émile Augier's *Les fourchambault*, his final play, which had just had a celebrated debut in Paris. Center stage now, playing a well-written part in a proper, indoor theater, Eleonora felt fully supported for the first time in her life.

A key part of Eleonora's style was a sense of freedom and abandon—not just in the way the words rose up within her, but also in the way she used her body. Actors were largely responsible for their own costuming. Duse had thrown away her restrictive corset and adopted loose-fitting gowns that flowed with her movements onstage, sometimes clinging to her body. This was provocative and sensual—and a time when actress and courtesan were often synonymous. Though not quite classically beautiful, Eleonora appeared striking onstage, with dark languid eyes that would suddenly light up with each new intention, and thick brows that were equally expressive. Her jaw was strong, her lips full. In Naples, she was the most alluring she'd ever been—and not simply because the romantic seaport had a way of rose-tinting everything. It was also a matter of technology.

Neapolitan theaters had recently installed gas footlights. Prior to gas, stages were lit with oil lamps—a fire hazard and also far dimmer, emitting thick black smoke that further contributed to the obscurity. More than twenty rows back, you'd be hard-pressed to read a subtle change in expression—hence the need to act with one's hands and to enhance the face with strong makeup. Gas illumination allowed for the subtle choices Eleonora was making onstage to be noticed—which is why the Neapolitans were so riveted.

One of her first admirers was Giovanni Emanuele, a fellow actor, also considered "modern," and ten years older than Eleonora. He couldn't take his eyes off her. "Here was a young woman who could grip your heart night after night in the theater and crumple it like a handkerchief," he once told a colleague. Emanuele was connected to a local principessa, who had recently acquired the best theater in Naples with the intention of forming a new company. Emanuele proposed that Eleonora be invited to join, along with her father.

Giovanni Emanuele would be *primo attore* in the new company; the *prima donna* was Giacinta Pezzana (no relation to Luigi), an established actress of some fame. It was thrilling for Eleonora to share a stage with Giacinta, particularly since the star was not threatened by the newcomer and even became something of a mentor to her.

They began performing in early 1879, in direct competition with Eleonora's former company. At one point both companies mounted rival productions of the same play. That play was *Hamlet*, and, just as Eleonora had soared playing Shakespeare in Verona—heartbreak and human tragedy worked well with her interiorized style—she likewise shined in Naples as Ophelia, gaining national attention from the press. The theatrical review *L'arte drammatica* reported on April 5: "Eleonora Duse was as ideal as a vision, courtly as a princess, sweet as a maiden, beautiful as Ophelia. She *was* Ophelia!"

Echoing Eleonora's own words about her prior encounter with The Grace ("I was Juliet!"), the Italian publication seemed to have picked up on the actress's sublimation of her own ego, which was at the heart of what Duse did. Eleonora would disappear, to be "visited" by something else—the spirit of Juliet one time; another time, Ophelia. This was disquieting to many. The theater was an extravagance for the middle class. So when they put down good money to see, say, the great Giacinta Pezzana, they paid to see a star, not to watch her disappear into the character. They expected the queen of Denmark to have a Giacinta Pezzana overlay. But when Giacinta Pezzana and Giovanni Emanuele watched Eleonora receive five curtain calls that first evening in Naples, they sensed the old style was on its way out.

Eleonora's work was singled out by Italy's leading theatrical newspaper: "her way of acting is the truest and most natural that can be imagined." Another Neapolitan critic wrote: "We trembled, a shudder ran through our body . . . we had not even the courage to applaud. The old doorman of the Teatro dei Fiorentini that evening said to me: '*Signurì, chesta è essa!*' [Sir, she is it!]"

— — —

Eleonora may have been an old soul, but, at age twenty, she was still a typical young woman with romance on her mind and lust in her heart. One night, after a show, Eleonora wandered until sunrise through the streets of Turin. "It was because I needed love!" she explained, "I was seeking love. The thought of returning to my lonely room was impossible. So I walked and walked . . . until dawn broke and fatigue compelled me to seek my bed."

She had roamed all alone through the shadowy streets, putting herself both in danger of being accosted and at risk of arrest; an unaccompanied woman was presumed to be a prostitute. One doubts that her father knew about it at the time—but even if he had, it's unlikely that Alessandro would have tried to stop Eleonora. He had learned long ago that he could no longer control his willful daughter. At sixty, his body was tired—too tired even to defend his daughter's honor, should it come to that. And it did.

Eleonora was smitten the moment she set eyes on him. He came backstage to congratulate her, like the many other would-be Romeos, but there was something different about Martino Cafiero. At thirty-eight, he was worldly, sophisticated. He dressed elegantly in dark tones, not like the typical Neapolitan dandies with their brightly colored cravats. Martino was brilliant, and supremely literate. An entrepreneur, he had founded *Corriere del mattino,* one of the most popular newspapers in Naples. He worked as its editor and wrote a lyrical daily column, which Eleonora read religiously. This was the first true writer she had ever met, and Eleonora adored writers almost as much as she adored reading their words.

As a man about town, Martino escorted Eleonora to places she had never been—the yacht club, the museum. From a childhood of abject poverty, Eleonora suddenly found herself in opulent salons with liveried servants pouring the most expensive wines—it was head-spinning. But what really impressed Eleonora was when Martino took her to the newspaper offices, which every night became a sort of literary salon of writers and journalists, with lively discussions about the affairs of the day. Though unschooled, Eleonora was bright and enjoyed the stimulation. She felt honored that Martino had taken an interest in her, initiating her into a world of ideas. As a colleague noted: "There was always an element of worship in Duse's love affairs."

Eleonora could not have avoided hearing about Martino's reputation as a philanderer. She had made her first female friend in Naples: Matilde Serao—a successful journalist and writer whose work had appeared in Cafiero's *Corriere del mattino*. Matilde knew of Martino's reputation, but there was nothing she could say to diminish Eleonora's infatuation with him. A common attitude among affluent young men was that ingénues could be bought—enjoyed for a season and discarded. But Eleonora felt that in his heart Martino was an artist like she. She trusted him. It ended badly.

The breakup began with the dissolution of Eleonora's acting company—following the sudden departure of the lead actor, Giovanni Emanuele. Giacinta Pezzana, now a free agent, had suitors from other companies lining up to entice the *prima donna* away. She chose to go with Cesare Rossi, who ran the most prestigious acting company in Italy. Giacinta persuaded Rossi to take Eleonora, too, along with her father.

Duse was thrilled but also torn, for it meant leaving Naples. Martino assured her that they would stay in touch, and she believed him. She could not afford to be too sentimental, after all—if she and her father missed a season, they would go hungry. So Duse signed a contract with Cesare Rossi. She and her father would be traveling north to Turin's Teatro Carignano, one of the oldest and most famous in Italy.

Martino wasn't at the train station to see her off. Duse was devastated. She hadn't told a soul about the child on the way, certainly not her father. It began as a suspicion; she hadn't known for certain until after agreeing to join Rossi. Eleonora had hoped, however improbably, that Martino would show up at the last moment to take responsibility. But she boarded the train alone.

As she began rehearsals for the new season with Rossi's company, Eleonora grew more and more anxious. She wrote Martino a series of increasingly desperate letters:

"Save me from the solitude of my silent room . . ."
    "Speak to me with truth, with sincerity, like a man . . ."
    "Think of what is in me that is yours. Oh Martino, Martino! Is this love! Is this—a father?"

She received no response. By June, her pregnancy apparent to all, Eleonora had to leave the stage and quietly disappear. Unlike in Paris where social conventions were far more relaxed, to have a baby out of wedlock in Italy brought disgrace to both the mother and her family. It was even a crime, in some parts, punishable by flogging and imprisonment. With reports to the newspaper that she had taken ill, Eleonora secretly departed to a sleepy seaside town in Tuscany where she could deliver the child without scrutiny. She gave birth to a boy at the *ospizio*, a foundling home to which she would be forced to surrender the child, although still required to pay for his care. It was a difficult labor that left her spent.

Still in love with Martino despite his indifference, and dreaming, perhaps, of an eventual reconciliation, Eleonora named the boy Mario, his father's pen name. She arranged for a photograph to be taken of her and the child, which she promptly dispatched to Naples. But Martino returned the photograph to her with a single word scrawled upon it (*commediante*, "comedian"), implying that Eleonora was putting on an "act"—the way a whore would. To add to her heartbreak, the boy lived only a few days.

As was often the case in an *ospizio*, Duse had been largely prohibited from interacting with her child. The newborn had been handed off to the wet nurses, who typically saved their best breast milk for their own children, feeding the orphans afterward. Many died of neglect. Mario's death was another blow to an already despairing and sickly Eleonora, who became suicidal and may well not have survived were it not for the arrival of her friend Matilde Serao.

Some years later, Martino, true to his scoundrel self, published a roman à clef about his affair with Duse and the unwanted pregnancy in his newspaper.

Following her Tuscan convalescence, Eleonora returned to Turin, where she found herself promoted to *prima donna*. Cesare Rossi had little choice in the matter; he had lost Giacinta Pezzana, his star, to another company. Eleonora did not, however, receive a raise, as Rossi had the Duses (both father and daughter) locked into a fixed contract of 7,250 lire per annum (about $25,000 today). Eleonora had no say in her repertoire and was forced to play melodramas—they drew the largest crowds but depressed her.

Desperate for stability and support, Eleonora sought comfort in the arms of Tebaldo Checchi, a fellow actor in the company who had been with Eleonora in Naples, where he had witnessed her humiliating tryst with Cafiero. Unlike the dashing writer, Tebaldo was not particularly intelligent, nor sophisticated—but he was caring and kind, which is exactly what Eleonora needed. As Tebaldo described their relationship in a letter: "seeing her so alone, so sad . . . fighting poverty . . . I paid her court, and fell in love for the first time in my life."

Though never more than a competent bit player, Tebaldo had worked steadily over the years and managed to save some money, which he happily spent on his new love, purchasing a wardrobe befitting a *prima donna*. "What can humanly be done to make a woman happy, I did," he wrote immodestly, "and I did it with love."

Though Eleonora did not return Tebaldo's feelings, she agreed to marry him. They were wed on September 7, 1881, to her father's relief. Alessandro was freed of the burden of chaperoning his head-strong and passionate daughter—who was, once again, pregnant. Now she would be Tebaldo's problem.

The Neapolitan did his valiant best for a number of years, but the marriage was doomed from the start. Eleonora soon acquired other lovers—and it was Tebaldo whose reputation suffered for it. As Matilde Serao wrote: "How much whispered slander and open ridicule fell about Tebaldo Checchi's ears on account of this marriage! In secret he was called 'the pimp.'"

Tebaldo maintained his dignity by becoming ever more devoted to his wife, convincing himself of the nobility of his role as "watchful protector of that chosen creature." In an account he wrote some time later, Tebaldo explained how he "stood before her, protected her with his body, and took on himself all those troubles, which are unavoidable for a rising actress." They were still viewed as playthings for moneyed bachelors.

Their child, a girl, was born on January 7, 1882: Enrichetta Checchi Duse. Though her baby was healthy, Eleonora became gravely ill after the birth, sinking again into postpartum depression. Less than two years had passed since her tragic liaison with Martino; Eleonora still had vivid memories of her poor, unbaptized dead son. When Tebaldo saw his new wife withering, he dispatched the newborn to the countryside where she would be suckled by a surrogate—successfully this time—while he nursed his wife back to health. Little by little, Eleonora began to feel better; then, after a few weeks, she heard some news that had her practically leaping from her bed.

Rossi would be giving them some time off—the entire month of February, in fact, an extremely long hiatus for a repertoire company. Tebaldo explained that Rossi had leased out the Teatro Carignano for the month to a touring company.

"Which one?" asked Eleonora.

"It's Bernhardt," replied Tebaldo.

Duse was speechless.

CHAPTER FIVE

Friends thought Bernhardt had gone mad. They didn't understand what she saw in her new lover. The woman who had been with princes and emperors was now on the arm of Aristides "Jacques" Damala, a midlevel military attaché from the Greek embassy. The scion of a wealthy shipping family, Damala had squandered his inheritance on gambling, prostitutes, and an increasingly pricey morphine habit. With his pirate mustache and trimmed beard, he had a reputation as the handsomest man in Europe. Damala's womanizing had led to several divorces, a suicide, and a string of broken hearts—which is what made Sarah so curious to meet him.

It happened after her sold-out tour of America continued onto its European leg in 1881. They were introduced by Sarah's younger sister Jeanne, who ran in Damala's morphine circles. Each was keen to seduce the other. As Madame Pierre Berton wrote in her biography of Sarah:

> Bernhardt prided herself on her ability to conquer men, to reduce them to the level of slaves; Damala vaunted his ability as a hunter and a spoiler of women. . . . Damala boasted to his friends that, as soon as he looked at her, the great Sarah Bernhardt would be counted in his long list of victims; and Bernhardt was no less certain that she had only to command for Damala to succumb.

When they met, Bernhardt, accustomed to fawning admirers, was appalled by Damala's cool reserve, which Sarah took for insolence.

Yet she was still strongly attracted to him and soon fell in love with the Greek, who dropped his diplomatic job in early 1882 to follow Sarah's company with the aspiration of joining her on the stage. After meeting Sarah, the vain Damala had begun to take bit parts as an actor in the hopes of becoming a star—a laughable ambition, given his lack of talent, poor technique, and unintelligible Greek accent. But Bernhardt, blind to his shortcomings, installed Damala as her new leading man. Prowess in bed was as good a reason as any to invite a man onto the stage with her. Talent was secondary. In fact, Sarah preferred to surround herself with lesser actors, so she could shine more brightly. Having already toured the rest of Europe, Sarah was now heading toward the final Italian leg, which began in Turin.

The parade through the stage door was impressive. Racks of exotic costumes, oriental rugs, tapestries, a menagerie of animals from pumas to parakeets . . . Eleonora stared, giddy, from the backstage shadows. It was like a circus. Her little dressing room had been transformed into a boudoir befitting an empress. When would "She" arrive? The Divine One! It was a moniker her fans had given her early on, perhaps suggested by Sarah herself or by one of her cronies. "People spoke only of her in town, in the salons, at the theatre," Duse recalled. Bernhardt had spent considerable sums on advance publicity for this tour; Eleonora was impressed by what she had read. At thirty-seven, Bernhardt ran her own company, deciding everything from scenery to costumes, fellow actors to props. Most importantly, Sarah was now in control of her own repertoire.

To Eleonora's delight, Bernhardt planned to open her run in Turin with *La Dame aux camélias*, her most famous role. *Camille*, as Alexandre Dumas *fils*'s play was also known, had a plot that was deeply personal to Sarah: a courtesan attempts to give up her errant ways when she finds true love, but the bourgeois world will not accept her, and the courtesan dies alone. Parallels to Bernhardt's past were well known; in fact, she flaunted them, which had caused trouble for her in America—a moralistic backlash in certain quarters that only fueled ticket sales.

Duse didn't quite know what to expect as she took her seat at Turin's Teatro Carignano on February 25, 1882, to see Bernhardt act for the first time. She held her breath as the gavel sounded three times to mark the start of the performance. She watched the curtains part to reveal Camille's drawing room. The set was more lavish than the rudimentary scenery to which Eleonora was accustomed. As Sarah prepared to make her entrance, a hush of anticipation fell over the crowd. Then, suddenly, Sarah took the stage the way a general seizes his battlefield. Her power was palpable, and the house erupted into enthusiastic applause. Sarah blew kisses to the crowd and winked coyly, before folding into an exquisite curtsy. The ovation from the Italian crowd felt like it would never end.

Eleonora gazed at the diva's shimmering gown. Eleonora had imagined (and would one day use) a far simpler wardrobe, reflecting the struggles of a woman for hire. But, creative differences aside, Eleonora could not take her eyes off Sarah. Damala appeared opposite Sarah as her young bourgeois lover Armand, and his clumsy performance must have been distracting; but not enough to diminish from Sarah's radiance.

Despite ill health, Eleonora attended all of Sarah's performances. "I went every night and cried," she wrote. As an actress in residence at the Carignano, Duse would have received discounted seats—but still appearing nightly was an extravagance. It was also conspicuous.

Sarah's manager, José Schürmann, remembered scanning the crowd from the wings one evening and noticing Eleonora. He described her as "a dark young girl, her hair badly coiffed, the purest of Italian, not beautiful but with an extremely expressive face, which, in the grip of an emotion, almost becomes beautiful." Eleonora, apparently, was feeling every one of Camille's emotions— acting from her seat as the play progressed onstage. Though this

Camille was performed in the original French, Eleonora was familiar with the text and did not miss a word.

Schürmann, who would one day also represent Eleonora, did not see much hope for her at the time. In an interview he gave years later for a 1926 biography on Duse, he recalled thinking: "With that physique, I do not believe she will ever amount to much in the theater." Schürmann might very well have been right. Duse's frailty made her seem almost sickly at times. Sarah, too, was considered thin. By Victorian standards of feminine beauty, Bernhardt was practically emaciated—and yet she seemed statuesque and indelible. There was a power to Bernhardt onstage that transcended her petticoats and diamonds—an inner strength that aspiring actresses would be wise to emulate. It was one thing to gaze at Sarah on a souvenir postcard, which Eleonora had done for years, quite another to see her in the flesh. Indeed, crossing paths with Sarah in February of 1882 would be key to propelling Duse to her own stardom.

As Duse recalled years later, she was enthralled by Sarah's visit—not just by her star power, but also by her business acumen: "*A woman had achieved all that!*" Eleonora had finally discovered a female role model. And so, Duse explained, "I, too, felt myself released; I, too, felt that I had the right to do what seemed right to me, and something quite different from what I had previously been compelled to do."

But if Duse was inspired by seeing Bernhardt, the experience emboldened her to go in an entirely new creative direction. As the Rossi Company toured Italy in the years that followed, Eleonora began to take the stage quietly and in character, ignoring the audience altogether, sometimes pausing in the corner of the room to notice a speck of dust on the bookshelf. She kept her costumes simple. Her movements were never forced for the sake of blocking— they sprang from intention, an impulse from the "mind" of the character she was portraying.

Like Sarah, Eleonora had star power, but a quieter sort. She had a new sense of purpose that made Cesare Rossi and other theater managers wary. "They did not interfere with me after that," she wrote with evident satisfaction.

In 1885, the Rossi Company booked a South American tour. Duse would be playing to non-Italian spectators for the first time. As she boarded the ship in Genoa in late April, Eleonora felt excited. It would take three weeks for the ship to steam its way from the Mediterranean to the South Atlantic. "I'd like a sea journey in order to live twenty days alone," she wrote a friend, "breathing fresh and wholesome air that will renew my body and soul."

Though she and Tebaldo remained married, theirs was more of a professional relationship at this point—he managed her career and finances. They booked separate cabins on the ship: she in a state room befitting a *prima donna*, he in lesser accommodations.

Duse needed solitude. They had decided to leave their daughter in capable hands back in Italy, to spare Eleonora from the screams and entreaties of a three-year-old as she prepared herself to face her first overseas crowd. This would become a lifelong pattern. Though Eleonora was not nearly as heartless toward her daughter as Sarah's mother had once been, the rule was clear: art came first.

Eleonora had begun to write the word with a capital *A* in her letters—and she wrote many of them. Ever since seeing Sarah onstage, Duse had been pursuing her "Art" with a purpose; she, too, had begun managing her image and career. Acting as her own press agent, Duse would write to certain critics to explain what she had been trying to do onstage.

"I use everything that I pick up in my memory and everything that vibrates in my soul," she wrote to Francesco D'Arcais of *l'Opinione*. "I have never known and will never know how to act! These poor women in my plays have so entered my heart and my head . . . I stand by their side, *with* them . . . not because I crave suffering, but because *feminine compassion* is greater, more concrete, sweeter and more complete than the grief that men are used to allowing us."

Duse would one day be embraced by feminists and suffragettes, though this was never intentional. She simply strove to express the truth as she felt it—and those feelings could be profound. In an era when doctors like Jean-Martin Charcot, Josef Breuer, and Sigmund Freud focused on women's limitations, Duse attempted to portray females who were multidimensional, shaded, and complex.

One production that highlighted this was *Denise* by Alexandre Dumas *fils*, who had written the piece expressly for Eleonora. In fact, it was her story: when a young girl is seduced by an older man, she becomes pregnant with his child and is forced to give her baby to a foundling home where the newborn dies from neglect.

Eleonora had recounted the tragic episode to Count Giuseppe Primoli, an aristocratic admirer who fell deeply in love with her after seeing Eleonora act in Rome. Primoli, whose mother was a Bonaparte, was well connected in France and mentioned the incident to Dumas, who wrote a play about it for Duse to "create," which is to say to originate the role and thus set the standard for its performance. Eleonora must have been flattered; she was now like Bernhardt—an actress for whom playwrights specifically composed works. But this particular incident was so personal that it felt uncomfortable, an invasion of her privacy.

Dumas completed his play at the end of 1884, and in early January, Count Primoli arranged to read it to Eleonora at his palazzo in Rome. "You can well understand how her heart was beating," he later wrote Dumas. "The first act . . . charmed her, but she was still waiting for her part. The second act interested her, but she was still waiting."

Duse was waiting for the confession scene: the moment when Denise courageously admits her affair and its tragic outcome to another suitor—this one a decent man, who accepts her past and marries her nonetheless, a radical act of forgiveness in this stuffy Victorian era.

As Eleonora listened to the scene, "she remained breathless, her color changed; from her staring eyes tears fell on her cheeks. She got up suddenly . . . and was compelled to hear the end of the speech from behind a screen."

Yes, she would create the role.

What made the play even more poignant for Eleonora was the recent passing of Martino Cafiero, who had died of cholera (along with half the citizens of Naples). Eleonora still loved Cafiero in some way, and his death left her desolate. There was another loss, too. Some weeks before the premiere of *Denise*, Eleonora suffered a miscarriage.

Tebaldo Checchi was quite upset, particularly because he had reason to believe he was not the father. Throughout the previous year, there had been rumors of an affair between Eleonora and her leading man in *Camille*, Flavio Andò, for whom she displayed unabashed passion onstage, even kissing him on the mouth for a minute at a time. Her performance was scandalous, quite erotic, and drew sold-out audiences of men—sometimes as many as five in a box. Most were familiar with Sarah Bernhardt's histrionics in the role; now they were entranced by Eleonora's electrifying passion and subdued inner strength.

Eleonora ventured even deeper into a character's psyche in the role of Denise, a character she was unable to shake after each performance. The public was aware of the parallels to her own life—it was similar to the link between Camille and Sarah. But Bernhardt forgot the role with the first sip of after-stage champagne, while Duse wept in her dressing room for hours following each performance. "Oh, this Art consumes my life," she lamented—dramatically, as always.

One of the reasons Duse found herself sailing to tour South America in 1885 was that critics beyond Italy had begun to notice this quiet revolution on the Italian stage. A British reviewer for the *Atheneum* had traveled to Rome to watch Duse perform *Denise* at

the Teatro Valle, and praised her naturalism—although, to much
of the British public, the apogee of contemporary Italian theater
remained Adelaide Ristori, a distinguished tragedienne who had
played London in 1856, one of the first-name actresses to perform
outside her own country. After her tours in America, she became
known as "The Columbus of the Dramatic Arts."

Ristori, like her contemporary from France, Rachel, was an actress who attempted to act in a more natural manner on the stage.
In fact, this duo from the prior generation had their own Franco-
Italian rivalry, not unlike that of Duse and Bernhardt, though on a
far smaller scale.

Ristori had met Eleonora in Rome, even acted with her. She respected her younger colleague, whom she characterized in a press
interview as the archetypal fin de siècle woman "with all her maladies of hysteria, anemia and neurosis."

Though Ristori was herself in the natural school, she maintained
a certain regal dignity in her performance. Eleonora was entirely
uninhibited onstage, even wild at times—hence Ristori's descrip-
tors of "hysteria" and "neurosis," which had come into vogue,
thanks to Sigmund Freud, to label free-spirited women who did
not fit into the Victorian mold.

Duse was not alone in her deliverance. Others exploring this
new theatrical emancipation included Konstantin Stanislavski in
Moscow and Rachel in France. But one singular distinction separated Duse from all of them—including Ristori and Rachel. For
Duse, acting was spiritual.

Audiences were beginning to feel the energy Eleonora seemed
to emanate when she took the stage. As one reporter had noted,
there was a "mysterious . . . sympathetic communication" between
Duse and the audience that transcended language.

"I will make Art, always!!!" Eleonora wrote exuberantly to the
critic D'Arcais, using three exclamation points, as she often did. "I
will go to America . . . Spain. I will go to Vienna. I will go . . . I will
go . . . I will take my name as far as I can."

In these moments of mania, Eleonora was able to overcome the doubts that she certainly still had about her disruptive role in the theater. A critic like D'Arcais knew that Duse took the stage relying on her intuition in the moment and nothing else. Her performances could vary significantly from night to night. It was terrifying at times, and deeply fragile—which is why, save d'Arcais and a few others, Duse avoided journalists. She was very selective about those with whom she chose to share the mystery of The Grace.

So it enraged her when, landing in Montevideo for the first stop on her tour of South America, Duse learned that a series of interviews had been arranged by Tebaldo Checchi, her manager and husband. The two shouted at each other. He could not fathom why Eleonora would be so press-shy just when her career was poised to take off. She thought his attempts at publicity clumsy and inept. Tebaldo was jealous of the *primo attore* Flavio Andò, though it's unlikely at this point that Eleonora was still involved with him. "*Il était beau, mail il était bête,*"* she later wrote to a girlfriend.

The only man she had truly loved was Martino Cafiero—a cad, perhaps, but at least he had been a man of letters. Eleonora was desperate to meet another writer with whom she could collaborate and make "Art." Her poet would come soon enough, but for now she remained far from home in an empty marriage, which ended abruptly when Eleonora caught Tebaldo in bed with another actress in the troupe, a girl who was underage. Tebaldo agreed to leave the company and remain in South America. Eleonora fell into one of her bleak moods, and it seemed to spread—the tour unfolded poorly for all. Many of the Italians contracted yellow fever in the tropical clime; one died.

In Rio, the theater was huge, as big as an opera house—tier upon tier of boxes, with a constant murmuring coming from each, which threw Eleonora. "I felt small and helpless," she remembered

---

* He was beautiful, but stupid.

later. "For my voice to have carried, I would have had to say 'I love you' in the same voice that one says 'Begone!'"

"A complete *fiasco* for your little Nennella," she wrote to Matilde Serao, her girlfriend from Naples, using the diminutive that Martino Cafiero had coined. She was desperately lonely. She even missed her father, who had finally retired from acting and settled in Venice to paint, the avocation he had wished to pursue all along.

Eleonora had nowhere to turn, no one at her side. Her only ally was within. So one night in Rio, she prayed—she did that often, especially onstage. "There before those footlights, hateful and blessed, I said: 'Madonna, show us your Grace.'" Slowly, sweetly, it came.

Now weeping openly as she played Denise, she moved her Brazilian audience to tears and the local critics exalted her. "Dumas made *Denise*," wrote one, "and Deus made Duse."

The culmination came with a visit by Brazilian emperor Dom Pedro II, who saw Eleonora perform *La Dame aux camélias*. Deeply moved, he summoned her to his box after the performance.

Eleonora felt apprehensive. "It's hard for me to speak with a sovereign!" she wrote to Adelaide Ristori, who had given Eleonora a letter of introduction to the emperor.

Dom Pedro presented Eleonora with a heavy gold bracelet as the audience stood facing the imperial box in enthusiastic applause. Eleonora Duse had become an international star.

CHAPTER SIX

In February 1883, Sarah Bernhardt declared she was on the verge of bankruptcy and announced a "humiliating" public auction of her jewels. Imagine the stir—only a few years prior Bernhardt had headlined the most lucrative world tour in acting history, and yet now her reserves were fully depleted, or so she said. It was a good story.

The big difference between Bernhardt and all the stars that preceded her—including Ristori and Rachel—was that other divas received their press coverage in the theater section. Bernhardt's exploits usually made it to the front page.

Knowing there was no such thing as bad publicity, Sarah bragged about her extravagant lifestyle and constantly mounting debts, like the substantial sum she still owed to the Comédie-Française, which had sued her for reneging on a ten-year contract; the French court had no choice but to fine Bernhardt 100,000 francs (around half a million dollars today).

Bernhardt had plenty of treasures to sell. During her grand tour of Europe, she received gifts from kings and emperors, including a diamond brooch from the king of Spain, a precious Venetian fan from the king of Italy, and an emerald necklace from Archduke Friedrich of Vienna, who insisted that she stay in one of his palaces. An exchange of favors was expected in these circumstances, but Sarah apparently declined—out of loyalty, she said, to Aristides Damala. This was the story the press could not resist—the diva and her leading man, whose drug habit had now expanded to include cocaine. On one occasion, a doped-up Damala tore Sarah's dress midperformance, exposing her bare buttocks to the audience.

It was great theater. Not a day had gone by that past year without a piece of gossip about Sarah appearing somewhere in print. Every city in the world now had its daily tabloid; some, like New York, had several competing for headlines and market share. The name Sarah Bernhardt sold newspapers.

Sarah insisted to reporters that "this ancient Greek god is the man of my dreams." There was some truth to that. She had real feelings for him despite his many shortcomings. But the popular papers preferred to mock the couple. One cartoon featured Sarah holding Damala like a puppet, manipulating his limbs. The cartoonists had gotten it wrong, however; the roles should have been reversed. It was Damala who did what he pleased.

In spite of his addictions and infidelities, Sarah always forgave him and begged for his return. The gossip of Paris was that Damala seemed to be the only man who could satisfy her sexually, that Bernhardt had been unable to achieve orgasm until she met her "Greek god."

But even if it were true, her devotion to Damala went beyond the sex. Part of it stemmed from compassion. Sarah's sister Jeanne had also succumbed to morphine addiction, often lying comatose all day behind closed doors. Damala, for his part, avoided sunlight altogether. The writer Bram Stoker later admitted that Damala had been the inspiration for Count Dracula.

In the spring of 1882, after just a year as a couple, Bernhardt and Damala found themselves in London. Sarah had been corresponding with playwright Victorien Sardou, in preparation for her creation of the lead role of his new play, *Fédora*. She and Damala were having one of their frequent fights, which left Sarah depressed. She dispatched the following telegram to Sardou: "I am going to die and my greatest regret is not having created your play. Adieu."

Then, a few hours later, Sardou received a second telegram: "I am not dead, I am married."

The wedding had taken place on April 4, 1882, at St. Andrew's Church in London, which presented a convenient workaround for Bernhardt (officially Roman Catholic) and Damala (Greek Orthodox); they could not have been married in Paris unless Damala converted to Catholicism. The Church of England was far more lenient on the question of mixed weddings.

It seemed an impulsive decision. When asked later by Sardou why she had wed so recklessly, Sarah responded flippantly that it was the only thing she had never done. She was thirty-seven, ten years older than her husband. It was she who proposed to Damala, and he seized the chance of getting closer to her wealth. Sarah's son, Maurice, seventeen at the time, despised the man. But Sarah hoped to facilitate a rapprochement between her son and her new groom.

Upon the couple's return to Paris, Sarah purchased the Théâtre de L'Ambigu in Maurice's name and made Damala its manager, a disastrous decision that would cost her a half million francs.

Sarah's peers were baffled by her decision to dismiss professional actors so she could perform alongside an amateur. But Sarah was besotted. "Won't he make an excellent Armand?" she had asked the disapproving Alexandre Dumas *fils*. The two had already toured Europe together one year prior, ending in Turin, where they had crossed paths with Eleonora.

That fall, Bernhardt and Damala found themselves back in Paris, on separate stages this time. She was at the Vaudeville performing in *Fédora*, but Sardou had refused to approve Damala as her costar. So Damala was by himself at the Théâtre de L'Ambigu in a lesser play, *Les mères ennemies* by Catulle Mendès. His leading lady was Madame Agar, the veteran actress with whom Sarah had performed her breakout "trouser" role as Zanetto. Sarah triumphed in *Fédora*; Damala flopped. He disappeared for a few weeks on one of his increasingly frequent binges with drugs and women.

Damala would die of a drug overdose years later in 1889. Sarah had by then developed a separate career as a sculptress, and she carved a marble bust of Damala for the sarcophagus in which he was buried. The intricacy in the carving is exquisite: the folds of the cloth, his beard, rose petals, all immaculately rendered and polished to a soft sheen.

She had begun studying sculpture at age twenty-five under Mathieu Meusnier and Emilio Franceschi, two masters in Paris. Five years later, in 1874, Sarah was exhibiting her work at the very prestigious Paris Salon. Then Sarah commissioned an haute couture designer to create a special sculpting outfit for her—a pajama-like garment in white silk, complete with a *foulard*. But being the first woman of fame to wear a pants suit was not simply playacting for Sarah; she valued her time in the studio and took the work seriously. Bernhardt's fifty sculptures would eventually be displayed in museums across Europe and America.

She took special care in her portrait of Damala, still her husband at the time of his death. The elegance of the composition, the noble expression on his face, the dignity in the closed eyelids—all demonstrated her continued love for him, and her forgiveness. As Sarah once said: "We ought to hate very rarely, as it is too fatiguing, remain indifferent a great deal, forgive often, and never forget."

The auction of Sarah's jewels at the Hotel Druout in early 1883 raised 178,000 francs—not nearly enough to settle her many obligations. It wasn't simply her own debts that were crushing her. Her son, Maurice, now eighteen, had developed an insidious gambling habit and he certainly wasn't planning to get a job anytime soon. It was up to Sarah to produce income.

The first idea: what about mounting another production of *Camille*? The thirty-year-old warhorse had never failed her (she would revive it no less than twenty-two times over the next decades). But Sarah hesitated. Not another *Camille*, she sighed. Too tired, too old.

A bold and public revolution in the arts was taking place all around her. Impressionists had taken to the streets to paint in natural light. This new "naturalism" was not photorealism, but there was something more subjectively *truthful* in the intricate play of light and shadows, the painters said. By deconstructing reality in a radically new way, Monet, Renoir, and the other Impressionists had broken ranks with the Académie des Beaux-Arts and become the toast of Paris. Their paintings depicted scenes of everyday, contemporary life, not the mythological or historical scenes favored by the classical painters.

The same revolution was under way in the theater. While the old guard—Sardou, Rostand—still produced plays about queens and empresses, modern playwrights—Ibsen, Sudermann, Chekhov—were now writing about housewives and the alienation of the bourgeoisie. Sarah found this insufferable. People attended theater to escape their everyday lives, she felt, not to face a mirror. Bernhardt wouldn't know what to do as Nora or Hedda Gabler. She preferred mythic figures from the past: Cleopatra and Joan of Arc.

Yet Sarah prided herself on being thoroughly modern, too; her showy embrace of the latest technologies, whether motorcars or hot air balloons, sold many a newspaper. During the 1880 tour of America, Sarah had famously detoured to Menlo Park to visit the laboratory of Thomas Edison, where she immortalized her voice in one of the earliest phonograph recordings. Later she would become the first world-class actress to appear on film. But somehow Sarah resisted modernity on the stage.

Critics were starting to take note of Bernhardt's dated style. When she toured Russia in 1881, writer Ivan Turgenev had called her a "grand poseur." Anton Chekhov, still a medical student at the time, condemned her as "ultra sensational," her so-called art nothing more than "enchantment smothered in artifice [and] premeditated trickiness." In a private letter to Turgenev, he wrote: "the unbearable Sarah Bernhardt . . . has nothing except a wonderful voice—everything else about her is false, cold, and affected—together with the most repulsive Parisian chic."

The English actress Ellen Terry, a contemporary of Bernhardt, was more nuanced in her evaluation of Sarah's acting: "On the stage, she has always seemed to me more a symbol, an ideal, an epitome than a *woman*. . . . No one plays a love scene better, but it is a *picture* of love that she gives, a strange orchidaceous picture rather than a suggestion of ordinary human passion as felt by ordinary human people."

But just as Bernhardt had no interest in being ordinary, she rarely cared what the critics had to say. "The Divine One" was as popular as ever—and the public seemed never to tire of *Camille*, which is why the role remained Sarah's favorite. The play itself was at once both old and new. It was thoroughly modern—risqué, even—in bringing the audience into a demimonde boudoir. But its heroine, the love-struck courtesan Marguerite, is one in a line of mythologized women of ill repute going back to Mary Magdalene.

Sarah had begun to hear talk of this new Italian, Duse, who had adopted *Camille* into her own repertoire, performing the role in a radically different style; and certain critics had begun to favor Eleonora.

Sarah knew how easily she could be forgotten if she committed the cardinal sin of any artist: being boring. She needed to keep topping herself.

Then, a sudden thought—Victorien Sardou.

"She conducts business, like everything else, at breakneck speed," playwright Sardou told a journalist in 1884, "letting herself be robbed left, right and center, and taking on things that she cannot hold to. This leads to anger, rancor, and hatred which is all the more destructive for not always having an outlet."

When the playwright went to visit her, he found Sarah in a state of "violent over-excitement, writhing, rolling on and gnawing at the carpet, weeping in sheer exasperation." The scene, likely staged by Sarah and certainly embellished by Sardou, made good copy. The newspapers flew off the rack, as the public anticipation mounted: Bernhardt was collaborating again with Sardou, who had written *Fédora*—Bernhardt's last hit. Now a new play was in the works, the title strikingly similar: *Théodora*. Sarah had played queens, Sarah had played harlots. In *Théodora* she would play both within the same character—a combination she hoped would prove irresistible to her fans. Set in sixth-century Byzantium, *Théodora* tells the mostly true story of a brothel-girl-turned-empress-of-Rome whose improbable rise to power mimicked the trajectory of the play's leading lady.

Sardou was not a modern playwright by any stretch. George Bernard Shaw coined the term "Sardoodledom" to describe his baroque but well-meaning work. But his outsized, mythologized heroines were perfect for Bernhardt, and she knew it. She also knew her audience better than anybody.

While the play may have been larger than life, Sarah insisted that it be accurate in its details. Sardou did extensive research, determined to give nineteenth-century Parisians an accurate picture of life during late antiquity.

Théodora's father had been the bear keeper at the Hippodrome of Constantinople, where his daughter began her career as an underage belly dancer. Her most famous routine involved geese pecking seeds off her bare torso while she writhed suggestively on her back. Théodora used her eroticism to woo increasingly powerful men and was soon wed to Emperor Justinian. From her throne, she became an ardent champion of the rights of women, urging her husband to pass laws against pimping and sex trafficking. Like Bernhardt, she used her power to elevate the status of actresses, giving them more of a say in their careers. Théodora also granted women greater control of their dowries and inheritances. But her inevitable downfall came when she fell in love with a commoner, one who happened to be plotting against the emperor.

In the final scene of Sardou's play, the emperor Justinian catches them together and murders Théodora by strangling her with a silk scarf. It was a perfect death scene for Bernhardt, especially as staged by Félix Duquesnel. The former director of the Théâtre Odéon, where Sarah had her first success as Zanetto, Duquesnel had now assumed the directorship of a new theater: the Porte Saint-Martin. Though not as prestigious as the Odéon, it was an extremely popular venue, and enormous, which allowed for formidable sets and grand productions. Duquesnel brought in the showy Sardou as his house playwright.

Sarah had not performed in six months when she took the stage as Théodora on December 26, 1884. Her entrance was delayed, a clever calculation by Sardou to allow the public to first take in the sumptuous scenery. There were rugs of incomparable richness, a sofa of tiger skins backed by a peacock's tail of enamel and rare jewels. A journalist writing in the *New York Times* was awed by the "attendants, guardians, eunuchs, all in costumes of endless variety and color, but as exquisitely harmonized as if the tableau were a canvas painted by an artist of discretion." When Sarah made her entrance—wearing a dress of *bleu de ciel* satin, with a train four yards long covered in embroidered peacocks with ruby eyes and feathers of emeralds and sapphires—her subjects prostrated themselves to kiss her feet. If the entrance was calculated to produce an ovation, it worked.

Over 4,500 gems had been sewn by hand onto Théodora's gowns. The costume budget alone exceeded that of most productions. Sarah had supervised her wardrobe's design, traveling to Ravenna to make sketches from the mosaics of the Byzantine empress at the Basilica di San Vitale. It had taken an army to construct the sets, too, and the staging involved two hundred people at times to capture the teeming energy of Byzantium. The audience was dazzled.

Émile Perrin, director of the Comédie-Française, called it "the greatest achievement in mise-en-scène of the nineteenth century." A write-up in *Le Théâtre* declared unequivocally: "*Théodora* is the most beautiful and most complete creation of Madame Sarah

Bernhardt's career. . . . In it, she is both a tragedienne and a comedienne, energetic and supple, gracious and terrible. She is incomparable. She is extraordinary."

As a playwright, Sardou certainly had his detractors. Henry James referred to Sardou as "that supremely clever contriver." But Sarah was exonerated for *Théodora*'s convoluted plot. Wrote a critic: "The press is unanimous: Sardou's play does not exist, only Sarah exists!"

The press was not, in fact, unanimous. To increasing numbers of critics, Bernhardt's style felt hopelessly dated. But the public was slow to sway.

Théodora was an unprecedented success. The production ran for three hundred performances until Christmas of the following year, returning Sarah to her rightful place in the spotlight, where she had every intention of staying.

CHAPTER SEVEN

Sailing back to Italy in 1886, Eleonora felt the weight of the world. It was thrilling, on the one hand, to be coming into her own power—a power that would soon give her freedom to pursue her "Art" in the manner she saw fit. But her personal life was empty. She admitted to her manager Rossi that she had begun to feel "a sadness without a name."

As a Catholic, Duse could never divorce; she and Tebaldo would be permanently separated, which made Eleonora a single parent—something she, so often traveling and self-absorbed, was ill equipped to be. Enrichetta would soon be dispatched to an expensive boarding school.

In February of 1887, still part of the Rossi Company, Eleonora traveled to Milan. The city was abuzz in anticipation of Giuseppe Verdi's new opera, *Otello*, his first work since *Aïda*, written sixteen years earlier. Though Duse had met Verdi's librettist, Arrigo Boito, she was shy about asking him for a ticket to the premiere, since the event was apparently sold out. Still, she longed for a chance to meet the composer, and fortunately another writer who knew Eleonora secured her a spot in the coveted author's box, alongside Verdi and Boito. An unforgettable night, the opera was interrupted so many times by ovations that La Scala management would write an open letter begging the public to hold their applause until the end of each act. Eleonora was thrilled to share the company of true artists.

One week later, she invited Verdi and Boito to a play she was performing in Milan called *Pamela*—a classic, written in the 1750s by Carlo Goldoni, a man ahead of his time. Like Eleonora's grandfather, Goldoni had rebelled against commedia dell'arte tradition, writing more realistic roles and less predictable plots. He was considered the founder of Italian realistic comedy—a man close to Eleonora's heart.

Duse felt anxious as the gavel sounded to hush the crowd. The curtains parted; she glanced furtively toward the boxes, breaking her rule of not making eye contact with the crowd. There he was: the noble Giuseppe Verdi, along with his writer, Arrigo Boito, who smiled at her in encouragement. She needed it. She was about to perform a century-old play in a thoroughly modern style: a radical choice she hoped to showcase for Verdi—but even more so for Boito, to whom she was increasingly drawn, because he was both a writer and a spiritualist. *Pamela*'s story—the ennobling of a servant girl—was close to Eleonora's own. The patricians appreciated her performance, roaring with laughter from their first-tier box. Backstage at intermission, Boito and Duse were seen holding hands. Within a week they would be lovers.

Boito was forty-five to Eleonora's twenty-eight, which made him something of a father figure. They had met three years prior, when Boito saw her perform in *Camille* at the Teatro Carcano; already smitten, he had asked for a photograph. Boito was the son of an Italian painter and a Polish countess, a bespectacled, proper gentleman with a walrus mustache who had composed the opera *Mefistofole* and written librettos for many other significant works. In Boito, Eleonora had found the pedigreed partner she sought.

Eleonora called him "The Saint" for his quiet brilliance and loving guidance. "Boito seemed to have been sent to her by some higher power," explained actress and confidante Eva Le Gallienne. Certainly, he was wholly unlike her first love, Martino Cafiero. Though all three of her significant romances—Cafiero, Boito, and later d'Annunzio—were with writers, only Boito had a deep, spiritual inclination. Thus, beyond being a literary mentor, Boito also became her guru.

"Up, upwards toward the Vision!" he would tell her. Boito,

like Duse, believed that "Art" came from a realm beyond the human mind. The job of artists was to cast their egos aside in order to become channels for this higher inspiration.

Though Carl Jung was a mere teenager at the time, concepts like the collective unconscious were already popular in certain circles. Russian medium Helena Blavatsky had founded her Theosophical Society in 1875 and then published *Isis Unveiled*, mapping out an "Ancient Wisdom" that underlay all the world's religions. In America, the Transcendentalists had been exploring Eastern mysticism and its expansive embrace of indwelling divinity. As described in the essay "The Over-Soul," published by Emerson in 1841: "within man is the soul of the whole; the wise silence; the universal beauty, to which every part and particle is equally related, the eternal ONE."

Across continents, there was a movement under way to broaden the definition of "God." Far from a bearded man throwing down lightning bolts, the Divine for these seekers was intimate. In a letter written to Boito six months into their relationship, Eleonora promised to keep looking for spiritual inspiration. "You'll see," she wrote, "if I stay well, I hope to *see the Vision* every night. You'll see!"

In a subsequent letter, she wrote: "The supreme power spoke to me of what I must do in my life. I bowed my head . . . and said—so be it."

Boito inspired Eleonora to expand her repertoire. In a bold move, she formed her own theater company in late 1887 using her own funds, just as Sarah had done, which allowed her to handpick her fellow actors. She chose onetime lover Flavio Andò for her leading man, along with other actors she admired—ones, she thought, who would be open to the new style that increasingly obsessed her. Eleonora knew it would take time to get the others to shift their paradigm and was wise enough not to force the issue. Rather than lecturing her actors, she preferred at first to lead by example.

The greatest emancipation for Duse was the fact that she would now be choosing her own plays. While Ibsen had yet to be translated into Italian, Eleonora could now perform works by rising local playwrights like Giuseppe Giacosa, Giovanni Verga, and Marco Praga. She also ventured into comedy, a genre that Bernhardt generally avoided; other than the occasional revival of Molière and later *Cyrano de Bergerac*, Bernhardt chose to appear almost exclusively in tragic roles—better suited, she thought, to her style of acting. Comedy required more spontaneity, timing, and strong listening skills—all of which came quite naturally to Eleonora, which is why she liked to include comedies in her repertoire. If nothing else, comedies provided a way to help shift her mood, which drifted often toward the morose. Eleonora did not respond, however, to contemporary Italian comedies; she chose, instead, to revive classic Goldoni comedies from the prior century.

Shakespeare—at Boito's prodding—was also in the mix. Flush from his success in writing the libretto for *Otello*, Boito began adapting *Antony and Cleopatra* into Italian for Duse. A literary snob, Boito was contemptuous of popular theater, including most of the plays in Duse's current repertoire, with which she was touring with modest success around Italy. She had made very safe choices in her first season as a manager—a series of proven hits by Sardou and Dumas, all of them made popular by Sarah Bernhardt. Duse also added the deeply personal *Denise*. Though Boito joined her for a performance in Palermo, he was unimpressed. The only way to do justice to the theater was to put on impeccable plays— hence, his idea of translating Shakespeare.

While Duse revered him deeply, his mind at least, there were ways in which she and Boito were deeply incompatible. Boito was secretive: he insisted their affair remain hidden, conducted through a series of clandestine rendezvous in remote locations. They would never go out in public in major cities, where he (and even she, now) was likely to be recognized. The relationship had its challenges when they were apart, too. Eleonora, in Boito's eyes, was overly passionate and emotionally needy—writing three letters to him in a single day, on occasion. At times he would disappear on long retreats, which only increased Eleonora's anxiety. Boito, in fact, had another secret mistress.

Marriage was unlikely, for Eleonora could not divorce; she harbored fantasies, nonetheless, of a makeshift family with Boito and Enrichetta under one roof. She craved a sense of normalcy. Boito, however, hinted that Eleonora would have to give up acting for their relationship to become serious, something she would never consider.

Antonio e Cleopatra—or *Cleop*, as Eleonora called it—would be the first major test of their already complicated relationship. The role of Cleopatra was becoming a must for any rising actress in the late nineteenth century. Boito made significant cuts to the original text, but his translation was nonetheless ambitious. There were thirty-eight scene changes and twenty speaking parts. Eleonora only had a dozen actors in her company, so half were forced to play multiple roles.

Still secretive about their relationship, Boito asked for his name to be removed from the playbill and did not attend the 1888 premiere, which saddened Eleonora. But what doomed the play was the disconnect between the mythic grandeur of the Egyptian queen and the understated simplicity of Eleonora's style. It was a combination that the public could not accept. Critics panned the play, too; it would be the biggest flop of Eleonora's career. Take this excoriation by William Archer, writing for the *World*:

> It is said that Signora Duse understands no English; and this fact, if fact it be, is the explanation and excuse of her Cleopatra. If she could read Shakespeare's *Antony and Cleopatra* she would either drop the part from her repertory or act it very differently. She would realize that the play is not a badly constructed domestic drama in outlandish costumes, but a glorious love-poem. . . . Signora Duse's Cleopatra is never for an

instant that incarnation of love and luxury of all that is superb
and seductive in womanhood, which has haunted the minds of
men for nineteen centuries. She is simply a bright little woman
like her . . . [Goldoni heroine] Mirandolina. She is not Cleopatra, she is Cleopatrina, Cleopatrinetta.

The critics were likewise vicious on the matter of Boito's butchery
of the original text, where he had drastically pruned the role of
Antony and cut entire scenes. Boito was ashamed of the failure,
later writing to Eleonora: "We only thought about one thing and
that was: taking from this powerful poem all the divine essence of
love and pain and we shut our eyes to everything else. That was a
mistake."

Duse forgave him, but the failure stung. She was hurt that he
had forced her into a grand role, then disowned the play by remov-
ing his name. But what bothered her most may have been that she
had discovered her limits as an actress by finding a role she was unable to perform.

For Sarah, however, Cleopatra was simply another role that
confirmed her stardom. In 1893, her Queen of the Nile would
mark another triumph for the nearly fifty-year-old Bernhardt,
though the play was simply another *Théodora* in disguise—
sumptuous palaces and improbably elaborate costumes, trans-
planted from Byzantium to Alexandria and culminating with Sarah
clutching a live, writhing snake onstage for the suicide scene. The
Parisian audience was enthralled.

In Milan, however, Eleonora performed her *Cleopatra* only
twice before shelving it. To replace *Cleop* with something reliable,
she sighed and chose Bernhardt's standard: *La Dame aux camélias.*

In the fall of 1899, needing a change of scenery, Duse decided to
go on tour. It would be her first time overseas as the manager of
her own company, and Eleonora chose an unlikely destination:

Egypt. She was determined to give Boito's adaptation of *Antony and Cleopatra* another go—and what better place than in the land in which it was set? Better still, Bernhardt had toured Egypt herself earlier that same year. By performing in the same theaters for the same audiences and critics, it would allow Eleonora to gauge her artistry against that of her idol in a low-profile setting. In five short years, they would be plotting dueling productions in London; for now, Duse was content to test herself against Sarah indirectly.

Alexandria was a bustling port city under British rule, situated at the mouth of the Nile with access to the Suez Canal and trade routes to the East. One quarter of the city's population was foreign, primarily British, Italian, and French. Eleonora felt hardly rapturous upon landing in Port Said. "A hateful country," she wrote to Boito, "a hateful place to work . . . Alexandria is nothing but a *Bazaar*—with stupefied people who smoke from morning to night—dazed by the sun—asleep—huddled up." She was disgusted by the beggars, whom she saw as "dirty and wretched"—they reminded her too much, perhaps, of her now distant youth.

The French quarter of Alexandria was the largest, and its inhabitants largely avoided Duse's performances—out of snobbish allegiance to Sarah, who had played there some months earlier. The Italians showed up though, along with locals, who were much more receptive to *Cleopatra*, as Eleonora had hoped.

Duse rarely mingled with her actors on tour—preferring instead to keep a strict separation between her personal and professional side. But she detested meals in solitude, so she had recruited a French traveling companion on this trip: a young Parisian named Marthe, who had been introduced to her in Palermo by the Marchesa di Ganzaria, and could provide interesting conversation; it also gave Duse a chance to practice her French. A much-discussed topic, of course, was Paris, a city Duse was starting to take an interest in.

The tour moved on to Cairo, where Eleonora marveled at the Pyramids. But she was taken ill with influenza after a few shows and had to cancel the rest of her engagement. While Sarah's tour earlier that year had included Egypt, Turkey, Sweden, Norway, and Russia, Eleonora's was far more modest; once she was well, the company set off for Spain, their last stop.

Spaniards seemed to understand her. Perhaps it was the similarity of Italian to Spanish—a factor that had assisted her popularity in Latin America. Her run in Spain proved a success, both commercially and critically; Duse was pleased that audiences were beginning to appreciate what she was bringing to the stage. Between shows, she attended bullfights and fended off Spanish gentlemen. But this leg of the tour was cut short, too, when cholera broke out in Spain.

As her company returned to Italy, Eleonora decided to take a side trip to Paris, Sarah's hometown. Though it would be years before she gained the confidence to play on a Parisian stage, Eleonora wanted to see why the City of Light was considered a theatrical mecca. She secretly attended a performance at the Comédie-Française and was horrified by what she saw, describing the actors as being "hacks," the actresses "painted dolls."

While in Paris, however, Duse had an experience that moved her to tears: she met the sixty-five-year-old Alexandre Dumas *fils*, who had written *Denise* for her, the play that told the story of the death of her infant son. The playwright felt honored to meet Duse and offered her roses from his garden—the feeling was mutual. Duse knew she was at her best when she could connect to the women she portrayed; she yearned for an Italian writer who could create the parts that she craved. Boito, it seems, was not he. But there was another playwright in their circle who showed promise: Giuseppe Giacosa, the man who had brokered her ticket to the premiere of *Otello*.

Giacosa was one of the few playwrights working in the new style of realistic narrative. Eleonora had acted in his last play, *Tristi amori (Sad Loves)*, about a married woman who must choose between her husband and her lover—similar in some ways to the melodramas of Dumas. But the text felt entirely different in its details and execution. It begins with a kiss on the mouth (specified in the stage directions) between the heroine and her lover, who declares his undying love to her. But do you *like* me, she responds. Fending off his kisses, she poses the question three times. Do you like me?

Later in the play comes a scene where the wife, even as her marriage risks collapse, must go over the household accounts with the maid. The combination of scandalous passion and humdrum daily life was very new, and Duse loved it.

She did not perform in the play's 1887 premiere. It opened with another actress who failed to grasp its modernism—and the play bombed. Duse loved taking on parts in which other actresses had had a misstep; she liked that challenge. And she felt a kinship with Giacosa's heroine, Emma.

The name was a clear reference to Emma Bovary, the similarly adulterous heroine of Flaubert's novel. When *Madame Bovary* was first published in 1856, it had caused a scandal. A story of a woman who tries to escape her suffocating petit-bourgeois life through an illicit love affair, the novel was an outright rejection of romanticism. *Madame Bovary* became the subject of an obscenity trial, in which the prosecutors argued not only that the novel was immoral, but also that *realism* in literature was, in itself, an offense against art and decency.

Flaubert prevailed against the prosecutors in France, but the novel remained banned in Italy for nearly a decade. While Flaubert's tragic heroine took arsenic in his finale, Giacosa's Emma, one generation later, would make the more practical choice to try and save her marriage. Her husband takes her back, despite himself, for the well-being of their daughter—a simple, painful compromise that is impossible to act with poses and artifice, which is why the play initially flopped.

Eleonora mounted her own production of *Tristi amori* in Turin later that year. The house was enormous, with a seating capacity of two thousand, but every seat was filled, and people even stood in the aisles, many of them students eager to experience Eleonora's new style of performance. As a critic described the play, "There are no scenes written for effect, no tirades, no display of fine sentiments or ostentation of wicked passions. . . . A glance, a gesture, a silence—and the state of her soul appears to the public in its true light." It was a modern drama for a modern audience. Yet it failed, ultimately, to win a broad audience beyond the rapturous opening night crowd in Turin.

Two years later, to Duse's shock, Giacosa announced that he would be writing his next play in medieval verse—for Sarah Bernhardt.

"Does he have a fungus on the brain?" Eleonora wrote incredulously to Boito. She could not fathom why, when most artists in their circle were experimenting with new forms, Giacosa would favor an arcane style and a bygone star. "Ask him if he wants me to send him Dr. Morisani," she wrote. Morisani, her gynecologist, had been treating her for a fungal infection.

Boito was equally flummoxed. "It's true," he responded. "The Hebrew seductress has seduced our friend."

But by encroaching on Duse's domain, Sarah was also paying Eleonora a compliment: their rivalry was now official.

The icy winter was just beginning to thaw in March of 1891, when Duse arrived in St. Petersburg for her first tour of Russia. It was exactly ten years after Sarah had traveled the country, when Turgenev and Chekhov had mocked her as "a grand poseur."

The idea of touring Russia had come to Duse from Count Alexander Wolkoff, a wealthy expatriate living and painting in Venice. Eleonora had traveled to Venice several years earlier in the hopes of a romantic weekend with Boito. But the librettist, who had begun work on Verdi's *Falstaff*, failed to show; so Eleonora occupied herself with the allure of the canals and the attentions of the foreign aristocrat. She had become frustrated with the dispassionate and noncommittal Boito and was yearning for a new source of inspiration. Though Wolkoff was married to an Englishwoman at the time, he and Eleonora became lovers.

Wolkoff was handsome, moody, and complex—a philanderer, very charming, and well connected. Praising Eleonora's sensitivity and her beauty, Wolkoff promised to make introductions for her to Russian society: "a cultivated audience" with which she was sure to have success.

With the exception of America, perhaps, no country was more primed to latch on to realism than Russia. Serfdom, the system that tied Russian peasants to their landlords, had been abolished by Tsar Alexander II in 1861, just a few years before Lincoln's Emancipation Proclamation. With this came a rapid rise in literacy and an eightfold increase in the number of university students. Though socialism had its roots in romanticism, the Bolsheviks, in their desire for art to reflect and impact social reality, adhered to realism in theater and literature. Dostoevsky, Tolstoy, and Turgenev were early proponents of this form. Maxim Gorky, who had become a vagabond at age eight after being thrown out of his grandparents' home, wrote fourteen plays in which he depicted the most miserable of human lives so realistically that audiences were afraid to sit in the front rows. Anton Chekhov, another abandoned child, whose abusive father deserted the family to avoid his creditors, wrote plays thick with tension and subtext.

Wolkoff was convinced Russia would be the ideal place to recognize Eleonora's subtle genius. She selected *La Dame aux camélias* for her debut on the Russian stage—the very play that Sarah Bernhardt had used to open *her* first Russian tour. While radicals like Chekhov and Turgenev had sneered at Bernhardt, certain Moscow critics had been effusive. Following a command performance at the Winter Palace in St. Petersburg, Sarah had curtsied before Tsar Alexander II, who had cut her short, saying: "No, it is *we* who must bow to you."

By opening with *Camille*, Duse threw down the gauntlet in a competition that was becoming evident to all; the *New York Times* was already calling Eleonora "Bernhardt's Italian rival." Rivalries among stars were common in the theater world, sometimes even within families. But this showdown would become larger than all those that had preceded it—Bernhardt and Duse's rivalry would change the art itself.

Despite successes in Spain and Latin America, Duse was largely unknown in Russia; her first few performances were marked by half-empty houses. Part of the problem was the language barrier. While French was a second, if not first, language for many Russian aristocrats, Italian remained incomprehensible. That was another reason Duse had chosen *Camille*—a play that everyone knew. Eleonora hoped her features and gestures would convey universally recognizable emotions. Latvian/Norwegian writer and psychologist Laura Hansson certainly thought they did, noting that Eleonora acted "in such a natural . . . and lifelike manner, that a knowledge of the language was not absolutely indispensable to the enjoyment of the piece."

Gradually, the Russians began to take note. Alexey Suvorin, the most influential critic in St. Petersburg, wrote in the conservative *Novoye Vremya*: "La Duse is a truly remarkable artist. She does not command Sarah Bernhardt's gift for advertising, but she surpasses her in talent, in extraordinary rightness of tone." Suvorin's review was widely read and caused Duse's next performance, four days later, to sell out. It was Boito's *Antonio e Cleopatra*, the second of sixteen plays in Eleonora's current repertoire. Among those in attendance was Anton Chekhov, who had begun writing his own plays, though still without acclaim, due in large measure—he contended—to the boring, wooden actresses who were unable to interpret his plays.

Watching Duse perform, he had an epiphany. "I have just seen the Italian actress Duse in Shakespeare's Cleopatra," he wrote that midnight in an impassioned letter to his sister. "I do not know Italian, but she acted so well that I felt I was understanding every word. What a marvelous actress! Never before have I seen anything like it."

Eleonora's success in Russia stemmed from her being embraced not merely by the aristocracy but by the proletariat as well, who saw their own struggles in the complex heroines she portrayed. Her immense capacity to express anguish seemed to touch the heart of even the most cynical Russians—"purifying our souls," proclaimed Aleksandr Kugel, one of the most articulate critics of the day. As Catherine Schuler wrote in *Women in Russian Theatre*: "Duse's emotionally lacerated heroines touched a chord in the Russian spirit that Bernhardt, with her callous calculations, Parisian cynicism, outrageous fashions, and scandalous escapades, could not."

There was an apparent "selflessness" with which Duse took the stage that got misconstrued by some of her local admirers. For certain men, Duse's art seemed to align perfectly with the Russian concept of *zhenstvenost*—an idealized notion of femininity that required women to be passively subservient in both public and private life so as to maintain the integrity of the family and the nation. Something about the way Duse behaved in the presence of her male costar prompted a Russian reviewer to write: "Duse devotes herself to men with the sincerity and heartfelt conviction of her whole feminine essence."

True, in all of her performances, Eleonora's commitment was absolute—but it was a commitment to her own role, to The Grace, to the women she hoped to channel, not to any man. Certain Russians knew exactly what she was doing. When the Duse Company moved from St. Petersburg to Moscow later that spring, her talent was beheld by a man who would go on to influence generations of actors: Konstantin Stanislavski, the father of "method acting."

Actors had an even lower status in Russia than in the rest of

Europe—until recently they had been serfs, quite literally the property of the nobility. Born into one of the wealthiest families in Russia, Stanislavski, like Eleonora, was determined to elevate the profession to an art. He pioneered "living the part," staying in character for days at a time and going out in public disguised, for example, as a tramp or a drunk. "When you play a good man, try to find out where he is bad," he once advised an actor, "and when you play a villain, try to find where he is good." This became known as Stanislavski's Principle of Opposites, a technique for creating multidimensional characters.

Eleonora gave nine performances in Moscow over several weeks in May 1891, and Stanislavski attended every one, along with several of his best students, who were riveted by her nuanced performances. Each moment seemed like a spontaneous creation, unpremeditated and unrehearsed. On a different night, she might play the same line in an entirely different way. And it was clear she knew how to create the space between the lines: the pauses, the glances, the character's inner thoughts, which seemed almost audible.

Then there was the novel concept of the Fourth Wall, an invisible barrier between Eleonora and her audience, which made her appear to be unaware of anyone but the actors on the stage. It was revolutionary.

CHAPTER EIGHT

The Bernhardts had finally arrived.

Sarah's dilettante son, Maurice, had wed a princess from Poland, and now there was a royal heir. Sarah doted on her new granddaughter for exactly two seasons. Then in 1891—the same year that Duse was in Russia—Bernhardt set off for a tour of her own: but west, not east. She was scheduled to open on Broadway.

Sarah was not the first grandmother to headline an American tour, and she would not be the last—the Italian Adelaide Ristori acted well into her sixties, England's Ellen Terry had a career spanning seven decades. But these women were by far the exception. Most actresses "past their prime" were shunned by managers because of their diminished drawing power.

Sarah knew that fame was elusive and worked daily to stay relevant, both on the stage and off. She courted the press at every opportunity with tales of her exotic, over-the-top life, prompting the *New York Times* to print: "To hear Mme. Bernhardt tell of her tour is like hearing a French comedy." The enchanted journalist concluded: "She enters into the spirit of each recital with the eagerness of a child, and as she talks [she] sometimes breaks into quaint English, which makes her story all the more piquant."

Bernhardt had equal fervor on the boards. In her indomitable style, she had recently played a teenager when she took the stage in 1890 as Joan of Arc and brought down the house as inquisitors demanded that she state her age.

"Nineteen," declared Sarah, winking conspiratorially at the delighted crowd. But Bernhardt was not ageless; and she injured herself during *Joan of Arc* by falling repeatedly to her knees, as called for in the script. Her right knee became so inflamed that she was ordered to two months of bed rest—a near impossibility for the mercurial Sarah, who routinely ignored doctors' orders. She chose, instead, to go on tour.

Bernhardt was well aware of Duse by now. *La Dame de Challant,* the play she had selected for her 1891 Broadway opening, had been written by Duse's friend Giuseppe Giacosa, who had composed it in French expressly for Bernhardt. He had hardly kept it a secret from Duse, or the rest of Italy for that matter. In a series of very public lectures before departing with Sarah for America, Giacosa had attacked the Italians for not supporting local playwrights, suggesting he had been given no choice but to fashion his play for a foreign star—an idea that infuriated Duse. Prior to Sarah's tour, Eleonora had cajoled Giacosa into translating the play into Italian for her; she had tried to upstage Bernhardt's Broadway premiere by mounting her own Italian production two months earlier.

Duse's *La Signora di Challant* opened on October 14, 1891, in Turin, and critics came from all over Italy for the sold-out premiere. The production was an expensive one, with opulent medieval sets reminiscent of Sarah's productions, quite unlike Eleonora's usual aesthetic—she seemed to be anticipating how Bernhardt might soon be staging her production on Broadway.

But Duse's lavish scenery was singled out by critics as "distracting," and the public had a tepid response. In translating his verse play from French into Italian, Giacosa had reverted to prose—a form more appropriate, he thought, for Eleonora's modern style. But the play lost its lyricism; Duse's *Challant* was a failure.

Bernhardt's turn came two months later, and she performed it in the Symbolic style—more suited to verse. Sarah had yet to see the new theatrical style—Duse's *verismo*—that had everyone talking, and it didn't particularly faze her just yet. While an increasing number of prominent actors had started to experiment with a more naturalistic style—Stanislavski in Moscow, the American Edwin

Booth, the English actress Ellen Terry—Sarah felt it was simply a fad that would come and go. Good acting was a subjective matter, after all, and legions of fans, along with numerous critics, continued to embrace Sarah.

While still "great"—the greatest, in the mind of many—Bernhardt was seldom thought of as a "serious" actress. Ellen Terry had made a career of acting in plays by William Shakespeare; Sarah gravitated toward more commercial fare. Even in weighty roles like Joan of Arc, Sarah might lighten the mood with a wink to the crowd. She relied on sensationalism such as carrying live snakes in her version of *Cleopatra*, which had been streamlined and heavily abridged.

And yet every time Bernhardt took the stage, she moved people deeply, even with the poses—for the public had been trained for millennia to accept the conventions of stylized acting as true.

"By all means see Sarah Bernhardt as la Comptesse de Challant," exhorted the *New York Times*. "Go to medieval Italy by way of the Standard Theatre and see the romance and intrigue of that era illumined by genius. . . . Bernhardt's acting has never been finer." The unqualified rave went even further: "No one could ask to see a more exquisite portrayal of the mind distraught than she gives in the short fourth act. The pathos of that cannot be resisted. It leaves the spectator with something very like heartache, and there are tears in his eyes."

Sarah was still making them weep. Even the men.

The grand tour made her the wealthiest actress in history. Sarah had insisted on being paid in cash before every performance, and her bags of gold sovereigns became the stuff of legend, appearing in caricatures in newspapers across the world. These cartoons were often anti-Semitic, portraying Bernhardt with a long, hooked nose, greedily hoarding her loot. As always, Sarah took the criticism in stride, even flaunted it. "This cherished blood of Israel that runs in my veins impels me to travel," she declared to a reporter. "I often take the train or steamer without even asking where I'm going. What does it matter to me?"

This devil-may-care Sarah was irresistible; she never allowed herself to be a victim.

Sarah was fêted at every port by emperors and kings. And they were not her only admirers—impetuous young men fought duels over her, others wrote sonnets. In Buenos Aires, Bernhardt had amused herself by taking two lovers in their early twenties. "Ah, Sarah! Sarah!" rhapsodized one eighteen-year-old poet. "Sarah is grace, youth, divinity! I am beside myself. My God, what a woman!"

She was showered with gifts. In Argentina, they bequeathed her thirteen thousand acres of land; in Peru, a cartload of guano (more precious, to some, than gold). In Australia, she had picked up a koala, a possum, and a wallaby to add to her growing menagerie, which traveled with her on tour, requiring a full-time zookeeper.

Red carpets met her at every stop, along with cannons, marching bands, and countless renditions of "La Marseillaise." In Bucharest, a command performance before the queen of Romania was abruptly interrupted because Sarah had reduced the exiled queen of Serbia to convulsive sobs. Such was the Bernhardt effect: fainting women, swooning men. Among the many who idolized her was the young Oscar Wilde.

If every writer has his muse, for Oscar it was Sarah. She represented ideals that were very dear to him: defiance of authority and seizing control of one's destiny. Whether playing trouser roles, sleeping in a coffin, or having a stuffed bat perched atop her hat, Bernhardt made no attempt to hide her eye-popping self-expression—even in sexual escapades, where she was open to both genders. She had an ongoing affair with the androgynous, suit-wearing artist Louise Abbéma. While the term "bisexual" had been introduced in 1886 by Richard von Krafft-Ebing in his landmark *Psychopathia Sexualis*, it was still risqué for Sarah to flaunt her relationship with a woman.

Abbéma painted Sarah on numerous occasions. She was talented, a regular exhibitor at the Paris Salon, and one of a handful of female artists from France to have their work on display at the 1893 World's Fair in Chicago. Another was, fittingly, Sarah Bernhardt, who chose to exhibit a bust of her fellow honoree Louise Abbéma. It had been bold enough to sculpt a well-known homosexual in the first place; now choosing to exhibit that bust at a World's Fair—the most visible place imaginable—was scandalous.

Oscar Wilde, who had been observing Sarah for some time, was now officially enthralled. He had begun thinking about writing a new play attacking the prudishness and repressed sexuality of Victorian London. But Wilde needed a vehicle for his message, and a way to disguise it. He chose the story of Salomé.

Wilde completed his play in the spring of 1892, writing in French expressly for Sarah Bernhardt. He was giddy when the diva, back from her epic tour of the Americas, accepted the part. Sarah relished biblical figures, but it was not to be—at least not in London. The London Examiner of Plays, Edward F. Smyth Pigott, banned *Salomé* on the grounds of blasphemy, citing an obscure sixteenth-century statute, rarely enforced, that prohibits the representation of biblical characters onstage. In a letter to a colleague, however, he expressed what truly disgusted him:

> It is a miracle of impudence . . . [Salomé's] love turns to fury because John will not let her kiss him *on the mouth*—and in the last scene, where she brings in his head—if you please— on a "charger"—she *does* kiss his mouth in a paroxysm of sexual despair. The piece is written in French—half biblical, half pornographic.

Artists like Oscar Wilde were determined to shed light on the sexual hypocrisy of his Victorian times. In 1865, Edouard Manet had famously painted *Olympia*, a reclining naked prostitute. Exhibited briefly at the Paris Salon, Manet's painting had caused an uproar.

Society was even more repressed across the English Channel, which is what brought about the ban of Wilde's *Salomé*.

Undeterred, Oscar and Sarah reconvened in France, where Wilde threatened to exile himself for good. As they began rehearsals for a French production in 1893, the *Times* of London ran a scathing review of the text, which had been published in England, although not yet performed:

> It is an arrangement in blood and ferocity, morbid, bizarre, repulsive, and very offensive in its adaptation of scriptural phraseology to situations the reverse of sacred.

Yet this production, too, came to an abrupt halt, when Sarah bowed out before the play was ever staged. Though no documentation remains to explain Sarah's sudden departure, it is possible she decided to distance herself from sensationalistic roles. As the *Times* had scathingly noted, *Salomé* was "not ill-suited to the less attractive phases of Mme Bernhardt's genius."

In other circumstances, Sarah may well have taken that affront as a challenge. It would have been easy—and likely quite lucrative—for Sarah to have gone ahead with *Salomé*, a surefire hit, given the titillation surrounding it. But because of Duse and others, Bernhardt had changed; she was tired of simply being a provocateur.

Oscar Wilde, for his part, felt bewildered by the sudden loss of his muse. He returned in disappointment to England, where he would soon be convicted of sodomy. After his prison time, Wilde would attempt to resurrect *Salomé* with a different actress. "Eleonora Duse is now reading *Salomé*," he would write hopefully in 1897 to a friend. "There is a chance of her playing it. She is a fascinating artist, though nothing compared to Sarah."

Yet, ultimately, both Bernhardt and Duse passed.

— — —

It was almost by chance that Sarah and an obscure Czech illustrator crossed paths; and the encounter would turn both into archetypes of Art Nouveau. His name: Alphonse Mucha.

Mucha worked at a print shop, where he was given a crack, one day, at a Bernhardt poster when a fellow artist got sick. With less than a week, he went to work immediately. The Czech artist had been developing a distinctive style in his illustrations, framing his subjects with wavy architectural curves—the language of a new style that would soon sweep Europe. It would be named "Modernism" in Spain and Britain. In France, they were calling it Art Nouveau.

Art Nouveau was a "total art style," its adherents professing that art should be a way of life, surrounding us in everything we do—from architecture to utensils, jewelry, furniture, textiles, even lighting. This is the period when Louis Tiffany began producing his distinctive stained glass lamps in New York. In Paris, there would soon be Métro stops with curvaceous metal designs. But it was in graphic design, specifically the collaboration between Bernhardt and Mucha, that Art Nouveau became the fin de siècle rage.

When Alphonse Mucha presented his poster to Sarah in late 1894, it left her breathless. "From now on you will work for me, close to me," she declared. "I love you already."

Mucha had made her appear regal, like a goddess—but in a thoroughly modern way. First of all, the layout: he had chosen a very tall vertical rectangle, several meters high by one across, proportions that allowed for a life-sized portrait of Sarah's full body with space above and below for titles and text. This alone was revolutionary. Posters by Toulouse-Lautrec and others of the time were far squatter rectangles, often horizontal rather than vertical. Then there was the striking line work.

Mucha had employed heavy lines in deep blue to delineate the figure and separate color fields, like the lead between panes of stained glass. Modern printing techniques allowed for a broader range of colors, and Mucha had chosen soft pastel hues, which stood in startling contrast to his deep blue lines.

Sarah was depicted in an exotic Byzantine full-length gown, her costume from the finale of the play *Gismonda* by Victorien Sardou. Framed in a mosaic arch, she wears a headdress of orchids and holds the frond of a palm. The effect is like a Tarot card—indeed, she is "The Priestess."

Mucha had captured the beauty and dignity of her stage presence rather than representing her realistic features. It was as modern as Impressionism in its absolute rejection of classical photorealism. And yet there was something deeply romantic about this poster of a full-standing figure placed in a raised shallow alcove like a saint.

Both old and new, it was perfect for Bernhardt. She offered him a five-year contract on the spot. Not only would Mucha design Sarah's posters, but he would also consult on her sets, costumes, and jewelry, and serve as a general artistic adviser for the theater.

Mucha's *Gismonda* posters were up all over Paris on the morning of January 1, 1895, and they immediately became objects of desire for collectors, who used clandestine methods to obtain them, either bribing bill stickers or simply going out at night and cutting them down. Though the Art Nouveau craze would last only until 1910, the several dozen posters that Mucha and Bernhardt created together have remained iconic for more than a century, influencing graphic art to this day.

Poster design was not the only way in which Bernhardt had decided to be bold. She had recently leased her own theater—a rococo gem named the Théâtre de la Renaissance—that would be her new home as producer, director, and star for the next five years. To add gravitas to her endeavor, Sarah made the choice not to fall back on her repertoire of melodramas, but to launch with a classic seventeenth-century play by Racine. She also decided to surround herself with great actors this time, not lesser talents who ran little risk of upstaging her. One of her young costars, Edouard de Max, the son of a Jewish doctor and Romanian princess, would one day be known as "the male Sarah Bernhardt" for his theatricality and powerful impact on the stage.

Sarah asked de Max to play opposite her as Hippolyte in Racine's *Phèdre*, the French classic in which she had performed in 1879 as a young ingénue in London with the Comédie-Française, where stage fright had nearly paralyzed her, before helping her pull off a spectacular performance. But would Sarah be able to repeat the triumph fifteen years later?

"Did you ever see such a get-up?" asked one old dowager when Sarah took the stage in Paris as Phèdre in 1894. "She's too old; she can't play the part; she ought to have retired ages ago."

Others felt differently. Marcel Proust would one day memorialize Sarah's performance as Phèdre in his seven-volume novel *Remembrance of Things Past*, where the protagonist is floored upon seeing the diva onstage, gushing:

> Her poses . . . had melted into a sort of radiance in which they sent throbbing, round the person of the heroine, elements rich and complex that the fascinated spectator took not as an artistic triumph but as a natural gift.

Whether Proust's is a true eyewitness account of Bernhardt's acting or an embellishment for his novel we will never know. But his description is precious, suggesting that Sarah, while still using the traditional poses, had achieved a sort of transcendence with them.

Photographs of her grand gesticulations as Phèdre appeared in the *Revue Illustrée*: Sarah swoons, she raises her arms, she wails, she beseeches. The photos were accompanied by an article by journalist Adolphe Brisson, the son-in-law of legendary critic Francisque Sarcey, an early champion of Sarah and author of an astonishing two thousand reviews. The younger Brisson, trying to make his own name as a critic, itemized an impressive range of emotions captured by Sarah as Phèdre: "Love sensual and tender, hope, shame, hurt pride, anger, despair, dejection, bitter jealousy and, finally, resignation." Quite an impressive range. There was clearly something unique about this performance.

"The idealized Phèdre at the *Renaissance* heralded Bernhardt's middle or 'iconic' period," noted scholar John Stokes, who has written several books about Bernhardt and nineteenth-century theater. "No longer the impersonation of characters so much as of presences, her performances were increasingly viewed as ritualized events."

In the carefully choreographed pageantry, there was something almost ceremonial or Mass-like, which is how people described the silences in Eleonora's performances. This was not by coincidence; Bernhardt, at fifty, was trying to recast herself. Sarah told a reporter: "The moment I have put on the veils of *Phèdre* I think only of Phèdre, I am Phèdre and I am left shattered by the performance."

She was starting to sound a lot like Duse.

CHAPTER NINE

The *Challant* fiasco had been disheartening to Eleonora. She realized that she could not beat Bernhardt at her own game; she needed her own material. That's why Duse had been so eager to discover a new playwright whose work spoke to her soul. In Italy, she had yet to find such a writer, at least not an Italian one. But there was a Norwegian.

Henrik Ibsen, with his stern face and muttonchop sideburns, had been living in Italy for decades. He was aware of Eleonora's groundbreaking work though they had never met. Still, Ibsen chose to use "Nora"—a diminutive of Duse's Christian name—for the protagonist of his play *A Doll's House*. Ibsen despised the old, Symbolic style of acting. "No declamation!" he had once admonished a young actress. "No theatricalities! No grand mannerisms! Express every mood in a manner that seems credible and natural. Never think of this or that actress whom you may have seen . . . present a real and living human being."

While he would later be recognized as the greatest European playwright since Shakespeare, Ibsen's "realism" was considered radical in his day. He was nominated three times for the Nobel Prize in Literature, but never won; Alfred Nobel's instructions specified that the literary prize be given to "the most outstanding work in an ideal direction," which was interpreted to mean conservative idealism—church, state, and family. Chekhov, Tolstoy, Joyce, and Zola would likewise be snubbed by the Nobel committee. It's no coincidence that many of these writers were the first to recognize Ibsen's genius. Among the growing contingent that greatly admired the Norwegian, George Bernard Shaw wrote: "It was held that the stranger the situation, the better the play. Ibsen saw that, on the contrary, the more familiar the situation, the more interesting the play."

A Doll's House, perhaps his best-known work, concerns a housewife who feels trapped by her bourgeois existence and makes the radical decision—unheard of at the time—to walk out on her marriage in order to "find herself." The play had been published in 1879, but Duse read it more than a decade later, when she was involved with the much older and somewhat stuffy Arrigo Boito; her exuberant reaction to Ibsen became a source of friction between them.

The play had astounded Eleonora. Not only did its plot reflect what she herself had done in abandoning her husband, Tebaldo, in South America, but she also recognized the suffocation of her present relationship with Boito, who did not share her enthusiasm for Ibsen: "an old Norwegian pharmacist" is what he called him. Boito's opinion notwithstanding, Eleonora added *A Doll's House* to her repertoire, introducing the Italian public to Ibsen in 1891.

Duse and Ibsen were made for each other; his plays were bold and modern. Delving into the psychology of his characters, Ibsen's work forced actors to play the moments between the lines—the places where Eleonora's craft shone most brightly. This was material that Sarah would never touch, which certainly figured in Eleonora's embrace of it. She would rehearse the plays for hours at a time, refining the pauses, perfecting the nuances—leaving the members of her company perplexed and exasperated.

Certain intellectuals began to take note of Duse's *A Doll's House.* Scandinavian author Laura Hansson, who would profile Duse in her book *Six Modern Women* (1896), was deeply affected by her portrayal of Nora, calling her a "complete woman." Hansson detailed the scene in which (Eleo) Nora realizes she no longer loves her husband:

She stands by the fireplace, with her face towards the audience, and does not move a muscle until he has finished speaking. She says nothing, she never interrupts him. Only her eyes speak. He runs backwards and forwards up and down the room, while she follows him with her large, suffering eyes, which have an unnatural look in them, follows him backwards and forwards in unutterable surprise, a surprise which seems to have fallen from heaven, and which changes little by little into an unutterable, inconceivable disappointment, and that again into an indescribably bitter, sickening contempt. And into her eyes comes at last the question: "Who are you? What have you got to do with me?"

When Nora finally says "no" to her husband—telling him the marriage is over—she says it quietly, almost to herself. As Hansson describes it: "I never heard anyone say 'no' like her. It contains a whole world of human feeling."

With divorce still illegal in Italy and other parts of Europe, the play was deeply poignant—an impossible fantasy for those trapped, as Eleonora had been, in a loveless marriage. The courage of Ibsen's heroine would one day be a source of inspiration for proto-feminists overseas. But the Italian middle class went to the theater to be entertained, not challenged. "There was enough horror, woe, and misery in the world without thrusting more of it upon us in places of amusement," commented the *Dramatic Mirror*. Thus, as a leading Italian critic was to comment: "Ibsen very soon went out of fashion in Italy, without ever having been in fashion." Eleonora realized she would have to travel abroad.

Eleonora took Ibsen to Moscow, and it was there, on January 11, 1892, that she received news that her father was dead. Having retired from acting many years ago, he had been living alone in Venice, where Eleonora had had little contact with him. As with her mother's passing, the telegram had been delivered backstage between acts—the play, in this case, was *A Doll's House*. With rattled nerves, Eleonora completed the show, then canceled the next two performances. She took the stage again three days later, but it was premature. Throughout *A Doll's House*, there are references to Nora's absent father, such as when she reminisces wistfully in act one: "My dear, kind father—I never saw him again. . . . That was the saddest time I have known since our marriage." Eleonora found herself uncomfortably emotive while performing the line, and again, later, during this exchange:

KROGSTAD: Your father was very ill, wasn't he?
NORA: He was very near his end.
KROGSTAD: And he died soon afterwards?
NORA: Yes.
KROGSTAD: Tell me, Mrs. Helmer, can you by any chance remember what day your father died?

Eleonora found herself weeping onstage, the opposite of how she would have wanted to play the moment in the modern style. She would have preferred to have been understated, subdued—instead she found herself out of control and embarrassed by this rare inability to modulate her instrument.

After a few moments, Eleonora composed herself and carried on; the lapse was far more noteworthy for the actress than for the Moscow audience. The Russians may have thought it was simply part of the show—even virtuosic, perhaps. Genuine tears, genuine emotions.

But Eleonora was clearly shaken. As a spectator reported, when Duse took her curtain calls on that Moscow stage, "she came out always pale, tired, and sad. She did not reply with a smile or a kiss of the hand, or any other gesture. She remained grave, still, and only as she went off, she bowed." There was a new and brooding power to the actress in mourning.

When Eleonora moved on to play *A Doll's House* in Vienna, here is how writer Hugo von Hofmannsthal, only eighteen at the time, recorded his impressions:

> She plays the gaiety that is not happiness, and with a light laugh, she plays all the arid darkness behind the laugh; she plays the state of not-wanting-to-think and the state of not-being-able-to-help-thinking . . . she turned pale, cast down her chin, and her tormented eyes screamed at us in silence.

For years Duse's black moods offstage had seemed to feed and enhance her performances. But it had been an unfocused malaise, a brooding baseline that she carried onto the stage as Camille or another overwrought heroine from the past. Now, in playing Nora, a flesh-and-blood modern heroine pushing back against millennia of patriarchy, Eleonora's profound sadness had made her exquisite.

Tänczer, a German-Turk who went by one name and the tour manager who had cajoled Duse into playing Vienna, was one of those irresistible impresarios—obstinate yet charming, young but ambitious, clearly on the rise, ferocious, audacious, and always immaculately groomed. Vienna had proved successful for her—and now he told Eleonora it was time for a tour of the United States. The arm twist was firm, but so was the resistance. Something still spooked her about America—a forward-leaping land, certainly, but one still mired, on some level, in its puritanical roots. Duse wasn't sure how they would respond to her work.

They will adore you, insisted Tänczer; the actress remained unconvinced. You can't ignore America, Tänczer hammered—they will think you are scared of them. Bernhardt had already conquered America—twice—in her smash tours of 1880 and 1891. As Mark Twain had said, "There are five kinds of actresses: bad actresses, fair actresses, good actresses, great actresses—and then there is Sarah Bernhardt."

Sarah provided plenty of gossip for the papers too. The tabloid newspapers of Joseph Pulitzer and William Randolph Hearst were in constant need of provocative headlines, and Bernhardt was more than happy to oblige—any publicity, whether good, bad, or indifferent, was still publicity. In Philadelphia, Sarah had a laugh attending the cabaret show of a famous female impersonator appearing as "Sarah Heartburn." In Boston, Bernhardt good-naturedly climbed atop a beached whale for photographers. "Are you a Jewess-Catholic-Protestant-Mohammedan-Buddhist-Atheist-Zoroaster-Theist-or-Deist?" asked one breathless reporter.

While Sarah relished the attention of the American press corps, Eleonora dreaded it. Despite consenting to Tánczer's tour, she sailed to New York in early 1893 with trepidation, and was dismayed by what she observed, writing: "When I set foot in America, after a stormy and painful crossing and saw the great city—nothing but railroads, automobiles, and business, nothing but spectacular buildings, colossal billboards, noise, and hubbub, without a single glimmer of art or repose for the eye or the soul—I thought of entrusting myself again to the stormy sea and coming straight back to Italy."

Tánczer had partnered with a pair of New York impresarios, Carl and Theodor Rosenfield, and they had high hopes for a media blitz upon Duse's arrival. But the Italian foiled their plans by arriving furtively one week before her company and quietly checking into the Murray Hill Hotel.

Eleonora had always been press shy. Just as she disappeared in plain sight on the stage, she preferred anonymity in the newspapers. She found that reporters, invariably, would ask about her work; Duse wished it to stand on its own merits. In rare moments, Eleonora wrote carefully composed letters to select critics, explaining what she was trying to do onstage but always insisting that her private affairs remain so. As a media strategy, it was bound to fail.

In Vienna, she had shunned reporters altogether, which prompted theater director and drama critic Paul Schlenther to speculate as to "whether she is silent or talkative, whether she is 'nice,' to whom and how long she has been married, what skeleton she keeps in her closet and what are her favorite dishes." It was the kind of gossip that drove Eleonora mad. While crossing the Atlantic, she had written a preemptive letter to the Rosenfields, her American tour managers:

> I have always found it possible to succeed in my work
> without having to resort to methods, which are, alas!
> generally adopted. I intend to adhere to my resolution, even
> in a country like America, where, I am told, exaggerated
> advertising is absolutely necessary. I believe there is in
> the United States a public that is cultured, educated, and
> impartial, and that is the only public which interests me.

American journalists did not appreciate being stymied, and began labeling Eleonora as "neurotic," "temperamental," and "egotistical." Mocking her desire for seclusion, they called her "the hermit of Murray Hill."

When a reporter who spoke Italian managed to corner Duse at her hotel by joining her in an elevator ride, Eleonora's only words to him were: "Sir, I do not know you, neither do I wish to know you. I have received no callers up to now, and my desire is to receive nobody. On Monday night I shall appear in public, and I will be seen upon the stage. Away from that I do not exist." Her behavior was wholly antithetical to that of Sarah Bernhardt, for whom there was no distinction between offstage antics and onstage spectacle—her whole life was the performance. Sarah lived her American tours so publicly that Henry James remarked: "She may, indeed, be called the muse of the newspaper."

After the uncensored and highly amusing shenanigans of Sarah Bernhardt, Eleonora's insistence on personal privacy was considered selfish and, apparently, took a toll on audience turnout. This was an era in which Americans relied on newspapers to tell them what was important. Without her name in print, Duse was less talked about. Indeed, Duse's penchant for invisibility, both onstage and off, would eventually cause her to disappear from our memories. It began in New York.

"She opened," sighed fellow actor Le Gallienne, "to a half empty house." Duse had brought it upon herself; why should the public bother to get to know her if she remained unwilling to be known? Duse made a second miscalculation in a last-minute switch of repertoire.

Though *A Doll's House* had been announced, Duse, in a change of heart, scrapped Ibsen from the American tour. Instead she chose to open, once again, with Sarah's signature play: *Camille*. While New Yorkers had gone berserk for Bernhardt in the role, they didn't quite know what to make of the Italian. The *New York Times* ran its assessment on January 24:

> Signora Duse could only seem to be voluble rather than eloquent in many of those long speeches that cannot be conveyed well from the conversational French of Dumas to the Italian language. Her speech was of the sharp and *staccato*, where we had been used to the soft, melodious running together of French syllables.

This criticism—favoring "melodious" French over "staccato" Italian—hits upon one of the essential quirks of these tours by foreign divas: the play was given in a language the audience often did not understand. At times, the language barrier took on comedic proportions. During a Bernhardt run in Hartford some years earlier, the audience was supposed to have been given an English translation of *Frou-Frou* to follow the action as Sarah performed the play. By mistake, copies of *Phèdre* had been handed out instead; but no one noticed they were reading one play and watching another. The absurd situation would have been a nightmare for Eleonora, whose performance depended on the audience's focused attention on her, not their *Playbill*.

This is the reason why Eleonora had chosen *Camille*, a play Americans knew well, and also why she had spent so much time perfecting her expression of the subtext, acting the pauses between the words in a way she felt was universal. But these gestures and expressions didn't translate well, it seems. To a public unaccustomed to naturalism on the stage, they were their own kind of foreign language. According to the *Times*, Duse's "mannered gesticulation would probably seem more effective, because [it was] more appropriate, in conventional tragedy than in prose drama of everyday life."

When Eleonora read that criticism, it must have felt brutal. Quite the opposite of the modernism to which she aspired, her "mannered gesticulation" seemed to the *Times* more appropriate to the dated classics written in verse. "There were too many motions," wrote the *Times*, "too much uplifting of the forearms . . . it suggested too sharply a pose for a picture." It's hard to imagine Duse *posing*, but that's what this critic seemed to be suggesting.

Was she using too much muscle, perhaps, in attempting to impose her new style on an old play? It's called "pushing" in acting circles, and it happens, on an off night, to the best of them. As the review concludes: "She fusses too much in her attempt to be natural."

There was more to his comments than simply implying that Duse was overacting; the critic was also playing into a common stereotype of the era: that Italians gesticulated wildly when speaking. Even more pernicious, Italian immigrants in America were seen as intellectually inferior to their northern counterparts, being darker-skinned and Catholic. Bigotry led to hatred, and just two years earlier, eleven Sicilians had been lynched in New Orleans—a shameful, ghastly episode that remains the largest lynching in U.S. history.

Prejudice against Italians could certainly be seen in this quip from the *New York Dramatic Mirror*: "For giving us Eleonora Duse, we can forgive Italy for the organ grinders, the mafia, and for Burt Haverly's 'Banana Song' [a reference to a racist but popular song of the time called 'The Dago Banana Man']." While terribly small-minded, this reporter had at least noticed something worthy in Eleonora's art. It was becoming something of a pattern. When Duse first arrived in a country unfamiliar with her work, there was some initial head scratching. Then, with word of mouth, theaters began to fill—and the critics soon followed.

By being natural on the stage, Duse appeared lifelike and approachable. Her Camille was a real woman, misunderstood and mistreated by the men around her, which is why American women were among her early champions. As described in the New York *Evening Sun*: "She seems to say for them the word they dare not or cannot speak. She shows them the beauties of love and self-sacrifice, the horrors of remorse, the power to suffer in silence."

Duse was human; she was *them*. Only hers was a version of femininity, in its raw emotion, that prim and proper society women could never quite express. Though this was never her intention, Duse became a poster girl for American suffragettes. Given her impoverished upbringing, Eleonora felt more akin to working-class women toiling in sweatshops—those who could never afford to see her onstage. Even with accolades and material wealth, the feelings of being an underdog never left Duse.

It was the opposite of the entitlement with which Sarah had entered the world. Bernhardt, from the earliest days, saw herself as royalty, which is why she thrived playing queens and empresses, expecting absolute submission and loyalty from her subjects. As the *Chicago Tribune* had reported in 1880 when Sarah went to Amsterdam, her family's hometown:

It was set down in the agreement that she would not be obliged to play unless received at the railroad terminus by the Burgesses and Burgomaster, and escorted to her hotel in a

carriage drawn by four white horses, by the Royal Guard, and
the students of the University in their caps and gowns.

She had the clout to demand what she pleased—but it came at a
price. As the *Evening Sun* critic delighted in pointing out: "The
tantrums of the divine Sarah prevented her from ever shining as an
exemplar, even in her most illuminated moods." The problem went
beyond Sarah's self-indulgence, however. As a bastard and former-
courtesan with a bastard child, Bernhardt could never be a role
model for the proper American suffragettes.

But, curiously, it was Bernhardt, more than Duse, who actually cared about the issue—at least she said she did. In 1892, Sarah
had announced briefly her intention to leave the stage and run for
a seat in France's Chamber of Deputies. Appealing for support to
the French League for Women's Rights, Sarah's declared intention
as a candidate was "to obtain special legislation for women." The
irony, of course, was that members of the league, which had been
established ten years prior, would need to persuade their husbands
to cast ballots for Sarah, since French women could not vote—it
would take another half century for that. And while Sarah certainly
cared about the rights of women, her short-lived candidacy was,
of course, a publicity stunt. Even the papers knew it. One headline
following her announced candidacy read: SARAH BERNHARDT'S
LATEST FREAK.

They never wrote sensational headlines like that about Duse,
who projected an image of saint-like purity to the media, despite her failed marriage, messy affairs, and the fact that she was
an absentee mother. Duse was focused on her work and nothing
else—that was the story she had managed to sell. So the American
press eventually overcame prejudice against Italians to laud her as
an artist—despite not really understanding what she was up to onstage. And American women fell in love with her.

The suffragettes may have placed Duse on a pedestal, yet puritanical clerics called for a boycott of her *Camille* on moralistic

grounds. There had been no such boycott the previous season for the *Camille* played by Sarah Bernhardt—even when, on her first tour of America, she had been denounced by local clergy. The Episcopal bishop of Chicago called her the modern version of the biblical Whore of Babylon. Sarah promptly instructed her manager to send him a note saying:

> Monseigneur:
>   I am accustomed to spending $400 on publicity when I bring an attraction to your city. But since you have done the job for me, I am sending you $200 for your parish's needy.

Sarah's run was sold out. But in 1893, Duse's *Camille* was deemed too real. While Sarah was playing, in effect, a version of her own sordid past, which made it very real in one sense, the way she acted it in the Symbolic style made it "pretend" real. No need to boycott *that*.

And the Duse boycott backfired, of course. Now everybody wanted to see her shockingly real *Camille*.

Among the other plays in Duse's rotation was *Francillon*, also by Dumas *fils*, and summed up as follows by a reviewer from the *San Francisco Call*: "Like all French plays, it borders on the immoral." In *Francillon*, Duse was portraying Francine, a woman who tells her cheating husband that she plans to have an affair of her own—then actually carries out the threat.

"The delicate subject is discussed with an abandon that is shocking," declared the titillated reviewer. The play and its plot seemed more exciting to many because in Duse's rendition it felt very immediate. "Her acting . . . was most beautiful in all its details," said the *New York World*, which continued: "A player less truly inspired might have made Francine more immediately and theatrically effective, and would not hesitate to sacrifice truth to that end."

Truth was suddenly a commodity in the theater, when only years before, it had neither been valued nor expected on the stage.

The *New York Herald* identified her "latent power" as being the greatest charm of her work, saying: "We feel that the woman has given vent to only a part of the tremendous passion, anger or grief that fills her." There was a sense with Duse that she had vast reserves of hidden treasure that would slowly reveal itself over time. This reviewer, like many caught between the old style and the new, was speculating that Duse's restraint onstage could be a form of modesty. Given the potency that radiated from her when she took the stage, perhaps Duse was capable of acting more powerfully. In the meantime, a new word entered the American vernacular as a result of Eleonora's presence on the stage: *doozy*, based on a mispronunciation of her surname, and meaning something outstanding and thoroughly unique.

When Eleonora sailed to England to continue her tour, the London press corps, which had kept its distance when she first performed in the West End ten years earlier in 1883, now joined in singing her praises. The topic du jour: comparisons to Sarah Bernhardt. Critic William Archer wrote with gusto that experiencing Eleonora's novelty after the contrivance of Bernhardt was like "passing out into the fresh air from an alcove redolent of patchouli." As Ibsen's English translator and champion, Archer had come around from his earlier dismissal of Eleonora and was now unapologetic, declaring Duse to be "the most absorbingly interesting actress I ever saw."

Archer had been confused initially, like others, by Duse's use of realism in melodramatic plays; it was an entirely new language that took some getting used to. Now, with Ibsen, it made perfect sense—and Bernhardt suddenly felt very dated.

The London leg of Eleonora's tour had been planned as a brief extension of her run in America, where the impresarios hoped she would be critically embraced, predisposing favorable press on the other side of the Atlantic. The strategy worked, prompting thoughts of an encore season in London the following spring. But first, Eleonora needed a long break.

While running her own company gave Sarah energy, for Eleonora, it was depleting. "You know that next year I am resting," she wrote to Cesare Rossi, the well-regarded manager of the company she used to tour with, before setting off on her own—a decision she was beginning to regret. Being in charge of thirty people took an enormous toll on Duse: "If my health does not . . . *'reflower'* as that stupid *Marguerite Gautier* [Camille] says, I will never manage a company again." She italicized "reflower" in the letter to Rossi, underscoring the fact that she took offense to *Camille's* romanticized notion of illness. Lung disease was a touchy subject for Eleonora, who had lost her mother prematurely to tuberculosis, and whose own health remained compromised. It's the reason why Duse was inviting Rossi into a partnership—to join her company as an actor and comanager. She would lead creatively, he would fuss with all the details that drained her.

"I will write you later from the country at length, from *Switzerland*, where I plan to take refuge at the beginning of July," she went on. "There—we will speak with peace and confidence of what (if I live) we can do in the future."

Eleonora did live and began rehearsals with a company assembled by Rossi for the spring season in London. The best way for people to understand the new style—she had decided this in America and remained convinced of it—was to see *verismo* applied to plays they already knew. Thus, the carefully curated repertoire for Duse's 1894 season in London would consist largely of dated Bernhardt vehicles, including *Camille*.

Duse insisted her fellow actors be entirely off-book—as *she* always was—because prompters were frowned upon in the West End. So she drilled her company to exhaustion—herself, too. If another period of recovery was later required, so be it.

— — —

When Bernhardt heard the news, she plummeted: Duse would be giving a command performance for Her Majesty Queen Victoria. Sarah, too, had played galas for royalty, but she had never been accorded this particular honor. Curious though Queen Victoria may have been to see the world's most-talked-about actress, Sarah's illegitimacy proved problematic—she could not very well invite a bastard to Windsor Castle. Such exclusion was maddening to Sarah and reflective of great societal shifts happening across Europe as the nineteenth century waned—Sarah's bastard son could marry a Polish princess, yet she could not play before the English queen.

Queen Victoria's daughters were the ones who had prodded the sovereign to request a performance by Eleonora, whose radical work came up frequently in London society talk. Duse had wanted to present *Camille*, but that was quickly vetoed by the royal princesses as being too risqué. So she settled instead on a classic play by Carlo Goldoni. The event, by all accounts, was a smash. As Her Majesty's diary notes pleasantly (although with less florid enthusiasm than the fawning press): "She is nice-looking, with a most attractive voice and way of speaking, and her acting is admirable."

The royal endorsement guaranteed continued success for Duse's London engagement. And so, in June of 1894, Sarah Bernhardt quietly crossed the English Channel to observe Duse onstage for herself. Duse had been in London for six weeks, giving only twenty-three performances, which seemed paltry to Sarah. During Bernhardt's last English tour, she had performed at double that pace.

"If I played *Camille* twice two nights in succession, especially the death scene, I should die," Duse had told a reporter, sounding remarkably like Bernhardt. "I am sure I should die; the part is so real to me."

Bernhardt must have chuckled. Here was her rival, taking a page from Sarah and finally courting the press. But what melodrama to imply that the death scene from *Camille* actually sapped her life away. Bernhardt had played the scene a thousand times, sometimes twice in the same day. She still made them weep, still got the ovations—and, after a quick champagne flute backstage, she was done with it. That was *true* acting, for Bernhardt—this new *verismo* remained a mystery to her, and it was clearly unhealthy. The toll it appeared to take on Duse was precisely why theater scholar Denis Diderot, in his 1830 essay *The Paradox of Acting*, had admonished actors not to exhaust themselves by "feeling" their parts internally, but "to act" them from the outside in by feats of mimicry. This was Sarah's forte—the talent she had honed and perfected; for three decades, it had made her the most-talked-about celebrity/actress in the world.

But Bernhardt was no fool—she knew the arts were changing. It was time to see this *verismo* for herself. That's why she had obtained tickets, without fanfare, to attend Duse's closing night performance of *Camille*.

Eleonora received word backstage that Sarah was in the house and, apparently stimulated by the presence of her rival, gave the performance of a lifetime, sweeping her audience away "in a whirlwind of emotion and enthusiasm," according to William Archer.

Sarah's reaction was not recorded—but she avoided the role for the next two years.

In 1895, en route to her third consecutive season in London, Duse stopped in Paris, where she crossed paths with Bernhardt, although not socially; they had yet formally to meet. Duse simply returned Sarah's favor by obtaining a ticket to see Bernhardt onstage with the great actor Benoît-Constant Coquelin at the Théâtre de la Renaissance. Duse's escort was fellow Italian Giuseppe Giacosa, her writer friend, now a Bernhardt worshipper. Afterward, Duse wrote a bitter note to Boito:

Five-year-old Eleonora stood proudly in the one dress she owned for this 1863 photograph with her mother, Angelica, who recognized her gifts early and supported them.

Youle's indifference to her daughter's aspirations tormented Sarah and contributed to a lifelong battle with stage fright.

While Eleonora was crushed by her mother's premature death, Sarah, seen here at age twenty in an 1864 photograph by Felix Nadar, could not wait to leave home and start life on her own.

Both Bernhardt and Duse had their dresses made by Paris designer Jean-Philippe Worth. Sarah adored wearing elaborate gowns onstage, which in her mind added to the theatricality and importance of her roles.

For Eleonora, the stuffy costumes she was forced to wear as a young ingénue were stifling. As her fame grew, she abandoned corsets and gowns in favor of free-flowing garments that allowed her to move without inhibition onstage.

Sarah played male parts—so-called "trouser" roles—throughout her career, from the breakout role that launched her (Zanetto in *Le Passant*, upper left), to Hamlet (upper right), Pierrot (lower left), and Daniel, a doomed morphine addict (lower right), which was the last role she ever played in a theater.

Eleonora walked the stage without makeup so as to not obscure her facial expressions and to allow for greater subtlety in her performance.

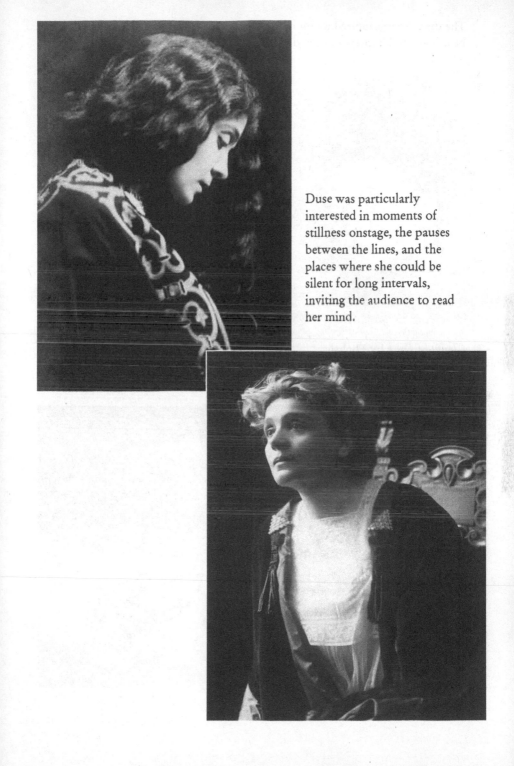

Duse was particularly interested in moments of stillness onstage, the pauses between the lines, and the places where she could be silent for long intervals, inviting the audience to read her mind.

The divas were captured by numerous artists. Paintings of Duse tended to be moody and impressionistic; those of Sarah, opulent and lush.

Eleonora Duse by Michele Gordigiani, c.1885.

Eleonora Duse by John Singer Sargent, 1893.

Sarah Bernhardt by Georges Clairin, 1871.

Drawings revealed the essence of each actress. Duse seemed chronically fatigued, often depressed and sickly; Bernhardt appeared indefatigable. Many sketches were done while they were touring, which Duse found exhausting. For Sarah, it was exhilarating.

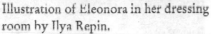
Illustration of Eleonora in her dressing room by Ilya Repin.

A sketch by Henri de Toulouse-Lautrec of Sarah as Phèdre, restrained by her nurse as she finds herself unable to control her lust for Hippolytus, her stepson.

Mixed media portrait of a wistful Duse by Franz von Lenbach.

Dynamic charcoal portrait of Bernhardt by Giovanni Boldini.

Sarah became a gifted artist in her own right, studying sculpture at age twenty-five under Roland Mathieu-Meusnier and Emilio Franceschi. Her evocative work was exhibited multiple times in the prestigious Paris Salon, as well as the 1893 World's Fair in Chicago.

Après la tempête (After the Storm), 1876, depicting a heartbroken mother holding the corpse of her drowned son, in the vein of Michelangelo's *Pietà*.

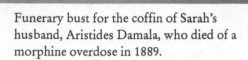

Funerary bust for the coffin of Sarah's husband, Aristides Damala, who died of a morphine overdose in 1889.

Both Bernhardt and Duse fell in love with men who were cruel to them, both hedonists and serial philanderers.

Warrior-poet Gabriele d'Annunzio (above and below) boasted that he had slept with one thousand women—the same number of conquests claimed by Bernhardt.

Aristides "Jacques" Damala, a midlevel diplomat from Greece, became an actor after meeting Sarah. He was wooden onstage, but apparently quite skilled in the bedroom. (Pictured below with French actress Jane Hading.)

Eleonora suffered postpartum depression after the birth of her daughter, Enrichetta, whom she raised as a single mom, as did Sarah (pictured above) with her son, Maurice. Duse was largely an absentee mother, while Bernhardt took her bastard son everywhere with her.

Duse left Enrichetta's father, Tebaldo Checchi, after four years of marriage, and was constantly surrounded by male admirers. (Pictured below with girlfriend Matilde Serao.)

While Eleonora was very private about her interest in mysticism, Sarah flaunted and exaggerated her fascination with the occult, claiming to sleep in a coffin to better understand death and dying and wearing a hat adorned with a stuffed bat.

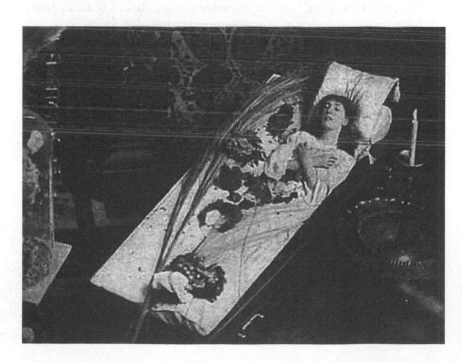

The role of Cleopatra, based on adaptations or translations of Shakespeare, became de rigueur for nineteenth-century actresses of all nationalities. Duse (above) played it in 1887, Bernhardt in 1890.

While Eleonora shunned publicity, Sarah invented the culture of celebrity, the first actress to lend her name to a series of product endorsements.

Despite being press shy, Duse became the first woman to grace the cover of *Time* magazine in 1923.
TIME MAGAZINE

Modernist Henrik Ibsen (left) was Duse's favorite playwright. Bernhardt preferred Victorien Sardou (right), who had one foot in the past. Yet even when his plays were grand and operatic, he did his best to encourage Sarah to embrace a more natural style of acting.

Though Bernhardt clung to traditional poses, she attempted to elevate them to high art.

When Duse retired temporarily from the stage in 1909, it allowed her to spend more time with friends and family. She entrusted her finances to a German banker friend, Robi Mendelssohn (pictured in center, gazing at Duse). They had had an affair—even though he was married to a good friend, Giulietta Gordigiani (pictured to the right of Robi). Giulietta and Robi felt so close to Duse that they named their two daughters (pictured on chair and with Duse) Eleonora and Angelica, after Duse's mother.

After the Great War, the deutsche mark collapsed and Duse lost all her savings. Forced out of retirement, she turned to cinema, which was still in its infancy. In 1916, she was cast to costar in *Cenere* (Ashes) opposite Febo Mari, who also directed the film. Duse asked him to keep her face in shadows—more cinematic, she thought.

Sarah starred in a number of films based on her most famous roles, such as Camille and Hamlet—but they were essentially filmed versions of the plays, fairly crude and static. Then, in 1923, Bernhardt was offered the lead in *La Voyante* (The Fortune Teller). Too old to travel at seventy-eight, she insisted they shoot the film in her own apartment.

Bernhardt had to wear dark sunglasses between takes to protect her eyes from the harsh lights, and was forced to act alongside a trained monkey. But Sarah died of kidney failure halfway through the shoot and the movie was never finished.

Nearly a million people lined the streets for Bernhardt's funeral procession, which was filmed as a Pathé newsreel and distributed around the world.

> Giacosa—and others of your friends—have declared those
> Two [Bernhardt and Coquelin] "unparalleled"—true,
> unparalleled in everything, in nonsense, too. . . . A man like
> Giacosa, so limited in heart and in talent, *bourgeois* to the
> roots of his hair—*must find* that whole world *in excellent
> taste!*—Well, that's their business!

Bernhardt had performed a two-hundred-year-old play by Molière, *Amphytrion*, a choice Duse may have found pretentious. But what certainly galled her was the next title in Sarah's rotation: *Magda*, a play that Eleonora had "created" a year earlier. Even though playwright Hermann Sudermann had modeled his flamboyant heroine, to some degree, on Sarah Bernhardt, he had been bowled over by Duse's premiere performance of *Magda* the previous season in Berlin. "To describe her art is something I am incapable of doing," he wrote the next day to his wife. "Imagine our ideal Magda and add thousands and thousands of surprises and revelations."

Featuring themes to which the times were sympathetic—the rise of the "New Woman," the revolt against patriarchy—*Magda* was a perfect vehicle for both Duse and Bernhardt. Indeed, the play, about a woman who becomes pregnant and walks out on her tyrannical father to make a career for herself as a singer, would become the most successful drama of the nineteenth century's final decade. And, just as Duse had appropriated *Camille* as a featured part of her repertoire, Bernhardt was now taking her own shot at *Magda*. But was it really a threat?

Eleonora must have been secretly amused by the thought of Sarah attempting this complicated, modern role in the old style—and even more so when Bernhardt's production bombed. "The Parisians had little patience for its Ibsenesque theme," concluded Bernhardt biographers Arthur Gold and Robert Fizdale. What made this especially delicious for Duse was that *Magda* was the very play with which she planned to open her London season.

When Sarah learned of Eleonora's plans, however, she dialed her recently installed rotary telephone to inform her impresario that they, too, would be performing in London in June.

The first play in rotation: *Magda*. The premiere? Two days *before* Duse's opening.

CHAPTER TEN

There was a rush of anticipation as London prepared for the arrival of the dueling divas. Tickets to the competing premieres quickly sold out and the London papers readied their best critics for what promised to be the theatrical event of the decade. For the London *Times*, that meant sending George Bernard Shaw. Not a playwright quite yet, the thirty-eight-year-old was London's most eloquent and acerbic critic, read religiously by all true theatergoers.

Notebook in hand, Shaw went first to Daly's Theater to watch Sarah's performance of *Magda*. Then, he trotted across the street to Drury Lane to see Eleonora's version of the same play two days later. His review promised to be the definitive comparison of the two most-talked-about actresses of their time. Printed on June 15, 1895, just five days after Sarah's performance, it began:

> The contrast between the two Magdas is as extreme as any contrast could possibly be between artists. Madame Bernhardt has the charm of a jolly maturity, rather spoilt and petulant, perhaps, but always ready with a sunshine-through-the-clouds smile. . . . Every dimple has its dab of pink. . . . But the incredulity is pardonable, because, though it is all the greatest nonsense, nobody believing it, the actress herself least of all, it is so artful, so clever, so well-recognized as part of the business, and carried off with such a genial air, that it is impossible not to accept it with good humor. One feels, when the heroine bursts on the scene, she adds to her own piquancy by looking you straight in the face, and saying, in effect: "Now

who would ever suppose that I am a grandmother?" That, of course, is irresistible.

Thus far the review appeared to be an underhanded compliment. Then Shaw lashed out.

> The childishly egotistical character of her acting . . . is not the art of making you think more highly or feel more deeply, but the art of making you admire her, pity her, champion her, weep with her, laugh at her jokes, follow her fortunes breathlessly, and applaud her. . . . And it is always Sarah Bernhardt in her own capacity who does this to you. The dress, the title of the play, the order of the words may vary; but the woman is always the same. She does not enter into the leading character: she substitutes herself for it.

Nothing in his critique, while more vivid and persuasive perhaps than most, was terribly new. Papers had been writing this for years—certainly since Duse appeared to rival the Divine Sarah. But Shaw was not done. The review then pivoted to Eleonora:

> All of this is precisely what does not happen in the case of Duse, whose every part is a separate creation. When she comes on the stage, you are quite welcome to take your opera-glass and count whatever lines time and care have so far traced on her. They are the credentials of her humanity; and she knows better than to obliterate that significant handwriting beneath a layer of peachbloom from the chemist.

Ephemeral though it was, Shaw was determined to convey, as best he could, the actual experience of watching the actresses onstage.

> I grant that Sarah's elaborate Mona Lisa smile, with the conscious droop of the eyelashes and the long carmined lips coyly

disclosing the brilliant row of teeth, is effective. . . . And it lasts a minute, sometimes longer. But Duse, with a tremor of the lip, which you feel rather than see, and which lasts an instant, touches you straight to the very heart.

There was one moment in Eleonora's performance that most astonished Shaw:

> She began to blush; and in another moment she was conscious of it, and the blush was slowly spreading and deepening until, after a few vain efforts to avert her face or to obstruct his view of it without seeming to do so, she gave up and hid the blush in her hands. . . . After that feat of acting I did not need to be told why Duse does not paint an inch thick.

While Duse had spent years nipping at Sarah's heels, she had never quite shaken Sarah's reputation as the preeminent actress of the age—until now. Bernhardt's miscalculation had been to take her rival head-on, to allow audiences to see the two back-to-back. It was the comparison that ruined Sarah forever in the eyes of George Bernard Shaw, who had seen the future and knew theater would never be the same:

> I doubt whether any of us realized, after Madame Bernhardt's very clever performance as Magda on Monday night, that there was room in the nature of things for its annihilation within forty-eight hours by so comparatively quiet a talent as Duse's. And yet annihilation is the only word for it.

The verdict was unequivocal: "I should say without qualification," Shaw wrote, "that [Duse's] is the best modern acting I have ever seen."

— — —

Sarah wasn't nearly as done for as some believed. Shaw's scathing indictment notwithstanding, Sarah had a number of distinguished supporters in the London press. One of them, twenty-two-year-old Max Beerbohm, who had succeeded Shaw as theater critic of the *Saturday Review*, had written a piece that was in complete opposition to Shaw's. For Beerbohm, it was Bernhardt who possessed "majesty, awe, and beauty," while Duse's performances were all the same, "so many large vehicles for expression of the absolute self." He found her work indulgent and repetitive.

That these two opposing views appeared the same week in competing papers conveys a sense of the intensity of the debate. There was bias, certainly, on both sides. It's possible that Shaw, a longtime bachelor, was intimidated by Sarah's overt sensuality. As biographers Gold and Fizdale speculate: "One suspects that the man who made love chiefly through the mails could not find attraction in a woman who, had she been Eve, might have devoured the snake along with the apple."

For Beerbohm, it was Duse's quiet power that proved off-putting: "My prevailing impression is of a great egoistic force." American writers had used that phrase, too, in describing Duse; her quiet strength onstage seemed to intimidate certain types of men like Beerbohm, who went on to express the sexism typical of the era: "In a man, I should admire this tremendous egoism very much indeed. In a woman, it only makes me uncomfortable. I dislike it. I resent it." Not so much egoism, perhaps, as the aura of one who radiates an unwavering certainty that her compass is true. Bernhardt projected that same quality, of course, while steering her performance in the opposite direction.

The polarity in the reviews by Shaw and Beerbohm underscored what no one could deny: Eleonora and Sarah asked theatergoers to profess profoundly different faiths. "Art is Bernhardt's dissipation, a sort of Bacchic orgy," wrote American author and critic Willa Cather. "It is Duse's consecration, her religion, her martyrdom."

Put in dualistic terms, Sarah became a kind of priestess of

materialism and sensual gratification. Her sets and costumes radiated opulence; she was paid in gold and seemed surrounded by it.

For Duse, redemption lay in other realms. The material world was a place of deep suffering—so said the First Noble Truth of Buddhism and other mystery schools to which Eleonora was increasingly drawn. It was in transcendence of materialism and communion with The Grace that Duse found her peace. That's what she offered to her audience on a good night: a secret doorway into a space where we glimpse ourselves in the other, and realize we are not alone. This, for Duse, was theater's true purpose.

Bernhardt arrived in New York harbor aboard the steamer *La Champagne* in late January 1896, brooding about something that had happened a few months prior, when Duse had blithely poached her longtime manager, José Schürmann, one of the best impresarios in the business. Schürmann had thought little of Eleonora early in her career; now he wanted to take Duse on another grand tour of America. Far from discouraged, however, Bernhardt booked her own tour of the United States, scheduled to arrive in New York one month before the Italian. It was London redux.

From the dock, Sarah was chauffeured to the Hoffman House, where apartments had been prepared for her on the second floor. More determined than ever, she got to work—beginning, naturally, with the press.

"The great French actress looks in decidedly better health than she did the last time she came to this country," wrote one reporter. "She also looks a few years younger."

Sarah, deeply satisfied, joked flirtatiously with the pressman: "If I came again five years hence, I would be too young . . . Americans would not recognize me."

Bernhardt, as always, gave them plenty of copy, chatting about her love of bicycling, and offering the requisite update on her menagerie of animals. But there was something new in her stump speech this time: Bernhardt had started talking to reporters about her art. And the words she used sounded remarkably like Duse's:

> I like all the characters that I play, but I do love Camille. I can cry every time I play the role. Oh, I feel the character so much in the pathetic parts of it that after a while I fancy I am participating in a drama in real life. You know, there are many such scenes in real life.

Then the reporter noted "a suggestion of a sigh," hinting perhaps at memories of her own sordid youth; Sarah was working him like a sorceress.

America, like England, remained deeply divided about the Duse-Bernhardt rivalry, and so, in a calculated move, Bernhardt decided to feature a new play, which she had never performed in the country, called *Izeyl and Prince Siddhartha.*

Like Camille, Izeyl is a courtesan—but hers is a tale of sin to salvation, set in the Himalayas five centuries before Christ, where, after attempting unsuccessfully to seduce the royal heir, Izeyl surrenders to Lord Buddha and becomes his spiritual disciple. It was a role more suited to the mystical Duse, which is certainly one of the reasons Sarah chose it. If Bernhardt had been on the defensive since the showdown in London, she showed no signs of it. Not only had Bernhardt once again upstaged Duse by arriving one month earlier in New York, but she was also attacking Duse at her core in a tale about the mysteries of the Orient. But it also played just fine in the Christian West, for, beneath the exotic veil, the biblical reference was clear: Sarah was Magdalene to the Hindu Christ. The part required reverence, devotion, even stillness; Bernhardt somehow pulled it off. In fact, the *New York Times* found her performance exalted:

> She is still the greatest of living actresses, as powerful in great climaxes as ever, as strong and fascinating in repose, as

strikingly original, and as wonderfully graceful in her gestures and poses.

When Sarah first premiered the part in Paris two years earlier, the newspaper had been equally ecstatic, calling *Izeyl* "the greatest of her many triumphs," and adding: "The role takes her to the extreme limit of every shading of her art; an art so perfect that it seems living." The words may well have been written to describe a performance by Duse. Coming from the *New York Times*—not known to dispense superlatives—there's only one explanation: Bernhardt must have been deepening as an actress.

She was also picking more timely plays. Eastern mysticism had come into vogue after Swami Vivekananda from Bengal made headlines for his 1893 address to the World Parliament of Religions in Chicago. Like Siddhartha, Vivekananda had renounced great wealth in order to lead a spiritual life. An enlightened man, he was also, like Sarah, gifted with great charisma.

Swami Vivekananda had brought the crowd to its feet by opening his talk with: "Brothers and Sisters of America!" After the ovation, Vivekananda went on to introduce the United States to yoga—the idea of attaining a "union" between body and soul. It was akin to Duse's state of Grace.

One night while performing *Izeyl*, Sarah became intrigued by a turbaned gentleman in her audience who turned out to be none other than Vivekananda. She told her stage manager to invite the swami backstage.

Vivekananda was entranced by going behind the scenes to reveal the artifice of the theater. It recalled a central idea in Vedic philosophy: we live in a world of maya, a cosmic trick or illusion, in which we are but players in a spiritual pageant of karma in service of a greater purpose.

The diva, charmed by the swami, invited him to a dinner party she was hosting after the show, where Sarah would facilitate one of the great meetings of the minds between East and West, by introducing the swami to another notable guest: the brilliant physicist Nikola Tesla. They had crossed paths once before at the World Parliament of Religions, but this evening in 1896 gave the two luminaries a chance to exchange ideas.

Translations of sacred Sanskrit texts had been in circulation for decades, and Tesla was well versed in them. He knew of Prana, the energy field, according to Vedic cosmology, in and around creation, which can be accessed through yogic breathing and meditation practices. Tesla had wild dreams of building a machine to harness this Prana as an infinite source of energy for all of mankind. Vivekananda might have laughed—such a machine already existed: the human mind.

One wonders if Sarah, having heard that her rival was drawn to just this type of mysticism, was intrigued. Was *Prana* just another word for Duse's *Grace*? Was this the secret to the new style?

When Schürmann learned of Sarah's plan to upstage their arrival on American shores, his delight only increased. He knew the battle of the divas would boost ticket sales. He also made the calculation to bypass Broadway and start Duse's tour in the nation's capital, where Eleonora had never been; and she liked its Jeffersonian architecture far more than the skyscrapers of Manhattan. President Grover Cleveland and the first lady attended Eleonora's premiere, along with a number of dignitaries, a sizeable Italian contingent among them.

When Bernhardt had thrown down the initial glove with *Izeyl*—a Duse vehicle if there ever were one—she was saying, effectively, if she can do it, so can I. Now in her Washington debut before the president and first lady of the United States, Duse returned the favor by performing the French play she had hijacked from Bernhardt: *Camille*.

Neither diva had any intention of backing down. Duse had been making the play her own for over a decade now, and, apparently, she brought her A game on this presidential soiree. "The almost hypnotic power of the remarkable actress eclipses everything," wrote the *Washington Post*. "She is at times a tiger, a panther, a snake fascinating its victim, and the eyes are compelled to follow her every step." Animal magnetism was a quality associated more with Bernhardt than with Duse, which makes one wonder if Eleonora's stage presence hadn't taken on a new dimension, influenced perhaps by her rival. Whatever fueled it, Eleonora's performance so mesmerized President Cleveland that he returned for every one of her shows. According to theater historian Thomas Bogar:

> The moment the curtain descended each night [the president] initiated the applause and signaled for the audience to join in. On the second night, presumably with Frances' blessing, he filled Duse's dressing room with sprays of white roses and chrysanthemums. At the end of the week he hosted a White House reception in her honor.

It was a first. No actor—and certainly no actress—had ever been invited to the White House. Schürmann felt a deep sense of satisfaction—the Washington ploy had worked brilliantly. From a publicity point of view, its worth was beyond measure, with Duse vaulting from the theater pages to page one of every major paper in America.

As she sailed back to Europe in June, after five long months in America, Sarah began plotting new ways to upstage her rival. Night after night, she had dutifully put on her makeup and taken the stage, playing twice the number of shows as Duse. But Eleonora's *Camille* had consistently drawn greater revenue due to higher ticket prices and, yes, higher demand. It made Bernhardt want to rethink her *Camille* entirely—which is precisely what she did. Never one to back down from a fight, Sarah returned to Paris and mounted another run of *Camille*, with significant changes in the way she staged the play.

In prior productions, Sarah had made Camille's boudoir and costumes as lavish as possible to showcase the extravagant lifestyles and latest fashions of the Parisian rich and famous—which is to say, of Bernhardt herself. Part of the evening's entertainment would be a fashion show of Sarah's most ostentatious gowns; she used to have fun blurring the line between her offstage persona and Camille.

The 1896 production was far more realistic, stripping down the sets and employing authentic period costumes from forty years prior, when the original story was set. Bernhardt chose simple, flowing garments for Camille, just as Duse had. A newspaper clipping wrote that they gave her "the sad and innocent look of a street-girl."

For someone who relished appearing in public like an empress, "street-girl" was an enormous shift. There can be no doubt about it—she was trying to be like Duse. How humbling that must have been for the Divine One, now fighting daily to keep her increasingly fickle audience—an audience that showed up to this staging of *Camille* for the novelty of it. (The production also benefited from even more media attention than usual, for this run marked Sarah's thousandth performance in the role.) But in attempting to sway with the times, was Sarah going against her own fundamental instincts? Or had those instincts changed? Impressive either way for a woman of fifty-two, who'd been wowing them for three decades in sequins and jewels.

Sarah had begun spending time at mortuaries, too, to help her work onstage. So many of Bernhardt's plays ended with the heroine's tragic death; so she studied the expressions of the corpses on their slabs and the limpness of their bodies, taking mental notes, sometimes sketching even. If Sarah was going to die onstage, she wanted it to be real.

— —·—

In late 1896, her fellow actors in Paris decided to host an event that would become "Sarah Bernhardt Day," for despite her many laurels overseas, Sarah had yet to be honored at home. Bernhardt accepted the honor with great dignity, writing an open letter to *Le Figaro*:

> I have ardently longed to climb to the top-most pinnacle of my art. I have not yet reached it. By far the larger part of my life is behind me, but what does that matter? . . . The hours that have flown away with my youth have left me courageous and cheerful, for my goal is unchanged, and I am marching towards it.

After the recent defeats by Duse, Sarah showed a newfound humility, evident in the gracious, albeit Duse-like, conclusion to her letter:

> French courtesy was never more manifest when—to honor the art of interpretation and raise the interpreter to the level of other creative artists—it chose, as its symbol, a woman.

It was not the first time Sarah had made the front page, and it certainly would not be the last. Festivities on "Sarah Bernhardt Day" included a "Hymn to Sarah Bernhardt" performed by a choir, along with five sonnets written in her honor and read aloud. Sarah was deeply moved by the tribute. According to one guest, "She stood with heaving breast. . . . Her trembling lips tried to shape themselves into a smile, but the tears gathered in her eyes. Her hands were clasped over her heart as if to keep it from bursting."

Of the five sonnets, the most powerful was that composed by not-quite-thirty Edmond Rostand, who would soon write the brilliant *Cyrano de Bergerac*, and then collaborate with Sarah on his next two plays. He read his sonnet to Sarah like a lover.

. . . In this dim age, you light a torch for us:
You speak verse; die for love; expiring stretch
Arms of pure dreams out, and then arms of flesh.
Your Phèdre turns us all incestuous.

Avid for pain, you win hearts. We have seen
Flowing down your cheeks—for ah, you weep!—
Tears of our souls' inmost sufferings . . .

But, Sarah, you will know, during a scene
You've sometimes felt the touch of Shakespeare's lips
Bestow a furtive kiss upon your rings.

Testimonials like this would inspire the ever-intrepid Sarah, in a few short years, to stage *Hamlet*. She had played Ophelia once before, but this time, she would be wearing a black doublet as the male lead.

CHAPTER ELEVEN

"As if she were preparing for a new role, Duse imagined her love affair with d'Annunzio before she lived it," wrote biographer Helen Sheehy. Though five years Eleonora's junior, the warrior-poet Gabriele d'Annunzio was already a national icon. His mythic name had first captivated Duse's attention: Gabriel of the Annunciation, as in the Archangel who delivers to Mary the news that Divinity would soon manifest within her. This idea of indwelling Divinity would become something sacred between the two lovers: d'Annunzio saw The Grace within Duse and she would recognize the same spark inside him. But while this spiritual union was significant, their relationship was primarily sexual. "My soul is no longer impatient to go beyond my body," Duse admitted. "I have found harmony."

Duse was deeply in love with d'Annunzio when she sailed home from America in 1896. They had been lovers for over a year, and after months of separation, she was eager to see him. Duse did not expect monogamy from d'Annunzio, a proud hedonist. He had other women—courtesans, prostitutes—but no one she knew. So Eleonora could never have imagined, while she was overseas, that her lover, Gabriele d'Annunzio, had secretly visited the Paris boudoir of Sarah Bernhardt.

The first thing she fell in love with had been his mind. D'Annunzio, like Duse, had been a child prodigy, publishing five volumes of poetry by the time Eleonora became aware of him. She read his stanzas with keen interest. His words were sensual and beckoning, such as these opening lines from *Canto novo* (1882):

> *O strange little girl with the wandering eyes,*
> *mysterious and deep like the sea,*
> *beautiful child, in my poor songs*
> *you will not stop smiling!*

D'Annunzio seemed to use language that penetrated the hidden world of Duse's imagination—a realm that no one had truly entered.

In 1894, while in London the year before the showdown with Bernhardt, Duse had read d'Annunzio's fourth novel, *Il trionfo della morte* (*The Triumph of Death*). Like many readers of the best seller, Eleonora had been swept up by its erotic plot of two doomed lovers who find themselves in Venice sharing a gondola one early morning; later they make wild, rapturous love in a room at the romantic Hotel Danieli.

D'Annunzio's vivid writing bordered on the pornographic— one of the reasons he was so popular. Even more titillating was the fact that his novel apparently detailed actual intimacies from his past, a kiss-and-tell account of his relationship with a now-discarded woman. Eleonora should have taken this as a warning. But she couldn't help herself; she was falling in love with his words.

That *diabolical*—divine *d'Annunzio?*

That's how she opened a restless letter to Boito, who had mailed the novel to her in London.

> That book—I have finished it!— Ahi! Ahi! Ahi!!!
> —Each of us . . . poor women—think that it's *she* who's
> found all the words—
> That diabolical d'Annunzio knows them all! I would rather
> die in a ditch than fall in love with a soul like that!

Though d'Annunzio's depraved themes were often repulsive to her, she had succumbed. "I *detest* d'Annunzio," she wrote, "but I adore him."

D'Annunzio pursued his goals with a vengeance—a quality Duse admired greatly in others and one to which she aspired. He was likewise unapologetic about his dark side. As described by a reviewer in the *New Republic*, d'Annunzio was "the very personification of Italian decadence, a creature of unembarrassed and unbridled appetite—for fame, for luxury, for thrills of all kinds. He dubbed himself *L'Immaginifico*, the Great Creator or Image-maker, and offered himself as a Nietzschean sort of Renaissance man."

He was spiritual, too. Though the Tantric arts were largely unknown in Europe at the time, d'Annunzio seems to have stumbled upon the mystical practice of liberation through the world of the senses. A privately printed English translation of the *Kama Sutra* had been in circulation since 1883, and it's quite possible that d'Annunzio got his hands on a copy.

"He accepts, as no one else of our time does, the whole physical basis of life, the spirit which can be known only through the body," wrote British poet Arthur Symons, d'Annunzio's English translator. "He becomes the idealist of material things, while seeming to materialize spiritual things."

Eleonora succumbed to d'Annunzio like all of his other conquests: by falling under the spell of his oratory. Their first encounter had taken place in Rome backstage at a theater in 1887. Her performance that evening had been an aphrodisiac for d'Annunzio. "O Greatest of Lovers," the twenty-four-year-old poet is reported to have said, falling to his knees to kiss the hem of her skirt as Eleonora leaped back in alarm.

While Duse, then twenty-nine, had her share of stage door admirers, none seemed as entitled and determined as d'Annunzio. Duse had toured Italy and gone overseas to South America at this point, but she wasn't quite rich and famous enough for

d'Annunzio, a narcissist and shameless self-promoter who had
cockily faked his own death at sixteen in order to draw attention
to his first volume of poetry. At twenty, d'Annunzio had married
a Roman duchess with whom he would have three children, before
leaving for his next infatuation: a Sicilian princess. At twenty-five,
after his backstage encounter with Eleonora, he published his first
novel, *Il Piacere* (*The Child of Pleasure* in the English translation).
Duse read the book multiple times when it came out, the better to
know his mind, and she certainly took note of the following lines:

> Intellectuals such as he, brought up in the religion of Beauty,
> always preserve a certain kind of order, even in their worst de-
> pravities. The conception of Beauty is the axis of their inmost
> being: all their passions turn upon that axis.

She, too, worshipped at the altar of Beauty. Could this be the Italian writer she'd been seeking?

As improbable as it sounds, Duse and d'Annunzio became lovers
when a pair of gondolas happened to cross paths one misty Venice
morning in 1895. It may as well have been a scene from his book.
Indeed, Duse and d'Annunzio made a beeline for the Hotel Danieli, just like the lovers from *The Triumph of Death*, and neither
set foot outside the room for days. D'Annunzio would later write
about it.

"I have felt your soul and discovered mine," Duse had
said dreamily, according to his account. This was the moment
d'Annunzio would claim to have found his muse: "Your presence
alone is enough to give my spirit an incalculable fertility," he told
her. "I suddenly felt a torrent of music rush through the silence."

Just as Boito had guided the young Eleonora into a deeper understanding of the mystical source of inspiration, it was Duse who
now initiated d'Annunzio into The Grace. It happened just before

an address d'Annunzio was slated to give at the close of the inau-
gural Venice Biennale, his first public speech. While d'Annunzio
was pleased with what he had written, when the moment came to
face the crowd, he was overcome by stage fright. The panic came
suddenly and with grotesque ferocity. D'Annunzio imagined the
audience to be a colossal and repugnant reptile, "a gigantic creature
with a thousand eyes" that were the glittering jewels worn by the
aristocratic women throughout the crowd.

Eleonora took his hand backstage and spoke words that transformed him: his fear was merely a gatekeeper to the unseen realm
where art flows without effort. Push through the fear, she urged, let
go of the script; allow the truth to channel through you.

D'Annunzio would one day become the most compelling ora-
tor in Italy—a role model for Benito Mussolini—and this is where
it began. He spoke haltingly at first, but soon his words flowed like
a torrent. He felt a "communion between his own soul and the soul
of the crowd, a mystery was happening, something that was almost
divine." It was Duse's Grace.

D'Annunzio was ready, finally, to write for the stage; an idea
had come to him while sailing the Greek islands. He whispered
the thought to Duse after a night of lovemaking, and they made
a pact on the spot—he would write the play for her, she would
"create" it on the stage.

The Duse-d'Annunzio pact transcended the one play, however.
They would soon concoct dreams of an annual Italian theater
festival on Lake Albano modeled on Wagner's Bayreuth, which
had been launched in 1876. And while each was free to take
other lovers, they would commit to artistic exclusivity in their
relationship—he would write plays for her alone, and she would
act *only* in his plays.

This absurdly lopsided agreement is a testament to d'Annunzio's
power of persuasion. He was untested as a playwright; she, at the

top of her craft. It was unthinkable that Duse, who had helped bring Ibsen, Sudermann, and many other modern playwrights to the stage, would abandon them for d'Annunzio. Yet this is precisely what she agreed to do.

At the core of their partnership was a mutual desire to elevate theater to the sublime. For this, Eleonora was willing to sacrifice her own style in service of her poet's words. That's how much she trusted him.

There was only one problem. D'Annunzio felt that Duse, in her comparative purity, was the wrong vehicle for his oft-depraved, operatic themes. He needed a Tantric priestess. He needed Bernhardt.

Duse felt heartsick at the thought of a prolonged separation from d'Annunzio, less than a year into their impassioned affair. But they had no choice. D'Annunzio always lived well beyond his means and she was paying the bills for both of them. When the offer came in 1895 from Sarah's former manager, José Schürmann, for an extended American tour, Duse agreed, albeit reluctantly. She took some comfort in knowing that their separation would give d'Annunzio the ability to focus on the play that he had promised her.

While in America, Duse wrote daily to d'Annunzio, who responded a few times then suddenly stopped, which hurt her deeply. "I ask and *require* that my soul not suffer," she stated in one letter. In another, the tone became more dramatic: "So *unspeakable* is this suffering, this great sadness caused by your silence—that I cannot *live* in it."

One of the reasons for d'Annunzio's silence was that he was in the throes of writer's block and felt guilty about it, even slightly ashamed. He had promised Eleonora a play, and it already had a title, *The Dead City*, but little else.

D'Annunzio was secretly intimidated by Duse, which made

him resent her. He had never written a play, nor collaborated with an artist of her stature.

The problem was a stylistic one. He felt blocked because, as much as he may have wanted to compose something sparse and modern for her, it was not in his nature. D'Annunzio was a Symbolist, like Edgar Allan Poe. As his resistance to writing grew, so did his grudge. He detested the ordinary realism of Ibsen. For d'Annunzio, Art must be larger than life, the larger the better. That's when it occurred to him: he was writing for the wrong actress.

Sipping tea after lovemaking in the early spring of 1897, Eleonora told d'Annunzio that she was finally ready to perform in Paris—which would be the perfect place to launch his play. D'Annunzio blinked. He, too, had decided to premiere *The Dead City* in Paris, but not with Eleonora. Months prior, he had secretly signed a deal with Sarah Bernhardt.

From a career standpoint, it was not unreasonable that d'Annunzio would want to premiere his play in France with the actress whose theatrical style he thought would do it greater justice—his flowery words were more suited to Sarah's poses than to Eleonora's pauses. D'Annunzio's novels also enjoyed greater success, at the time, in France, where his translator, Georges Hérelle, had the good sense to make discreet edits here and there to d'Annunzio's purple prose.

It was during the winter of 1895, with Duse still in America, that d'Annunzio arrived in Paris to meet Sarah. This was his first visit to the capital. Count Primoli, Duse's friend and admirer, had brokered the introduction to Bernhardt—the same aristocrat who had presented Duse to Dumas. In his mind, Primoli was, again, simply introducing a worthy writer to a worthy actress. How could he have known of d'Annunzio's intent to betray Eleonora? D'Annunzio later called his scheme "a frightful conspiracy," a description that left it unclear whether he felt guilt or glee.

It should have come as no surprise that d'Annunzio and Bernhardt would be drawn to each other. There were, after all, more than a few similarities in their characters. Both were vain, with mirrors everywhere and legendary wardrobes. D'Annunzio's boasted suits by the hundreds, dozens of dressing gowns, and seven distinct pairs of white shoes (to say nothing of those in other colors). Both he and Sarah enjoyed extravagances they couldn't afford. And both took great pride in their ability to command headlines with publicity stunts and bawdy tales of their respective romantic exploits. Indeed, to Eleonora's dismay, the press had begun to cover their relationship. The high-profile affair between two of Italy's leading artists, both of them still married to others, became the gossip of the day.

D'Annunzio enjoyed it. He actually thrived on a certain amount of scandal. Duse was mortified. She felt exposed, a feeling she preferred to have only onstage, never off. Sarah, for her part, was dying to know why her rival's lover had made a discreet appointment to see her in the winter of 1895. But she made him wait; she always did. D'Annunzio fidgeted restlessly in the waiting room. When the last dab of rouge was exactly where it needed to be, Sarah signaled her maid to open the door and then dismissed her. D'Annunzio swooped in and bowed to kiss Bernhardt's hand. Despite Sarah's fifty-odd years, she came from the world of courtesans, with the skills to pick a bustier that would accentuate her bosom.

"You are sublime," d'Annunzio whispered. "Yes, Madame, you are positively *d'Annunzian*."

Sarah frowned—*d'Annunzian*? What impudence!

She bade him sit across from her, which he did, perched on the edge of the settee. Sarah rested her chin on her folded hands and stared at him without expression. It was a tactic she often used to unnerve her guests. As described by friend and biographer Madame Berton: "Few men, or women either, for that matter, could withstand the hypnotic appeal of those glorious blue eyes, which at fifty retained all the sparkle and fire of youth, together with the

mysterious inscrutability of approaching age." Bernhardt's magnetism was undeniable, and this is why d'Annunzio had wanted
her for his theatrical debut. He considered Sarah a "more sincere"
actress than Eleonora. What he meant was that though Eleonora
may have been the greater artist, Sarah's acting appeared more
genuine to him, more believable—as fantastical as that may seem.
D'Annunzio was not alone. In 1895, much of the public still favored the exaggerated but *familiar* conventions of the Symbolic
style of acting.

As a Symbolist-Decadent writer, d'Annunzio was one of
them. He pitched Bernhardt the idea for *The Dead City*, and she
pounced. D'Annunzio had yet to write a word, but Sarah, delirious
at the prospect of humiliating her rival, was more than willing to
sign the contract—which d'Annunzio conveniently had in hand—
for French rights to the play.

It was payback in Sarah's mind for Duse having usurped her
manager José Schürmann. Bernhardt assured d'Annunzio that
she'd produce *The Dead City* right away. She could already see the
headlines: DUSE'S LOVER GIVES PLAY TO BERNHARDT.

The plot of d'Annunzio's play could not have been a more perfect case of art imitating life—for it featured one of d'Annunzio's
favorite themes: the "eternal triangle" between a man and two
women. A wife who is blind—both metaphorically and literally—
discovers that her husband is cheating on her.

Duse was already fuming over an entirely separate matter when she
learned of this betrayal. She had been preparing to go on a tour of
Germany and Russia and, as always, had recruited a paid female
companion to accompany her. For this trip, she had hired Giulietta
Gordigiani, a young and gifted pianist who was quite alluring.
D'Annunzio, true to form, tried to seduce her.

While Eleonora tolerated many of d'Annunzio's infidelities, this
flirtation with her employee, Giulietta, had enraged her. To make

matters worse, d'Annunzio had begun pressuring Duse to announce the Italian premiere of his yet-to-be-written *The Dead City*. Unlike Sarah, Duse was reluctant to commit to an unfinished play she had not read. When she repeated her intention to premiere the play in Paris, d'Annunzio was forced to come clean. Eleonora slammed the door and left seething for her tour of Northern Europe.

In Berlin, Eleonora met with Robi Mendelssohn, a friend who was related to composer Felix Mendelssohn. Duse's male friends would invariably fall in love with her; Mendelssohn, an amateur cellist and professional banker, was no exception. Eleonora would eventually entrust Mendelssohn with managing her investments, but for now, she simply needed to divert his unwanted attention. She did so by introducing Mendelssohn to her traveling companion: Giulietta Gordigiani. The ruse worked; the two would soon marry.

Leaving Giulietta with Mendelssohn in Berlin was also a way of keeping her away from d'Annunzio. But that meant proceeding to Russia alone, a state Duse found unbearable. Lonely, she wrote to her aristocratic ex-lover Arrigo Boito: "I want to *see you* soon, soon." They hadn't spoken in months. There was desperation in her need for companionship. She proposed that he come meet her on the road: "make love to me and hold me tight and close all night."

Boito knew, like all of Europe, of her affair with the married d'Annunzio, a man and writer he considered beneath her. Yet Boito, who still had feelings for Duse, was pleased by her gesture of rapprochement. At her request, he agreed to write a new play for her. Despite their failure with *Antonio e Cleopatra*, Boito embarked once again on an adaptation of Shakespeare—a comedy this time, based on *As You Like It*.

D'Annunzio, for his part, had been using Eleonora's rage as a source of inspiration for *The Dead City*, channeling her passion into his heroine—a woman betrayed by the man she loved. The intensity of her fury had unlocked his writer's block. D'Annunzio seemed to thrive when she was in anguish.

For Duse, it led to illness. She caught a nasty flu in Russia and had to cancel all her Moscow performances. Confined to bed, alone and vulnerable, she finally wrote to d'Annunzio with forgiveness:

> I still have hope for you. . . . Speak to me again and give me *The Dead City*. . . . The heart, it *knows* you.

By the time Duse returned to Italy, both Boito and d'Annunzio had finished their respective plays. Boito mailed his, and Duse read it first in Genoa. Not unexpectedly, she found it unimpressive; Boito's work tended to be cerebral and dispassionate.

Next, Eleonora met with d'Annunzio in Rome. Knowing of the competition from Boito, d'Annunzio had wisely arranged to travel to Rome and read his play to her in person—which put him at an immediate advantage. D'Annunzio's mellifluous voice transformed his sometimes overwrought words into what seemed like poetry, and Eleonora was won over; she signed a contract to appear in *The Dead City*, accepting even that Sarah would have first crack at the play in Paris—Duse would be licensing only the Italian rights.

D'Annunzio, having managed to win over the two biggest divas of the day, collected checks from both Bernhardt and Duse. Meanwhile, the rejected Boito dashed off a bitter telegram to Eleonora, which she shared with d'Annunzio, before declaring with typical offstage melodrama that it was impossible "to live without making someone else suffer."

With her Paris season only two months away, Duse was feeling anxious. She was in fragile health—bedridden, coughing violently—prompting a bizarre regimen of strychnine injections. Given in microdoses, strychnine was meant to act as a stimulant, but it simply made Duse even more nervous than she already was.

It came down to this: She could hardly take her first steps on a

Parisian stage in a French play by Dumas or Sardou, in which her Italian (or, even worse, her highly accented French) could be seen as provincial. She urgently needed fresh material to energize her repertoire, ideally an Italian work—preferably something entirely new. That had been her wish for *The Dead City,* but the French rights now belonged to Sarah Bernhardt.

Playing upon d'Annunzio's guilt, Duse begged him to compose something else for her imminent Paris debut. D'Annunzio scowled in disbelief—impossible!

Not a play, coaxed Eleonora—a poetic monologue, a dream, perhaps. This avant-garde idea elicited immediate interest from d'Annunzio; poetry was something he could produce with ease. As always, the title came to him first: *A Spring Morning's Dream.* Eleonora felt a surge of elation as he departed to compose it.

"When will you give me the dream?" she wrote impatiently a few days later. He ignored the letter, which prompted her to send a follow-up: "I bless your silence because it proves that you're working." He actually *was,* this time—at an impressive pace. Just ten days later, at the end of April, he handed her the completed text: the mad ranting of a woman, Isabella, as she clings to the bloody corpse of her lover, slain by her husband.

It was a stylized piece, almost experimental in its mise-en-scène. D'Annunzio had been influenced by a new wave of "abstract" drama that was sweeping across Europe in reaction to the "realism" of the bourgeois theater in which Eleonora excelled.

Though she could have been put off, Duse became intrigued; *A Spring Morning's Dream* would stretch her as an artist. It would be entirely new, unlike anything she'd ever done. Duse felt certain that she and d'Annunzio had crossed paths for a reason. Something sublime was just waiting to manifest. Perhaps this?

CHAPTER TWELVE

"It was more of a collision than a meeting," reported Count Robert de Montesquiou about the moment, in the late spring of 1897, when Sarah Bernhardt and Eleonora Duse were formally introduced: "The two women grasped each other so tightly that it looked like a mad wrestling match." One of the best-connected hosts in Paris, *le comte* had arranged the encounter personally—an intimate afternoon gathering with a few select guests in Sarah's sculpture atelier.

In preparation for their arrival, the Italians had mounted a clever public relations campaign. Several of Eleonora's friends (Count Primoli and Matilde Serao, the writer from Naples) had published a piece in *La Revue de Paris* that, instead of singing Duse's praises, bestowed accolades on Sarah Bernhardt and French culture—shameless flattery in an attempt to lower expectations and sway public opinion to the "underdog." But Bernhardt concocted an equally cunning response—she would act "magnanimous," as if Eleonora were her protégée.

Even though Bernhardt and José Schürmann had not been on speaking terms since he abandoned her to oversee Duse's career, Sarah had decided to pay her former manager a visit. She knew that Schürmann had been searching for an appropriate venue for Eleonora's Paris debut, so Sarah offered them her own Théâtre de la Renaissance—at no charge.

It was an irresistible proposal for the impresario, who accepted it on the spot; soon all of Paris knew of Sarah's generosity. She would come to regret her decision almost immediately—but for now, at least, Bernhardt had regained the upper hand.

Then Duse announced her opening night's play: *La Dame aux camélias*. Bernhardt exploded. It was one thing for Duse to trot around foreign capitals performing the most famous of Sarah's signature roles. It was quite another for the Italian to announce *Camille* as her debut in Paris, where Sarah had played the part a thousand times—as recently as last season, in fact.

Eleonora had wanted to open with *A Spring Morning's Dream*, d'Annunzio's poetic monologue, but had thought better of it. It was customary for the author to be present on opening night—especially since this particular writer was also her lover—but d'Annunzio had decided to stay in Italy. He was running, audaciously, as a "Candidate of Beauty" for a seat in the newly formed Italian congress. He was also avoiding the scene that was sure to erupt in the volatile triangle he had created. Given the author's conspicuous absence, Duse decided to save d'Annunzio's play for last, and go all in by declaring her intention to open with *Camille*.

It was with clenched teeth that Sarah embraced her Italian rival two weeks later at the private afternoon reception arranged by Montesquiou. Duse arrived without makeup and simply dressed, which raised more than one eyebrow. Sarah looked ravishing, as always. This disparity was noted with glee by Montesquiou, a renowned dandy who would become the inspiration for Baron de Charlus in Marcel Proust's *Remembrance of Things Past*.

Count Robert de Montesquiou had attempted heterosexual sex exactly once in his life, simply out of curiosity—with Sarah Bernhardt. By his own account, the experience had left him vomiting for a week but did nothing to diminish his adoration of the actress.

The Italians had a count in their camp, too: Count Giuseppe Primoli, who was actually half French, which is why they had recruited him. Primoli knew everyone in Paris, including Sarah.

Nonsense and pleasantries were exchanged all afternoon, but there was no disputing the underlying tension. Day turned to night, and the guests left for the Théâtre de la Renaissance, where Bernhardt had invited Duse to watch her perform in *La Samaritaine*. It was a brand-new play written for Sarah by Edmond Rostand—"a 'gospel' in three tableaux" is how the author described it. Performed just four days before Easter, its main theme was identical to that of *Izeyl:* the conversion of a sinner by a saint—in this case, not the Buddha but Jesus in his encounter with the Samaritan woman. This was the play she chose to present to Eleonora on April 14, 1897—one can only speculate whether Bernhardt was being influenced by Duse's spirituality. It would be Bernhardt's final performance at the Renaissance before she turned the keys over to her rival.

The theater was packed with the Parisian elite. Eleonora was given a place of honor in Sarah's private box, which had been lavishly decorated with orchids—difficult, if not impossible to procure in 1890s Paris and exorbitantly expensive. The stunning effect did not go unnoticed by theater patrons, the very people who Sarah intended to impress with her noblesse oblige.

From his box across the Grand Loge, Montesquiou watched the Italian through his pearl opera glasses as she took her seat among the flowers. She seemed flustered; he nodded in satisfaction. When Sarah walked before the footlights, she appeared radiant, with sparkles dancing from every jewel of her gem-encrusted dress—illumination made possible by the latest technological innovation: electricity.

Duse rose immediately, and the house followed, erupting into an ovation. Sarah curtsied in seeming humility, then stood to blow a kiss to her honored guest, who remained standing for a very long time—so long that it became awkward. After a while, Sarah moved to take her first pose and began the scene, which prompted the audience to settle into their seats. Not Eleonora. She was still on her feet—she remained standing for the entire scene, in fact. Duse rose to stand every time Sarah took the stage.

One wonders what crossed Montesquiou's mind as he watched the charade unfold. On some level, it was brilliant. The feigned deference by Duse was diverting attention from the performance, so the audience spent the evening swiveling their gaze back and forth between the two divas, as if it were a championship tennis match.

One week later, the who's who returned to the Renaissance to see Duse's audacious Paris debut in *La Dame aux camélias*. Montesquiou realized the ingenuity behind Eleonora's decision to play Camille. For one, it would underscore the fourteen-year age difference between the two actresses.

It was a play, moreover, whose plot was well known. The French public could follow an Italian-language *Camille* without missing a beat. And because the Parisian audience had memorized Sarah's every pose in the part, Duse's performance would underscore their deeply antithetical acting styles.

Besides the obvious difference in technique, there was a fundamental contrast simply in the way each actress viewed the character. Eleonora saw Camille as a victimized woman whose lifestyle presented a constant struggle. Money came, money went; she had to make do on limited means. It made the part more poignant, she thought. For Sarah, that made the role pathetic; Camille's appeal was that she was a highly successful courtesan and therefore flush with cash. She was the queen of the demimonde with the best boudoir in France. To make her any less would rob the finale of its irony: once a courtesan, always a courtesan.

Eleonora commissioned her costumes from Paris designer Jean-Philippe Worth, who also outfitted Sarah, as well as royals across Europe. When Duse told Worth she wanted a very simple, modest wardrobe for *Camille*, it confused the designer, who became horrified when Eleonora admitted she had not brought any jewelry. "But, Madame, in Paris you must wear jewels for this play, we French could not imagine it without jewels," he protested. "We must see some material evidence that Marguerite Gautier was richly provided for." Duse succumbed and accepted a forty-thousand-franc pearl necklace on consignment from the House of Worth in a rare moment of self-doubt.

While Bernhardt and Worth were not on speaking terms—she

had failed to pay him some years earlier for several dresses she had ordered—Sarah found out nonetheless through the grapevine exactly what Eleonora intended to wear, and she made certain that her own costuming and accessories would overshadow the Italian in every conceivable way.

Bernhardt wore a crown-like wreath of roses when she entered the sold-out theater on Duse's opening night. Still seething that Eleonora had upstaged her performance, Bernhardt had her electricians install a small spotlight in her private box, meant to give Sarah an angelic halo and draw attention to her famous locks, dyed now to maintain their auburn pigmentation.

Bernhardt was playing a role herself as she took her seat, according to younger actress and Duse confidante Eva Le Gallienne, projecting the appearance of "the all-powerful, magnanimous artist who, in the generosity of her princely nature, stretched out a helping hand to this foreign actress—talented no doubt, but still in need of patronage."

Many of the "free" tickets to the performance—a custom on opening night—had been scalped at five hundred francs a seat, the average monthly pay for a member of the petite bourgeoisie. There were princes and princesses in the audience, dukes and duchesses. After the opening gavel sounded three times to indicate the beginning of the play, Eleonora's performance was not the only one set to begin.

From the box where she sat, Sarah, too, struck a pose. American theater-writer Victor Mapes recorded the moment:

> She puts one arm forward on the edge of the box, and after giving a nervous glance to see if she is still being observed, she leans her chin on her open palm and fixes the stage with her eyes.

Eleonora made her entrance unusually out of rhythm. Part of her trouble had to do with the conditions backstage. Instead of offering up her own sumptuous dressing room, Sarah had relegated Eleonora to cramped and stuffy quarters in the rear of the theater, an arrangement that forced the actress to exit into an alley and climb a short fire ladder to get to the stage. Duse tried to take the slight in stride, but it threw off her timing

"As the play goes on," continued Mapes, "her nervousness betrays her at every step. It holds her in an agony, which she tries in vain to dominate. Her voice sounds hollow, her fingers twitch, her whole form is trembling from head to toe."

Meanwhile, in a concurrent performance, Sarah was "going into ecstasies over the talent of her protégée."

By intermission, Eleonora retreated to her closet-sized dressing room and slammed the door. Sarah, meanwhile, held court with champagne and caviar. By the final curtain, Eleonora had been trounced. "The audience filed out," Mapes wrote, "after giving one final look at Bernhardt, there could be no doubt. . . . If someone had triumphed it was not Duse."

This disaster was confirmed by esteemed critic Francisque Sarcey, the one man whose opinion all of Paris awaited. His review appeared the following morning in *Le Temps*, and Sarcey mocked the Italian actress with a belittling stereotype:

> La Duse, either because she thinks of the character in that way, or because she cannot play it in any other, suggests a good little soul who ruins her lovers by making them buy macaroni for her.

While Count Robert de Montesquiou may have felt gratified, the match was not quite over.

As it turns out, Sarah's subterfuge had begun to backfire. The dressing room stunt, which had forced Eleonora to exit the heated theater into a drafty alley before taking the stage—going from "fire

to ice," as she reported in one of her daily letters to d'Annunzio—
had taken its toll on her health. The actress canceled and delayed
performances, extending her stay at the Renaissance to the increasing ire of Sarah Bernhardt.

Every additional day that Duse's company occupied the Renaissance prevented Sarah from putting on her own productions there—
her only source of income. Meanwhile, she still had to pay her
actors and technicians, even when Eleonora took to her sickbed for
an entire week and the theater went dark. Bernhardt suspected the
Italian of faking her illness to drain money from the Renaissance.

There was another problem, too: Sarcey's damning review
notwithstanding, Parisians were starting to talk about Duse's new
style—whatever they thought of its artistic merits, it was undeni-
ably "of the moment." They were intrigued.

One useful by-product of her relationship with d'Annunzio
was that Duse had become less shy about publicity; knowing that
journalists could not be stopped, she had realized she needed to
work with them. Thus while in Paris she scrapped her customary
press blackout and invited critics to her quarters for tea, so she
would remain in the spotlight even while convalescing offstage.
Jules Huret of *Le Figaro* paid the infirm Duse a visit in the apartment she had leased, and described the scene in fawning detail:

> A great fire burns in the fireplace, and from time to time the
> artist bends over a vaporizer to inhale the tar steam with which
> she treats her throat. Then the slender, mystical fingers are
> raised to pull back the rebellious locks, as she speaks ardently
> with friends surrounding her of the subjects that mean most to
> her, uttering in passionate accents the words *goodness, soul, life*.

Sarah was outraged at how easily critics bought into Eleonora's
"saint" mystique. She needed another ploy to sabotage her rival
and had an idea. Sarah had been organizing a gala tribute to honor
her cherished playwright, the late Alexandre Dumas *fils*, who had

passed away two years prior. Bernhardt felt confident that Duse would agree to join her in remembrance of Dumas—he had written *Denise* for her, after all, one of Duse's favorite roles. Each actress would put on a representative scene—and Paris would see them juxtaposed—which, Sarah remained convinced, would put her at an advantage. Sarah would be performing her Dumas in the original French, while Eleonora would use an Italian translation—this would sway the crowd in her favor, Sarah felt certain. At the very least, she would be able to watch her rival's performance up close, unnoticed from the wings. Was there a trick to it?

Bernhardt picked the perfect date for her showdown: June 14, 1897, one day *before* Eleonora was scheduled to premiere the final work of her Parisian run, the new play by d'Annunzio, which would guarantee its doom.

In preparation for its Paris debut, *A Spring Morning's Dream* had been translated by Georges Hérelle, and the text was published in the *Revue de Paris*. Sarah had read it along with everyone else and was baffled by d'Annunzio's hastily written verses. The bizarre and morbid Symbolist poem seemed both pretentious and infantile—the stream of consciousness ranting of a madwoman, better suited to some small art-house theater than the full-scale production that Eleonora planned. Sarah was confident that this d'Annunzian folly would fail—especially on the heels of an evening in honor of the wildly popular hometown hero Alexandre Dumas.

Eleonora, for her part, remained enthusiastic about d'Annunzio's stanzas. She found them staggeringly beautiful and challenging to act, which was, for her, an irresistible combination. "Never, never, never was *A Spring Morning's Dream* more sweet and cruel," she wrote to Boito, with whom she continued to correspond, hoping still to receive his blessing as her first mentor into the world of High Art. "*I* will be beautiful . . . and this *madness* will be played so sweetly."

— — —

It was Sarah's night; Eleonora accepted that, which is why she agreed to less time onstage than Bernhardt for the Dumas benefit. Bernhardt would be performing two acts from his most celebrated play, *La Dame aux camélias*, while Duse would be restricted to a single act from *La Femme de Claude* (*Claude's Wife*). There would be other names on the marquee as well, including the esteemed Comédie-Française veteran Coquelin, along with Yvette Guilbert, a racy Moulin Rouge headliner and one of Toulouse-Lautrec's favorite models. The soiree began with Bernhardt taking center stage facing a bust of Dumas, to which she recited an ode by Edmond Rostand. Recitation was a particular talent of hers, and the crowd showed their appreciation in an ovation.

Next came scenes by Coquelin and Yvette Guilbert, followed by Eleonora's turn onstage. Sarah had staked out the perfect position from which to observe her rival from the wings. Yet even backstage Bernhardt had to keep up the facade that the Divine Sarah was not terribly interested in the curious novelty of Eleonora's craft. Bernhardt had surrounded herself with admirers, who took turns mocking Duse's pretentions and giggling.

But Sarah fell silent. There was something powerful about what Duse was doing on the stage. It seemed so free. And terrifying. Like a high-wire act without a net.

Bernhardt bolted to the privacy of her dressing room to calm her nerves. She gulped down another glass of champagne and stared at her reflection in the looking glass.

When the curtain fell to rapturous applause, she rushed onto the stage to embrace Eleonora, and then, using her own epithet to underscore her supposed enthusiasm: "Divine! Dear, you were simply Divine!" But to Paris police commissioner Ernest Raynaud, who was also backstage that evening, "she looked very much as if she would rather have choked her than hugged her." It was an impossible act to follow.

Le trac—stage fright—came on more strongly than usual for Bernhardt that night. She had opened the evening reciting an ode, which was simple enough. But now as the "headliner," she was the final act, with everything that entails. Sarah battled through her fear to give one of the most memorable performances of her career. According to a retrospective piece written in 1925 in the *New York Times*, "It is a matter of theatrical history that Bernhardt surpassed herself that day, and followed Duse up with a performance that she never equaled before or afterward"—a significant claim, given that these words were written with almost thirty years' hindsight. Just as Sarah had been an early inspiration for the teenage Duse, it appears that Eleonora had now become something of an artistic mentor to the French diva—though Bernhardt would have been loath to admit it.

Countless dignitaries, including the president of France, attended Duse's performance of *A Spring Morning's Dream* the following night. But Sarah was conspicuously absent—busy, she claimed, with her upcoming tour. Whether still flustered by the previous evening or simply exhausted, Sarah, apparently, didn't miss much.

D'Annunzio's bizarre play received predictably poor notices, though most of the criticism was aimed at the writing, not at La Duse. D'Annunzio's text included elaborate stage directions, nearly as verbose as the dialogue, in which he indicated specific classical poses to be performed on given lines:

> *She touches her hair at the back of her neck and on her forehead with a shudder, then stares at her hands.*

Eleonora underlined that direction three times in her copy of the play: although she didn't usually map out her acting, this particular direction was one she could work with. Duse used her hands often and quite naturally touched her hair onstage.

Later, in the margin, Duse scribbled the words "all the perfumes in Arabia" from Shakespeare—reminding herself, in playing a madwoman, to recall Lady Macbeth, the greatest of them all. Eleonora had been toiling, it seems, to figure out how she might adapt her

singular style to suit d'Annunzio's text. He wanted theatrical tableaus, the antithesis of how Eleonora approached her craft. It was
far more suited to Bernhardt.

Indeed, after Duse's bomb, Sarah announced her own plans to
perform the *Dream* in its French translation—a direct challenge
that mystified even critic Sarcey, a longtime supporter of Bernhardt. "What fly is biting her?" he wrote. "If she wishes to engage
in a duel . . . she should take refuge rather in those inaccessible
regions which it would seem Duse could never penetrate, and act
Phèdre."

But Bernhardt had her talons in d'Annunzio's flesh, with no
intention of releasing him.

The Paris bout had been brutal on both of them. Duse had called
it a "prison of a city," in a letter to d'Annunzio. Sarah had likewise
been unnerved by the episode. She complained bitterly in a letter to
Count Montesquiou, who had introduced her to Duse:

> I was extremely courteous and polite to her. She was
> supposed to perform ten times in eleven days; instead she
> performed ten times in thirty days. This cost me a great deal
> of money.
>   You are aware of all the pettiness and infamy I have
> been exposed to since La Duse's arrival. I have had my
> apotheosis . . . now they want to bury me. All this is bad,
> including La Duse who has played a shrewd role—Oh how
> shamelessly shrewd! It's all ugly, despicable. The Italian
> artiste is an underhanded, ignoble creature. Imagine, she
> didn't even write to thank me or bid me farewell! It makes
> my heart sick.

To Sarah's dismay, even her own Sarcey, who had panned Eleonora's opening-night performance in *Camille*, was becoming

intrigued by Duse. He saw her a second time in *Magda*, then a third time in *Claude's Wife*. His verdict:

> La Duse then leaves victorious. . . . She has won us by the sheer power of the truth. . . . she leaves behind her an example which it would be well for all to profit by.

It was a hint, perhaps, for Sarah: learn from Duse's example or become passé.

The duel over d'Annunzio continued into 1898, when both actresses appeared onstage in his work. Duse was at the Teatro Valle in Rome, launching the Italian premiere of *A Spring Morning's Dream*. If the French reception had been cool, in Italy there was open hostility. The audience limited its show of disapproval to snickers and shuffling feet, however, because Queen Margherita was in attendance. Had the monarch not been present, they might have thrown objects at the stage.

In her infatuation with d'Annunzio, Duse seemed oblivious to the reaction. The play was ahead of its time, she reasoned. D'Annunzio didn't particularly care. Though he prided himself on commercial success along with his artistry—all his novels had been best sellers—d'Annunzio wasn't that invested in *A Spring Morning's Dream*. He knew that *Dream* had never truly been a play: it was a monologue in verse, built upon the thinnest of plots. He had written it in less than a fortnight. *The Dead City*, on the other hand, was a play for which he had high hopes.

One can only imagine how Duse felt as d'Annunzio boarded the train to be at Sarah's side for the world premiere of the play that should rightfully have been hers. In true Bernhardt style, it was a lavish production with evocative scenery of Greek ruins in Mycenae. *The Dead City* involves Leonardo, a young archaeologist, who inadvertently opens an ancient crypt and releases dark spirits, which are unleashed upon his party of companions: his sister, Bianca, a poet named Alessandro, and Alessandro's blind wife, Anna—the role to be played by Bernhardt.

Anna, a seer, is able to predict, but not stop, the machinations unleashed by the ancient energies of Agamemnon and his tribe. Both Alessandro and Leonardo become beguiled by Bianca. Alessandro is willing to betray his wife for her. Leonardo, when tempted to have an incestuous affair with his own sister, murders her in the bloody finale, designed to be controversial, as was often the case with d'Annunzio's work. And no one fueled controversy better than Sarah Bernhardt.

In the adrenaline leading up to the premiere, Bernhardt invited d'Annunzio back into her boudoir, where they were perfectly matched, it seems. D'Annunzio had boasted about having seduced a thousand women; Bernhardt claimed the same number of men. Sarah paraded her Italian writer about town in a series of soirees. Then came opening night. As reported by the *New York Times*:

> The first performances were accompanied by the excitements of intrigue and cabal. The rumors concerning [d'Annunzio's] private life did little to dispose the public more favorably towards him.

The gossip was everywhere: here was the world premiere of a play written for Sarah by the lover of her archrival, Eleonora Duse.

Eleonora's cohort convened in Rome that evening in Palazzo Primoli at the invitation of the count, who felt guilty for having brokered the initial encounter between d'Annunzio and Bernhardt. Eleonora's writer-friend Matilde Serao was there, along with another journalist, Ugo Ojetti, who wrote a vivid account of Eleonora's agitated state: "La Duse . . . dressed in gray . . . stretched out over a sofa, with a hot water bottle on her stomach, her hair already disheveled by her constant drawing her hand over her brow."

D'Annunzio's frequent betrayals were well known; Eleonora

forgave his infidelities as weakness of the flesh. But artistic duplicity was harder to take. And she hadn't yet realized that her lover had also been in bed with her rival.

The Duse camp had a spy embedded at the Renaissance—Matilde Serao's husband, Edoardo Scarfoglio, who had promised to sneak out between acts to send them updates by telegram. ACT ONE WELL RECEIVED came the first cable. All eyes turned to Eleonora, who, apparently, remained unruffled. As Ojetti reported:

> La Duse spoke calmly of the drama, scene by scene, at times quoting the words of the text as if she already knew them by heart. . . . We were all prepared to speak ill of Sarah Bernhardt, even Primoli, but Signora Eleonora drove chivalry to the point of defending her. Looking up at the ceiling, she declared: "Sarah is the mistress of the public because first and foremost she is mistress of herself."

On the one hand, it appeared to be a compliment. It was, after all, something that Duse admired in her rival. Bernhardt did things on her own terms, and never apologized—just like d'Annunzio. It's the way in which they approached their work, too: as dictators. This was where Duse parted ways with both of them. Yes, a healthy dose of ego was needed to navigate the world—especially as celebrities. But when it came to Art, one needed to surrender—Duse believed true Art could not come from ego. So the apparent compliment ("mistress of herself") was, in fact, derogatory, as Duse continued:

> "A hundred performances: always the same in every gesture, precise as clockwork. In *La Dame aux camélias* I saw her three times. When she asks Armand to go back to his father, she sits down at a table on which there is a coffer and she nervously starts twisting the little key. In all three performances, she turned it the same number of times: five. I counted."

More telegrams arrived reporting increasing success, and Eleonora launched into a eulogy in praise of d'Annunzio's poetry. Everyone wondered why she was being so forgiving.

"It was only when she fell silent," Ojetti recalled, "that I realized, as she had spoken, she had taken, one by one, all the flowers from a nearby vase and ripped off each petal with her nails."

The telegrams from Paris had been misleading, however. Though their spy, Scarfoglio, was a newspaperman—he and Serao had founded *Il Corriere di Roma*, Italy's first daily paper—he had reported only part of the story. The energy in the crowd that night had everything to do with witnessing the great betrayal of Duse by d'Annunzio and nothing to do with d'Annunzio's writing. The only person truly invested in the play was d'Annunzio himself.

As the tragedy built to its denouement, d'Annunzio felt a surge of adrenaline—the final scene was his favorite. Sarah was about to enter and come upon the slain body of Bianca. As the blind seer runs her fingers over the corpse, d'Annunzio's text spelled out explicit instructions for the acting he had in mind:

She shudders from head to foot at the clammy touch, then utters a piercing shriek in which she seems to exhale her soul. "Ah ... I see! I see!" she says as her sight is restored.

D'Annunzio was pleased when Sarah followed his directions precisely—the shudder, the shriek, the soul-exhale. Eleonora, he knew, would have chafed against them, then done things her own way. Bernhardt, on the other hand, gave his words the passion and size they needed. *"Je vois! Je vois!"* shouted Sarah, and the curtain fell. But the lively applause that d'Annunzio had expected did not come.

Sarah put on *The Dead City* a dozen times to half-empty houses, then dropped it from her repertoire. It was a fiasco; Sarah regretted ever having been intimate with d'Annunzio. His eyes, she said, "resembled little blobs of *merde*."

Chapter Thirteen

At nearly forty, Eleonora was more obsessed with d'Annunzio than ever. She'd written him letters from Paris beseeching a reunion: "I lose the *harmony* of my soul—and of the world . . . when I go away from you." Then, two days later:

> Where, where would I go, dear soul, without the great
> promise? . . . I cannot tell you! Only you know how to say
> beautiful things; I know only how to listen to you! This
> *anguish*, and joy, and *harmony* of *listening* to you . . . oh!—it
> must not be taken from me!

She was besotted. The "great promise" referred to the pact they'd made—the one d'Annunzio had already broken—to create great Art together and with no other. Duse still had faith in it; she was overjoyed, therefore, when d'Annunzio informed her in early 1898 that he was writing another play. He required privacy, however, to be productive. That's why, at Duse's expense, they rented not one but two villas in Tuscany—side by side, separated by a hedge. D'Annunzio spent a fortune (of her money) renovating and redecorating his villa in an over-the-top style that posed quite a contrast to Duse's spare and natural decor. His "d'Annunzian" motifs were martial and masculine—dark tapestries, swords and suits of armor, oversized heavy furniture painted in dark shades, busts of Wagner and his other heroes. His life of princely splendor included thirty-eight borzoi dogs, ten horses, fifteen servants, and two hundred doves.

Duse was happy to foot the bill. "I have earned a few pennies," she said philosophically, "I will earn more . . . what do you want me to do with them? Buy a palace? . . . Can you see me surrounded by liveried servants, giving the parties of an actress grown rich? No, no! Art has given me joy, intoxication and money; Art shall have the money back."

She was convinced that, despite the dual fiascos of his first outings in the theater, d'Annunzio was on the verge of making "Art" on the stage. They would cocreate it, in fact—which would finally bring Eleonora the joy she claimed to have received from her own work but had not, in truth, fully realized. Duse had high hopes for her poet and every reason to think his inspiration would come. Their villas were in the village of Settignano in the foothills northeast of Florence, with spectacular views of the Renaissance capital—where Dante was born and Michelangelo had carved his *Pietà*. In fact, they were living on the very street where Michelangelo had grown up.

D'Annunzio got down to work, which meant a lot of sex. He believed that intercourse with a variety of partners fueled his creativity—another of the reasons why he required separate quarters. He also liked to keep round-the-clock hours when he wrote, often fueled by cocaine or sugar cubes soaked in ether, which acted as a stimulant. He could be highly productive in these states. Just as he had dashed off *A Spring Morning's Dream* in ten days, it took him less than a fortnight to produce a new play, *La Gioconda*.

The plot involves another triangle: a sculptor, his model (mistress, also), and his wife—not blind this time but destined to become a cripple. The denouement has the two women coming to blows in the studio. When the sculptor's greatest work starts to teeter on its podium, the wife dives to save it. The bust is a depiction of her rival—yet the wife treasures it as his "Art." So the heavy marble falls upon her, destroying her hands.

D'Annunzio would go on to write three more plays for Eleonora, for a total of six, and in nearly all the central character suffers terrible calamity: blinded in *The Dead City*, mutilated in *La Gioconda*, driven mad in *A Spring Morning's Dream,* murdered in *Francesca da Rimini,* and burned alive in *Iorio's Daughter.*

Duse dutifully acted in all of them, with the exception of *Iorio*, which came after the two were no longer on speaking terms. She fully accepted the violent theme that d'Annunzio was exploring as an artist: the struggle between man's higher and lower natures and the destructive aspect to love. But the problems for Duse came when d'Annunzio acted on this conflict in real life, which was often.

"So poor deluded Duse has succumbed to that beast d'Annunzio," wrote philanthropist and art collector Isabella Stewart Gardner in a letter to art historian and fellow expatriate Bernard Berenson, who happened to be a neighbor of the lovers in Tuscany.

THE DUSE'S OWN SAD TRAGEDY proclaimed a Boston headline, with a subtitle: SHE LOVES WITHOUT HOPE D'ANNUNZIO . . . PASSION IS EATING HER AWAY.

In early 1899, Eleonora traveled to Egypt to escape the lingering winter. Enrichetta, now seventeen, accompanied her—one of the rare occasions in which Duse allowed her daughter to join her on tour. They would have plenty of time together on the boat and between shows, thought Duse, something the teenager badly needed and rarely got. Eleonora's letters to the girl, while loving, were always brief—a sentence, maybe two, in sharp contrast to the tomes she wrote to d'Annunzio.

While it was nice to be traveling with her daughter, it was not, for Duse, a vacation. She needed time with her scripts and fellow actors, she required space to prepare. And Enrichetta would not, of course, be attending the performances. That was Eleonora's rule. Duse never permitted Enrichetta to see her act, for fear of corrupting her young soul. Given her ancestry, it would not be surprising for Enrichetta to have had stage aspirations; Eleonora had no intention of feeding that. The actor's life, as Duse knew well, was one of suffering and indignities.

After she returned to Italy, d'Annunzio's third play, *La Gioconda*, had its world premiere on April 15, in Sicily, of all places—and the location was inopportune. In one of his more notorious affairs, d'Annunzio had bedded, then dumped, a Sicilian princess, which made for open hostility in Sicily toward the poet. Crowds of the princess's supporters packed Palermo's Teatro Bellini to hiss at the stage. The irony of the situation could not have been lost on Duse. Here she was, acting in a play where the heroine is caught in a triangle between an artist and his mistress, and ultimately she chooses to sacrifice herself in the name of his "Art."

"This is not a home," says La Gioconda to her rival in the play. "This is a place beyond all laws, beyond all common rights. Here a sculptor makes his statues."

Perhaps it's not surprising that the seven years that d'Annunzio spent with Duse mark the most fertile period of his career. By now, d'Annunzio had churned out three plays for Duse—his latest, a political diatribe entitled *La gloria*, which premiered in Naples two weeks after the disaster in Sicily, nearly incited a riot.

Scholars uniformly agree that *La gloria* was d'Annunzio's worst play, though its patriotic fervor and Nietzschean themes would go on to inspire the rhetoric of Mussolini. D'Annunzio was ahead of his time again, and the audience wasn't quite ready for it. Several cried out: "Death to d'Annunzio!" The play opened and closed on the same night. Yet Duse was still not ready to give up on d'Annunzio.

On the heels of Sarah's dismal failure in *The Dead City*—because of it, in fact—Eleonora became fixated on mounting what she hoped would be a successful Italian run of the play. Bernhardt's version had been criticized for its uninspired sets and costumes; Duse was determined not to repeat that mistake. In keeping with d'Annunzio's theory of "complete theater," every aspect of the production—from scenery to lighting, costumes to wigs—was to bear equal weight and contribute to an artistic whole. Even the actress herself was to be no more important than the decor. Eleonora respectfully complied with her lover's vision. "She plays a part of renunciation," wrote a reporter, "a part subdued and gray, in contrast with the brilliant opposing character." The Poet is the hero, naturally, in d'Annunzio's play; Duse's character, the blind seer Anna, plays more of a supporting role.

For the other cast members, Duse commissioned flowing costumes designed in monochrome hues to evoke Greek statuary. A stunning hip-length wig was woven for the actress playing Bianca, giving her the splendor of an Aphrodite. The silken hair flowed freely as she glided innocently across the stage, turning the heads of the married Alessandro and, far more ominously, of her own brother, Leonardo.

The opening night audience, while lulled by the sensuous scenery and lyrical lines, was shocked at the brutality of the finale, when Leonardo drowns his own sister so as not to succumb to her allure. *"Assassino!"* shouted an outraged man from the gallery. But the ending's devastation was by design.

As a journalist wrote: "The playwright effects a brilliant contrast by introducing one scene of pure joy before all are plunged into abysmal horror." Then Anna, the blind seer, has the final words.

While Sarah had shuddered and shrieked as she came upon Bianca's cold, lifeless body—those were the stage directions—Eleonora made a subtler choice. "Her eyes, which—though open throughout the play—had seemed dead, slowly came alive," explained actress Eva Le Gallienne. "One *saw* her see for the first time. . . . For several moments she was completely still, until the realization that she was actually able to see slowly penetrated her consciousness. Then she gave a cry . . . of wonder at seeing, of horror at what she saw, and mingled joy and anguish at the gift of sight coming to her at such a price." Her final line (*Vedo! Vedo!*) came in such a low voice, it was as though she could scarcely believe it.

It was powerful and deeply moving. Unlike the Paris run, which came and went within a fortnight, Duse's production of *The Dead City* had legs enough to warrant a tour of several cities, including Genoa, Bologna, Florence, Rome, and finally Venice, where d'Annunzio delivered a rousing, nationalistic address with belligerent calls to rearm the Italian navy.

Though he'd lost his reelection bid, d'Annunzio was still a well-known figure who was blending art and politics to impressive effect. Patriotic fervor helped to prime the local audience in his favor, and he was called to the stage again and again for countless curtain calls, accompanied by cries of "Viva d'Annunzio!"

Duse and d'Annunzio glanced at each other in incredulous delight as they took their bows hand in hand. This was the antithesis of the reception to *La gloria*, where the crowd had demanded the author's death. Suddenly d'Annunzio was no longer a pariah. Critics hailed *The Dead City* as "the most beautiful of d'Annunzio's plays."

Duse received surprisingly little credit for *The Dead City*'s success, even when the play had failed miserably in Sarah's hands. It was Duse's more subtle performance that had made his oft-belabored words more palatable. But d'Annunzio had a way of seizing center stage, so most of the adulation focused on the poet. One hagiographic review put the work in a class unto itself:

> *The Dead City* stands alone among recent dramatic literature for beauty of phrase and workmanship. . . . On every page . . . one may hold [a] festival. . . . I consider it to be of the most memorable and significant dramas I have read.

Emboldened by his triumph in Venice, d'Annunzio set to work on another play—this one even more ambitious. *Francesca da Rimini* was inspired by the famous episode from the fifth canto of Dante's *Inferno*. Francesca, the daughter of the lord of Ravenna, has been forced for political reasons to marry the crippled Gianciotto Malatesta. But Francesca is secretly in love with her husband's handsome brother, Paolo. When Malatesta discovers the affair, he kills them both.

The narrative was well known in Italy, having already inspired fourteen operas, numerous paintings, a symphonic work by Tchaikovsky, and an iconic sculpture by Rodin. (*The Kiss* was originally entitled *Francesca da Rimini*.)

While the plot was fairly straightforward, d'Annunzio's vision for his fifth theatrical endeavor was grandiose. Influenced by Wagner, who had mined Germany's medieval past, d'Annunzio dreamed up a historical pageant requiring twenty-six actors and an original musical score. He set his love triangle against the backdrop of a war between the Guelfs and the Ghibellines, a schism of rival political factions that had consumed parts of Italy for centuries. Though it had little to do with the central love triangle, the conflict allowed d'Annunzio to feature all manner of weaponry on the stage, including mortars, catapults, and heavy crossbows that actually fired. D'Annunzio's script called for molten lead to pour down from the battlements, along with "Greek Fire," an early form of napalm.

He had written the magnum opus while standing at a lectern, sometimes for fourteen hours at a stretch, interrupted only by the occasional horseback ride, which he often enjoyed naked. He had once singed the mane of his horse with a match to fill his nostrils with the pungent odor of burned hair in an effort to conjure the feeling of the battle scene he was writing.

D'Annunzio insisted on being involved in every detail of the production, from props to hairstyles. It was not uncommon for an author, particularly a celebrated one, to be part of a theatrical production of his work—but d'Annunzio began codirecting the actors with Eleonora, which led to rifts and confusion within the cast.

Still, the company appreciated d'Annunzio's tireless commitment; he was present at every rehearsal, whether giving fencing lessons, finding props, or even performing menial chores.

After two months of rehearsals—standard for Duse, but twice as long as Bernhardt would have taken for a new play, even one this elaborate—*Francesca da Rimini* opened in December 1901 at the Teatro Costanzi, Rome's newest and largest opera house, where Puccini's *Tosca* had recently premiered. It was the event of the season.

"All of Italy talked of nothing else," reported the *Giornale d'Italia*. Attendees included the great actress Adelaide Ristori, now eighty-five, along with gifted young playwright Luigi Pirandello, who would go on to win the Nobel Prize.

The first act went well enough. As was common practice, the audience summoned the writer to the stage for recognition. D'Annunzio received three curtain calls, and there was another one for the company. But what followed in act two, as recounted by d'Annunzio's secretary, Tom Antongini, was "unique in the annals of the theater."

During a siege, "a thick, acrid smoke, scientifically obtained by the chemist Helbig, blinded and left breathless some hapless spectators, who abandoned the theater, howling and booing." Worse was still to come, when "a big stone hurled by a mangonel [catapult] knocked down a wall of the stage."

As the extravaganza hobbled along, the audience became exhausted and confused. Though there were smatterings of applause, whistles and boos dominated, followed by cries of *"Basta!"* (Enough!). D'Annunzio hastily marked up his manuscript during intermission to cut portions of act five.

In the end, Luigi Pirandello wrote: "I believe I have never suffered so much in the theater." He was especially indignant about what d'Annunzio's text had done to Duse: "The art of the great actress seemed paralyzed, indeed downright shattered by the character the poet drew with heavy strokes. . . . For me, and I believe for many others, the impression then provoked a deep and sad nostalgia for the Marguerite Gautier [Camille] that Duse had brought back to life." Adelaide Ristori was likewise disappointed.

But d'Annunzio, as always, had his supporters. Future Nobel Prize recipient Romain Rolland called *Francesca* "the greatest Italian work since the Renaissance." Duse, undoubtedly relieved, went on to support the play vigorously in an interview:

> In the theater one has been content with bad translations or mediocre provincial dramas written in barbarous jargon. Now, on the old boards, between potboilers, one hails the unexpected reappearance of poetry. . . . As an artist and as an Italian, I consider it a great honor to be able to lend my name and my firm determination to this effort of renewal. . . . I am doing my duty, placing myself at the service of a beautiful and fertile idea.

Duse, ever the idealist, took d'Annunzio's leviathan production on a tour of Italian cities, and while it was by no means a hit, the public came, if only out of curiosity for the sheer spectacle. In a time of growing patriotism, there was a certain admiration for d'Annunzio's ambition to resurrect Italy to its former glory, both artistically and militarily. The ancient Romans, after all, had invented the ballista, the mangonel, and the other martial technology on *Francesca*'s stage. The theme likewise played well in the Germanic countries; when Duse took the play to Vienna and then Berlin, it was hailed as the theatrical event of the season. In a blizzard of flowers, Eleonora was summoned to the German stage over thirty times. They were hailing *her*, at last, along with the glorious play.

All of Italy was talking about it: d'Annunzio's new novel, *The Flame*, was on every bookshelf from Pisa to Palermo. Despite its fictionalized pseudonyms—Stelio (for d'Annunzio) and La Foscarina (for La Duse)—the protagonists' identities were clear. They were among the most celebrated couples in Europe: the poet and his world-renowned muse.

The Flame revealed some of their deepest secrets; d'Annunzio had been working on it clandestinely for years. He included detailed descriptions of their most intimate moments—in the bedroom, certainly, but also stories she had whispered to him after lovemaking, like her first encounter with The Grace at age fourteen. This was a deeply private matter for Eleonora. The Grace could be fragile, even fickle at times. She didn't want her spirituality to be the subject of gossip. But there it was on d'Annunzio's pages for everyone to read. Nothing was off limits for d'Annunzio. Duse, for her part, remained torn.

Writers, she believed, were entitled to draw upon details from their lives, particularly when the themes were worthy. And what could be more worthy than a narrative exploring the creative process, the source of inspiration, and the human struggle between flesh and spirit? Eleonora had read portions of early drafts, so she was aware of d'Annunzio's intentions.

"I know the book, and have authorized its publication," she wrote to her manager, José Schürmann, who had heard rumors about the novel and was rightly concerned. Like the heroine of *La Gioconda*, Eleonora appeared willing to sacrifice herself in the name of Art. "My suffering, whatever it may be, does not count," she told Schürmann, "when it is a question of giving another masterpiece to Italian literature." Instead of feeling betrayed, she appeared to be flattered.

In *The Flame*, writer Stelio has found a partner in his quest for "Art." And she, a celebrated actress like Duse, is no single archetype as a muse. La Foscarina is a shape-shifter who can channel the qualities of several mythic figures of antiquity: "the heroic fidelity of Antigone, the fury of Cassandra . . . the sacrifice of Iphigenia." In certain passages of the novel, these attributes seem to surge forth and overwhelm La Foscarina, who momentarily "becomes" one of those Greek heroines, and so fodder for her lover's plays; the two artists, thus, are almost cocreators of the works.

Eleonora was passionate about words and wrote copiously; her letters to d'Annunzio alone amount to 1,400 pages. But she didn't think of herself as a writer, so it was a distinct honor to feel she was actually contributing to a work of literature. That's why, at least initially, the publication of *The Flame* did not offend Duse as it did those around her. She felt the book was a shared offspring, a symbiosis of their energies, which had comingled in art, love, and life.

But the public read the novel like a tabloid. *The Flame* trumpeted d'Annunzio's serial infidelities, and, even worse, his disgust of Duse. Eleonora was only five years older than d'Annunzio, but he chose to exaggerate that age difference, making La Foscarina appear decrepit:

> . . . troubled by cruel dismay, and the impossibility of closing her weary eyelids again, for fear that he might observe her sleep, and see in her face the marks of the years, and be repelled by them, and yearn for a fresh, unaware youthfulness.

D'Annunzio knew these words would hurt Duse. He admitted to Hérelle, his French translator, that the book "would cause great sorrow." And many of Eleonora's friends and supporters were outraged by his humiliating portrayal of an aging actress struggling to hold on to her youthful lover. One critic referred to *The Flame* as "the most swinish novel ever written." As Adelaide Ristori, the Grande Dame of Italian theater, remarked: "Nobody would be surprised if it ended with a revolver."

Over time, the dismay and disgust of friends began to get to Eleonora. In rereading the novel, Eleonora came to see another meaning in the text: she began to see how La Foscarina was expendable in d'Annunzio's mind. She could easily be replaced.

D'Annunzio had inserted yet another eternal triangle into the novel's plot, introducing the virginal character of Donatella

Arvale, a striking beauty and singer of considerable talent, modeled after Giulietta Gordigiani, Duse's traveling companion whom d'Annunzio had tried to seduce. Donatella immediately captivates Stelio's attention; and it is not simply a matter of lust—Stelio sees in Donatella the potential for a new muse.

Duse hadn't connected it to her own life initially. In the whirlwind surrounding *The Flame*'s release, Duse had shut down emotionally. Now in rereading her lover's words, she felt heartsick. In one passage, Donatella begins to haunt the protagonist's dreams:

> Suddenly . . . the Song-maiden reappeared on a background of shadow, such as he had first seen her in the crimson and gold of the Great Hall holding the fruit of the flame in an attitude of dominion. . . . Her power over his dream seemed to return with her absence. Infinite music welled up from the silence that filled her empty place in the supper-room. Her Hermes-like face seemed to withhold an inviolable secret.

How easily she could become obsolete! Rather than become angry, however, Duse was deeply saddened by the whole affair. "I thought [the novel] was true art; I tried to defend it," she blurted finally to an acquaintance: "It's terrible, terrible."

Later authors have been more forgiving of the book than most of its readers at the time. Along with the scandal came plenty of praise. The couple's Settignano neighbor, art historian Bernard Berenson, was forced to admit "there are exquisite and sublime pages in this filthy book." James Joyce believed d'Annunzio had surpassed Flaubert as a novelist and took inspiration from his lyrical prose. Henry James, D. H. Lawrence, Marcel Proust, and Ernest Hemingway were also admirers. They found in d'Annunzio a writer who sanitized nothing. Intoxicated with the flesh, he was also disgusted by it and wrote about his revulsion with an unflinching and graphic candor that most writers avoided.

Twenty years later, Thomas Mann's masterpiece *Death in Venice* would bear striking similarities to d'Annunzio's novel. Venice is where the hero of both texts—a writer in crisis—encounters a beguiling object of desire that becomes his creative muse. For Stelio, it is La Foscarina; for Gustav von Aschenbach, a young boy in a sailor suit. But the plots diverge when—in the battle between erotic and artistic urges—Mann's writer succumbs to his obsession and therefore to death, while d'Annunzio's protagonist succeeds in sublimating Eros to Art.

It was this very ideal—the power of true Art to be transcendent—which Eleonora revered, just as she clung to the stubborn hope that d'Annunzio would meet her there and fulfill his promise.

And so the love affair dragged on. Duse wrote d'Annunzio in anguish from London on May 21, 1900; she wrote him *three* letters on Savoy letterhead that day, in fact, two months after publication of *The Flame*. The first was fatalistic:

> If you loved, then, the beautiful creature—I don't fault you—it was your right. I, first of all, (—and perhaps only I) understood. If you sang her praises in your book, you did well—this, too, was your right.

More than anything, Duse wanted to give d'Annunzio complete artistic freedom—the same emancipation she had worked so hard to earn. But this noble desire couldn't stop her from spending days in her hotel room, shedding tears. "If you are making Art, why should we cry?" she wrote d'Annunzio.

In spite of trying to justify her lover's many betrayals, she couldn't bear the thought that d'Annunzio could be seeking a spiritual connection with another. Her second letter became despairing, the third cut to the core of the betrayal:

The *only* great, deep sorrow . . . was just one: here it is:
—THE SECRET—*given so freely,* to the mob.
—Everyone talked about it, and knew about it.
You'll say, but no!—
—THE SECRET was OURS.
Now—it's done.

The Secret was sacred. It's what happened when two souls beheld each other with open hearts, made a pact, and Art flowed down from heaven. Duse realized suddenly that d'Annunzio wanted to find that Secret with someone else.

On the matter of *The Flame*, even Bernhardt closed ranks with her rival. When d'Annunzio sent Sarah a signed copy of his novel she pointedly returned it—apparently unread.

Drop d'Annunzio or I'll drop you, was the message from impresario José Schürmann as he and Eleonora discussed the potential for another tour of the United States. It had been six years since her last visit, and Americans were ravenous for their "Doozy." But d'Annunzio's scandalous novel had tarnished his reputation, and Schürmann did not want that to interfere with his client's tour. Duse had no intention of touring America without d'Annunzio, however. The last time she had done that, in 1896, he had snuck off to Paris to meet with Sarah Bernhardt. She wanted him at her side this time. Schürmann's ultimatum offended Eleonora, and the two parted ways.

It did not take long for another manager to swoop in—a Yankee, this time, named George Tyler. He, too, made the case for America, dispatching his European representative, Joseph Smith, to propose a six-city tour for the fall of 1902. But again, the same obstacle—d'Annunzio had, according to Tyler, "gained the contempt of every woman in the land." Many in America had read *The Flame*, and everyone had heard about it.

While Duse eventually acquiesced to the Americans' demands that he stay home, she informed the tour managers that she intended to perform exclusively in his plays—*The Dead City*, *La Gioconda*, and *Francesca da Rimini*.

D'Annunzio, in his narcissism, took this as a given—but woe to Duse if she dared to suggest her artistic fidelity to him should warrant sexual fidelity in return. Conversations of this kind quickly devolved into fights. It was in the middle of one of these battles that Duse set sail in September for her third tour of America; her company would follow on a different ship. Cherishing her solitude, Duse never traveled with her costars; and she had returned to her practice of shunning the press.

Duse docked two weeks later in New York harbor in a better mood. The ocean had calmed her nerves and Central Park shimmered with fall color. Arriving at the Holland House in midtown where she had stayed on her first tour, she was given the same room, which comforted her. Eleonora settled in, as always, by unpacking her trunk of books, which included d'Annunzio's poetry, accounts of Saint Francis and other mystics, esoteric books on the occult, and some French literature. She lit a candle and set up a little altar of mementos, crystals, photographs, and other memorabilia, a ritual that went back to her youth, creating a feeling of "home" wherever she happened to find herself. Meditating for a moment at the desk, Eleonora placed a sheet of hotel stationery on the blotter, picked up the quill, and tried to make peace with d'Annunzio. But he never wrote back.

As was typical for a tour by a foreign artist, Duse's run did not begin on Broadway—the thought was to build steam in lesser markets before tackling the biggest one. In this case, George Tyler had chosen Boston, thinking that America's intellectual capital might be most receptive to the heady d'Annunzian themes they were stuck with. The instinct proved wise; there appeared to be insatiable curiosity about the Duse-d'Annunzio collaboration. Tyler decided to capitalize on this excitement by offering the first week's seats at auction to the highest bidder. Tickets for the early shows were quickly bid up to an impressive twenty-six dollars. Among the Boston elite in attendance was the sister of soon-to-be Harvard president Abbott Lowell. No one could have guessed that shy and closeted twenty-eight-year-old Amy Lowell would become so smitten with Duse that she'd embark on a literary career that would be crowned one day by a posthumous Pulitzer Prize for Poetry.

Duse had been spellbound by the dazzling New England fall; the Boston Common, not far from her hotel, was almost numinous in its beauty. The Grace was all around her when she took the stage at the Tremont Theater.

Lowell, in the audience, was entranced. Like the other women in the patriarchal Lowell family, Amy had been forbidden from pursuing higher education. Yet she had dreamed since childhood of being an artist, which is what drew her to Duse. Later that evening, she composed "Eleonora Duse"—what many have called her first "adult" poem:

> *Seeing you stand once more before my eyes*
> *In your pale dignity and tenderness,*
> *Wearing your frailty like a misty dress.*

Lowell would later admit that the composition contained "every cliché and every technical error which a poem can have." But the act of writing it, after witnessing a magnificent performance by Duse, was life changing: "It loosed a bolt in my brain and I found out where my true function lay." This is how Duse preferred to share her Grace: onstage, in the work. Not in the pages of a salacious novel. Eleonora's artistry was something Amy Lowell would remember forever. Others, apparently, agreed.

"If you could see how many roses I have in my rooms!!!!" wrote Eleonora to d'Annunzio, with four exclamation points.

She had opened with the least controversial of his plays, *La Gioconda*, which, while it ended like the others in tragedy, avoided at least the spectacle of murder and incest. This choice had prompted the *Boston Herald* reviewer to advise his readers—to the relief of all—that *La Gioconda* carried "very little moral danger to the spectators."

When it came to *The Dead City*, however, the reviews turned scathing. A PLAY OF GREAT SUPERFICIAL BEAUTY, BUT FUNDAMENTALLY DECADENT was the *New York Times* headline. One critic called it "positively vile," while keeping circumspect about precisely why, for "decency forbids us to enter into more details concerning the plot of this play." Reviews only got worse when Duse took the play to New York, where the *Evening Post* printed the following excoriation: "[A] ghastly piece, the latest product of a diseased and morbid fancy."

But the bad press seemed to whet the curiosity of a sufficient number of theatergoers to make the tour, while not a smash, reasonably successful. Duse had promised d'Annunzio the generous royalty rate of 12 percent of ticket sales, which amounted to a small fortune. His share from *Francesca da Rimini* alone came to fourteen thousand lire, or ten years of rent on his Tuscan villa—and that was for just five performances.

As always, Duse, with her delicate constitution, needed to pace herself and therefore limited the number of performances on the road. Compounding her exhaustion was the fact that she gave her all every time she walked out on the stage, slipping like a chameleon into the different characters of her repertoire, a feat that didn't go unnoticed. As d'Annunzio's English translator wrote in an introduction to *The Dead City*: "this wonderful woman . . . seems to have effaced the boundary that separates nature from art."

When the road-weary Eleonora returned to New York at the end of 1902 to wrap up her American tour with a few farewell shows, she was no longer jubilant. The leaves had fallen long ago from the Central Park trees, whose bare branches seemed to match her somber mood. She stared despondently through the window as the carriage rattled along Broadway. They came to a tall building, nicknamed "The Yellow Brick Brewery," home to New York's largest theater—the Metropolitan Opera House. This was the original Met, built across from the Garment District, twenty-five blocks south of its current home at Lincoln Center. The building had been constructed in 1883 by a consortium of businessmen excluded from joining New York's former opera house, the Academy of Music at Union Square.

Tour managers George Tyler and Joseph Smith were there to greet Duse, and they escorted her through the stage door. Needing a moment to herself, Eleonora strolled onto the colossal stage to take in the empty house. The place was huge, with five tiers of balconies soaring up some eighty feet, and a capacity approaching four thousand.

Eleonora had planned to play *Francesca* on this storied stage. Standing on the boards, she pictured herself in the role, as she did often before performing—a quick mental flash through the narrative arc, from the first scene to the finale. In *Francesca*, the heroine is forced to marry a man she despises, who murders her in a jealous rage.

Not exactly uplifting. Eleonora, sensing a bleak mood descending, decided spontaneously to change plays. To the jubilation of George Tyler and Joseph Smith, Duse informed her American tour managers that she was done with d'Annunzio. She would perform *Magda*. Instead of getting slaughtered for her transgressions, Magda defies her controlling father. In the finale, he raises a gun to her head, but, unable to fire, he has a stroke that ends *his* life— and an emancipated Magda goes off to pursue her dreams. After months of nothing but d'Annunzio, it would be a relief, finally, to play a woman who felt empowered.

But shaking off d'Annunzio did not revitalize Duse. There was something missing in her Magda that night. Her timing was off; she felt disconnected.

"Time and again," wrote the *New York Times* critic in apparent exasperation, "she does absolutely nothing but wait for the last word or action to sink in more deeply."

Her novelty was suddenly old.

Chapter Fourteen

The sordid tale of the diva and the playwright made for good copy. However, this one was more of a fling than a serious romance. He was in his thirties, after all; she, almost twice that age, though there was no denying it—Sarah Bernhardt was aging brilliantly.

Just as she had launched herself by bedding Napoleon III, among others, Sarah continued to use her boudoir to advance her career. The current target: playwright Edmond Rostand. Duse's affair with d'Annunzio had resulted mostly in a series of failures. Bernhardt and Rostand, on the other hand, were a good match.

Many considered Rostand to be France's greatest living poet at the time. He had just written one of the masterpieces of French theater, *Cyrano de Bergerac*, and Bernhardt wanted to make certain she was first in line for his next play, which was all but assured. Rostand adored Sarah and was thrilled at the prospect of her performing in his latest work. To cinch matters, Sarah lured Rostand to her bed, which happened—this time—to be on a moving train.

It was the fall of 1899, the waning months of the nineteenth century. They were crossing the Austro-Hungarian Empire, where Bernhardt had been touring. As she and Rostand enjoyed each other's company one afternoon in a private salon in one of several train cars she had commandeered, Sarah noticed something passing in a blur outside the window: the word WAGRAM, on the dusty wall of a remote railway station.

Wagram, exclaimed Sarah. We are passing Wagram!

Rostand looked up with interest. Wagram was the site of a decisive, century-old victory for France in the Napoleonic Wars, where

Emperor Napoleon I had driven the Austrians back across the Danube. It was also the site of an important scene in the new play that Rostand was writing for Sarah: *L'Aiglon (The Eaglet)*, which told the story of young Napoleon II. Sarah was planning to don trousers to play Napoleon's exiled heir, who spent his short life under house arrest in Austria. The part would require a physical miracle from Bernhardt—who, in addition to switching genders, would have to shave three decades from her age. This is what Sarah lived for on the boards—the spectacular provocation, the supreme feat that only a true champion would attempt.

Sarah was obsessed with historical accuracy, along with correctness of wardrobe and design. It was among the reasons for this tour of Austria—part of Bernhardt's rigorous preparations for her new production.

Upon arriving in Vienna that evening, Bernhardt summoned her Austrian tour manager to her hotel suite and demanded he schedule an immediate tour of the famous Wagram battlefield.

"Organize a pilgrimage to Wagram? You cannot be serious, Madame," he protested. "There is nothing of interest in that dreary hole."

But there was no swaying Bernhardt.

"Most divine of living beings," stammered the Austrian tour manager, "you are demanding the impossible." The battlefield was miles from the train station. They would require horses, carriages, cooking equipment—even lights, since the days were getting shorter. And the whole thing would be pointless, insisted the manager: "There is nothing to see but beetroots and potatoes."

Sarah was adamant: she would visit Wagram.

The story, as recorded faithfully by Rostand, picked up one week later. After touring and performing in Brno to the north, they were back on Sarah's train, returning to Vienna and approaching, once again, the forgettable rural station—but this time the locomotive screeched to a halt.

You'd hardly recognize the place. Wagram station had been thoroughly transformed by hundreds of flaming torches, garlands of paper flowers, soldiers standing at attention in gleaming helmets and shiny boots. . . . An incredulous, bleary-eyed Sarah emerged from her carriage to a cannon salute as a portly gentleman stepped forward to kiss her hand—the mayor of Wagram, humbly begging for the honor of escorting her to the site made famous by her esteemed countryman Napoleon, a site that would now become even more sacred by the grace of her own footsteps.

Sarah caught a glimpse of the station clock, which read—it could not be true—two o'clock in the morning?

She frowned. "Is something wrong with the clock?"

"No, Madame," replied the mayor. "The clock is in perfect order."

Bernhardt glanced at her Austrian tour manager, who, grinning with pride, had clearly pulled off an exceptional feat. But her divinity notwithstanding, Sarah was an exhausted mortal on a demanding tour with another show that very evening in Vienna. To hell with Wagram, her sleep came first. Spinning toward the engineer, she commanded: "Start the train! *En route! En route!*"

"Oh the mayor and the officials!" lamented Rostand. "I shall never forget their faces when the train began to move, their stupor, their frightened round eyes as Sarah retreated while the mayor was still 'speechifying.' I can still see him, his dignity shattered, surrounded by his committee and those sad paper flowers." As the train gathered speed, Sarah sank languidly into her fabled chinchilla coat and fell asleep as though nothing had happened.

Despite the aborted trip to Wagram, Rostand completed his play, which culminated in a scene on the epic battlefield. While deeply patriotic, the play is also bittersweet in that Napoleon II would never soar to the heights of his formidable father. This plot was personal to Rostand, whose father was a distinguished economist and man of letters. The playwright had an equally daunting standard to live up to of his own making: *Cyrano*, a play that had received so much acclaim that many doubted whether Rostand could ever match it. The stakes were personal for Bernhardt, too, who had been once, but was no longer, the undisputed empress of the stage. Sarah needed a play like this.

When Rostand read his completed text to Bernhardt and her company of actors, they were moved to tears. The curtain rises on the Schönbrunn Palace in Vienna, the seat of the Austrian court, where the young Napoleon II and his mother, the Austrian duchess Marie Louise, are living, having been exiled from France. While his tutors have tried to avoid the subject of his father's colossal legacy, the lad dreams of glory. Secretly, with the help of Flambeau, a grizzled veteran of the Napoleonic Wars, he practices military maneuvers using chess pieces and toy soldiers in the hope of assembling an army to reclaim the imperial throne. In act five, a dramatic torch-lit scene takes us to Wagram where the Bonaparte heir awaits a militia of coconspirators willing to march with him on France—but no one comes. Instead, the boy, consumptive and feverish, has visions of ghostly soldiers from his father's campaign, a delirious glimpse of the glory that will never be his.

It was a story meant for Bernhardt, who, as the century turned, had lost some of her luster. And there was another reason that Sarah needed a patriotic role—she had been tainted of late in the eyes of her countrymen.

Just two years earlier, Sarah had slipped precipitously from national icon to national pariah when she stood all but alone alongside the infamous Captain Alfred Dreyfus, a French army officer of Jewish descent who had been accused of passing secrets to the Germans. She declared that he had been falsely accused.

Throughout her career, Sarah had been subjected to anti-Semitism. There were mean-spirited caricatures in the press, depicting her as avaricious with a hooked nose. She had been bombarded with rotten eggs onstage, had stones pelted at her carriage with cries of "Kill the Jewess." But Sarah was proud of her heritage and defended Dreyfus. It was she, according to playwright Louis Verneuil, who stirred writer Émile Zola to write "*J'Accuse*," his highly controversial open letter to the president of the Republic, which was printed on the front page of the paper in January of 1898. Zola's letter accused the French army of trumping up evidence of treason against Dreyfus in order to protect "one of their own"—that is, a gentile officer. After its publication, Sarah dispatched the following note to her dear friend Zola:

> Dear Grand Master,
> Allow me to speak for the intense emotion I felt when I read your cry for justice. As a woman, I have no influence but I am anguished, haunted by the situation, and the beautiful words you wrote yesterday brought tremendous relief to my great suffering. . . .

A surprisingly modest Bernhardt was suggesting she had "no influence" as a woman—but, if Verneuil is to be believed, it was she who had inspired Zola to begin with, in earlier letters, one assumes. Sarah's position on Dreyfus was so unpopular that even her own son, Maurice, was against her—they did not speak for months. When Zola's letter appeared in print, an angry mob descended on his small home in Paris's rue de Bruxelles, calling for his death. They threw rocks at the shuttered windows, until the wooden panes were flung open and a figure appeared—not Zola, but Bernhardt.

Sarah had been visiting Zola to commend him in person on his courage. Now, framed in the open window, Sarah was suddenly and unexpectedly "onstage." So she squared her shoulders to face the bloodthirsty crowd and addressed them in her distinctive, much-adored voice. The precise words Sarah used that morning were never recorded—but whatever she said, Bernhardt caused the crowd to return to their homes. Her position—and very public defense of it—were the most courageous acts she would perform, going well beyond what she had done for wounded soldiers during the Franco-Prussian War of 1870.

Newspapers the following morning put the incident on the front page. SARAH BERNHARDT AT ZOLAS, read one headline;

THE GREAT ACTRESS IS WITH THE JEWS AGAINST THE ARMY, went another. All week, there were angry demonstrations outside the Théâtre de la Renaissance—and it was around this time that Sarah Bernhardt decided to shutter it for good. Despite some artistic achievement, running the theater had been financially draining, with a series of flops culminating in the disaster of d'Annunzio's play earlier that year. So Bernhardt put her beloved theater up for sale.

Never one to quit, Bernhardt doubled-down a few months later, going further into debt by signing a long-term lease on a new theater, the Théâtre des Nations, which, at 1,700 seats, was nearly twice the capacity of the Renaissance. Sarah needed a new start—to resurrect the formula that had always worked for her: size.

The colossal backstage of the Théâtre des Nations afforded storage for multiple sets of scenery, allowing for a different play each night of the week. What's more, the elevated proscenium put greater distance between the aging actress and her public. At fifty-five, Bernhardt felt self-conscious about the thick makeup she needed now to conceal her wrinkles.

Sarah's new dressing room was beyond opulent—a five-room suite complete with electric chandeliers and a proper bathtub, the first ever in a theater. Bernhardt personally supervised every detail of the new venue's renovation, including a complete facelift of the foyer, adding paintings of herself by Mucha, Abbéma, and Orientalist painter Georges Clairin. Since she had signed a twenty-five-year lease on the place, Sarah felt it entirely reasonable to rechristen the theater with a new name: Théâtre Sarah Bernhardt.

Why not? she thought. One year earlier, Teatro Brunetti in Bologna had changed its name to Teatro Duse, and Eleonora wasn't even in residence there—it had simply been done in her honor. Sarah, on the other hand, would be putting sweat into her enterprise on a nightly basis. In fact, the Théâtre Sarah Bernhardt was to be the only Paris venue where the diva performed for the remaining two decades of her life.

In another courageous move, Sarah decided to launch her new theater by going where Eleonora didn't dare: performing as a man. It was a feat Duse never attempted; not that she didn't have the ability—she was an actor, after all. But wearing trousers held no appeal for Duse, whose sole focus remained her obsession to embody and articulate real-life female characters.

Sarah had launched herself at twenty-five by playing a man, or rather a boy, in *Le Passant*. Now, in her fifties, almost as if in defiance of her aging body, Bernhardt would add another *seven* young males to her repertoire, including *L'Aiglon*. But first Sarah tackled what is widely considered to be theater's greatest hero. On May 20, 1899, she strode onto the stage of the Théâtre Sarah Bernhardt with a sword and black cape—as Hamlet.

It was vintage Bernhardt: bold, controversial, and the hottest ticket in town. Sarah had rejected the standard verse translation and commissioned her own in prose, which preserved more of the original text than any of the productions of the day, whether in France or possibly even in England, where local theaters tended to abridge Shakespeare. Sarah's version ran for an astonishing four hours—very demanding for the audience, who nonetheless showed up in numbers. After two weeks in Paris, she took the production on the road, beginning boldly in London, where British critics were preparing to raise their sabers in defense of their bard.

The reaction was mixed. Longtime Sarah supporter Max Beerbohm was at a loss, writing: "The only compliment one can conscientiously pay her is that her Hamlet was, from first to last, [a] *très grande dame.*"

But actress Elizabeth Robins vehemently disagreed: "Madame Bernhardt's assumption of masculinity is so cleverly carried out that one loses sight of Hamlet in one's admiration for the tour de force of the actress."

For the writer Maurice Baring, Sarah was "a marvel, a tiger, natural, easy, lifelike and princely." But some thought she went too far in her attempt at masculinity, to which Sarah replied: "I am reproached for being too active, too virile. It appears that in England, Hamlet must be portrayed as a sad German professor. . . . They say that my acting is not traditional. But what is tradition? Each actor brings his own traditions."

Bernhardt's choice to tackle roles for young men was an anti-agist, radical feminist response to limiting and often demeaning professional and social opportunities afforded to women past their prime in Victorian Europe. She was saying, in effect, we can be anything. And yet it was Duse on the suffragette pedestal, not Bernhardt. Sarah simply couldn't win.

Not satisfied with stopping at the West End, Sarah took her *Hamlet* to Shakespeare's hometown, Stratford-upon-Avon. Then she ventured north to Edinburgh, where, because her costume failed to arrive on time, she was forced to play the role in a kilt to the bewildered amusement of the Scots. After sweeping across Europe as the melancholy Dane, Sarah returned to Paris for an additional fifty triumphant shows. A scene from the historical performance—the sword fight with Laertes—was even captured on film for the Paris Expo of 1900, and survives to this day on YouTube.

Just six years prior, the French Lumière brothers had won the race against Thomas Edison to produce the first viable movie camera. By 1900, visitors to the expo could pay one franc to see a series of short subjects, such as "Feeding the Baby" or "Fishing for Goldfish." But all of these shorts were silent and felt more like home movies than works of art. Sarah's *Hamlet* constituted the first attempt to capture high art on celluloid. What was truly groundbreaking was that technicians had also captured a sound recording of Sarah delivering her lines, which they ran in conjunction with the projector—using separate but synchronized technologies to make Bernhardt the first actress to speak on film.

While Bernhardt, so often a pioneer, would go on to have some misgivings about the medium of film, she also harbored nagging concerns about the nature of her art, which, unlike a painting, is ephemeral. For Sarah, celluloid held the promise of immortality.

— — —

One year after *Hamlet*, Sarah, at age fifty-six, took the stage in full military dress to play the twenty-one-year-old Duke of Reichstadt, heir to the throne of Bonaparte. It was one of the greatest moments of her career. People wept openly, the ovations were unending. If *Hamlet* had been an artistic tour de force, her turn as Napoleon II was also infused with patriotic fervor, which made it, by some accounts, one of the most triumphant events in theater history. As reported by the *New York Times*: "Everybody distinguished in the worlds of literature, art, and politics was present to witness her performance, and repeated bursts of applause proved that she had added one more brilliant success to an already long list. Melancholy, despair, irony, anger, enthusiasm, and tenderness—all found in the role of Reichstadt—she interpreted to perfection."

Rostand had written *L'Aiglon* in the same manner as *Cyrano*: rhymed alexandrines, the twelve-syllable couplets employed by classical French dramatists such as Racine and Molière. Though he composed it at a time when most modern dramatists, such as Strindberg, Ibsen, and Pirandello, were writing their plays in prose, Rostand, like d'Annunzio, had chosen a more classical form for his work. Both writers felt their text was elevated by the rhythm of the verse structure. As Samuel Taylor Coleridge had half-jokingly remarked, prose was "words in their best order," while poetry was "the best words in their best order."

But the movement toward prose in "realistic" theater was inevitable. Ironically, it had been Shakespeare—the master of verse—who had begun the prose tradition. Many of the Bard's lower-class characters break from iambic pentameter to distinguish their speech from that of the more noble cast members. Even Hamlet delivers one of his poignant, heartfelt speeches ("I have of late . . . lost all my mirth") in prose, and certainly shorter lines ("I pray you leave me") are that way so as to ground the words in reality. Goethe took up prose in his playwriting, and by the nineteenth century the practice had become widespread. Certainly, most of Sarah's repertoire (Dumas, Sardou, and others) was in prose. And yet, at the dawn of the twentieth century, both she and Eleonora had returned to classical forms.

L'Aiglon culminated with the night scene on the battlefield of Wagram, "an episode whose sharp pathos pierces the heart and the imagination like a rapier," wrote one critic. It was "Shakespearean in its character," remarked another, while a third compared it to the Waterloo scene from volume two of Victor Hugo's *Les Misérables.* Reviewers described the moment in vivid detail:

> In the obscurity of the night, you hear the voices of the dead legions rising from their graves. . . . And, when struck with terror before these apparitions . . . the heir of the Caesar, expecting some terrible malediction, his face blanched, his eyes dilated with horror, cries "Why do you open horror-sated lips? What will you speak?" The voices of the corpses utter a formidable cry in turn of "Long Live the Emperor!"
>
> It is the cry of pardon that the victims of the Corsican address to his son. And he then, in a sudden revelation, exclaims: "I understand. I am the expiation!"

France, reeling still from the Dreyfus affair—and earlier still, the humiliating defeat in the Franco-Prussian War—was in desperate need of permission to be proud of its military. And who should give it to them but Sarah Bernhardt, the Jew who had sided with Dreyfus? In that moment, she became the expiation for all of France; all was forgiven, and her position as supreme national icon became permanent.

After months of sold-out performances in Paris, Bernhardt took *L'Aiglon* to London, where it likewise proved irresistible. The young duke became one of her signature roles, and Sarah established the tradition of making it a part to be played almost exclusively, like Peter Pan, by women. Later that year, Maude Adams

would star in the play on Broadway, where Bernhardt was scheduled to return with *Hamlet*—her other cross-gender sensation.

There are similarities between the roles. Conventional wisdom
considered both Hamlet and *L'Aiglon* "inappropriate" models
for manhood—they were brooding, indecisive, even effeminate—
which is why they could, and perhaps should, be played by females.
But Sarah saw it differently: "There is one reason why I think a
woman is better suited to play parts like *L'Aiglon* and *Hamlet* than
a man. These roles portray youths of twenty or twenty-one with
the minds of men of forty. A boy of twenty cannot understand the
philosophy of *Hamlet* nor the poetic enthusiasm of *L'Aiglon*. . . .
An older man . . . does not look the boy, nor has he the ready
adaptability of the woman who can combine the light carriage of
youth with the mature thought of the man." And no one quite
had the adaptability of Sarah Bernhardt—a grandmother still agile
enough to play a teenager.

L'Aiglon proved successful for Bernhardt for another reason,
too: the play was perfectly suited for its time. It is no coincidence
that, within a year of each other, both Sarah and Eleonora starred
in patriotic pageants with militaristic themes and weaponry on the
stage. As the new century began in earnest, the European powers
entered a period of unrestrained nationalism that would soon lead
to the Great War.

SARAH BERNHARDT IN L'AIGLON MAKES GREATEST TRI-
UMPH OF GREAT CAREER.

So claimed a 1901 headline read throughout America, where
Sarah was back on the road. After 250 performances in Paris of
L'Aiglon, Sarah took the play on an extended American tour, which
would last six months, twice the length of Eleonora's overseas
tours. Just like Duse, Bernhardt would end her run at the Met,
but for two weeks instead of Eleonora's one. A key reason for the
tour's success was that Sarah had chosen, this time, to alternate

seasons with her rival rather than go head-to-head. Duse would be back again in 1902. Sarah would not return until 1905.

George Tyler, a colorful impresario who managed both Bernhardt and Duse in America, came up with the marketing gimmick of dubbing Sarah's outings, both in 1901 and the later one in 1905–1906, as "farewell tours" (she had surpassed the average life expectancy for a Victorian woman, after all)—but there would be two more. The farewell tours created a sense of urgency that led to a frenzied rush for tickets. During her late 1905 run in Texas, the indefatigable sixty-something Bernhardt made not one stop, but five—in Dallas, Waco, Austin, San Antonio, and Houston. When it became difficult to secure venues large enough to accommodate the unprecedented demand, Bernhardt performed in a circus tent.

George Tyler had, at first, proposed renting Barnum and Bailey's largest big top, but Sarah dismissed the idea—she'd been mocked once as "Sarah Barnum" in the gossipy 1883 biography by actress and friend-turned-enemy Marie Colombier. Sarah commissioned a custom tent instead—to be built in Kansas City with a staggering seating capacity of five thousand. The tent offered a full acre of seating in an area just shy of a football field

SARAH BERNHARDT'S TRIUMPHANT TOUR IN THE WEST, went a January 1906 headline in *Theatre Magazine*, whose story began:

> The present tour of Sarah Bernhardt is certainly the most remarkable one ever played in this country, not just by Madame Bernhardt, but by any other foreign or native player. Her receipts everywhere have been colossal, and the size of her audiences unprecedented.

In Kansas City, while waiting for her tent to be made, Sarah performed in Convention Hall to an audience of just over 6,500, with an astonishing till of $9,984—"the largest single night receipts from

a dramatic engagement ever known in the history of the stage,"
said *Theatre Magazine*. And Sarah made it look easy.

The play she had chosen for Texas was a classic that had never
failed her: *La Dame aux camélias*. She had taken breaks from the
role from time to time, most notably after seeing Duse play it, but
Bernhardt always came back to *Camille*.

While a drama about a prostitute was racy fare for many Texans
of the day, they devoured it—a reaction that inspired the *New York
Times* reporter to compose a rapturous poem, in iambic heptam-
eter, no less:

> *The Texans crowd into the tents and madly cheer and clap;*
> *The ceiling flounces to and fro; the walls bulge out and flap.*
> *Delighted cries of "Sarah!" sound amid the bravo! calls,*
> *Till Sarah smiles and sweetly bows and then the canvas falls.*

After opening night in Dallas, the tent and its attendant army of
roadies traveled one hundred miles south to Waco, and then onto
Austin. Rain was falling hard when the company arrived at the
state capital. After Sarah inspected the tent site and determined it a
muddy mess, she summoned her car and ordered the driver to take
her to the Hancock Opera House in downtown Austin. Bernhardt
had been barred from performing there; her tour hadn't made a
deal with the syndicate that controlled all the largest venues in the
state. Marching inside nonetheless, Sarah, according to a newspaper
report, "commandeered" the theater.

It helped that George Tyler had telephoned the Texas attorney
general and cited the decade-old Sherman Antitrust Act, suggesting
that the syndicate's stranglehold on Texas theaters might constitute
a monopoly, which would be a violation of federal law. Suddenly,
the Hancock's manager was jumping to fulfill Sarah's every request. But he couldn't, on such short notice, provide the team of
stagehands the diva required. So Sarah walked out onto Sixth Street
and personally rounded up a crew.

When the curtain rose that evening, attendees included the Texas governor, lieutenant governor, and distinguished members of the legislature, along with scores of adoring fans—people with every reason to revere Sarah for her determination to ensure the show went on despite the rains. That night she played the most sublime, glorious, pathetic, sickly, unfortunate, dignified, and ultimately heroic courtesan these Texas boys and girls had ever seen.

On nights like these, Sarah felt an "electricity" in the house—a current between the public and the stage. It flowed toward her, egging her on; and she may have wondered: was this Prana? Was this Duse's Grace?

Whatever it was, Bernhardt certainly knew how to harness it. There remained a power to her presence on the stage that could not be denied—even by Duse. Sarah had played her cards well. The recent alliance with Rostand, the bigger venues, reprising the old standards—each idea had been good. And Sarah still held a trump card.

She had recently challenged the aging Victorien Sardou to write another play for her. The author's previous Bernhardt vehicles had all been successes: *Fédora*, *Théodora*, and *La Tosca*—written for Sarah a decade before Puccini turned the story into an opera. Sardou, whose work Duse also performed, was independently wealthy and wrote for writing's sake alone. He accepted Sarah's challenge and created *La Sorcière (The Sorceress)*, a drama set in Spain, pitting an accused witch against the tyrannical Inquisition. The plot could not have been more perfect for Bernhardt, who found herself increasingly under fire by the intelligentsia.

The playwright was in his seventies by that time yet still utterly captivating. "Sardou looked a little like Napoleon, a little like Voltaire and a little like the smiling portrait of a malicious actress," joked Italian writer Edmondo de Amicis. "He wore a large black velvet cap, below which fell long waving gray locks. . . . My attention was riveted by his strange face, without beard and colorless . . . lighted up by two keenly sparkling gray eyes, full of thought, the glances of which correspond with the rapid motion of the thin and flexible lips."

Sardou loved to talk, which was generally charming—except when the playwright insisted on attending every one of Sarah's rehearsals. It did not take long for the thirty actors in her company to succumb to the playwright's charisma, and suddenly, to Bernhardt's chagrin, there were two directors on the set.

Marguerite Moreno, a young actress in Sarah's company, recalled an example of the frequent and storied bickering between the playwright and the diva during rehearsals for *La Sorcière*:

> Suddenly Sardou climbed up on a table. And what a sight he was in his eternal black velvet beret and white silk foulard. . . .
>
> SARDOU: [to Sarah] "I want you to sit still during this scene."
> SARAH: "But adored master, I'll look like a dead fish if I don't move."
> SARDOU: "Listen, *ma petite*, I'm not an idiot yet, and I tell you that if you move you'll ruin the whole scene."
> SARAH: "I'd rather ruin it than sit still."
> SARDOU: "Good God, Sarah, you *are* irritating."

The playwright must have realized his audacity in offering that particular suggestion, since sitting still was what Eleonora did onstage. Duse would be seated and do nothing but listen. Yet her listening was so alive that her thoughts became almost audible to the crowd. Duse was interested in having the character's thoughts arise spontaneously—meaning she never wanted to force them—so this was not a "pose," not something you could plan and rehearse in advance, which is why Sarah remained wary of doing it.

But Sardou, who had worked with Duse on plays like *Fédora* and *Divorçons*, was gently nudging Sarah precisely in that direction—to stop "performing" and start simply "being" in the scene. He was trying to bring his dear friend Sarah—the nineteenth century's greatest actress—into step with modern times.

CHAPTER FIFTEEN

The beginning of the end came in 1903, on Duse's return from America. Exhausted from her tour and wary of another reunion with d'Annunzio, Duse became acutely ill on the ship home. Her fever made the Atlantic crossing the worst she had experienced.

When Duse arrived at the twin Tuscan villas, she discovered that d'Annunzio, as feared, had a new mistress installed in a Florence apartment: the Art Nouveau dancer Loie Fuller, who had been an inspiration for Toulouse-Lautrec. An irate Duse stayed just long enough to regain her strength, then set off for a northern tour from which she sent d'Annunzio the following telegram:

> No more pain will come from me.
> I will tie myself to work

In the past—the moment her father died, the loss of her newborn son—Duse had used her pain to feed the work onstage. "I play them well," she had said of Ibsen's heroines, "because I am filled with sorrow." Now it appears Duse was counting on the stage as a means to escape her pain.

As was her pattern, she followed the telegram with a letter the same day:

> You are free towards me as towards life itself. I can no longer
> live beside you.

She had come to realize that d'Annunzio would never change and admitted her "blindness" to a friend: "It seemed to me that it would have been in vain to make a *new form of art* without a new form of life." In fact, d'Annunzio believed that the way he lived was itself a work of art. He did as he pleased, no matter the consequence— even if it hurt the one he actually loved. D'Annunzio saw no need to alter his ways, nor his politics. "I am beyond right and left," he had told the press: "I am beyond good and evil."

No longer artistically exclusive to d'Annunzio, Duse returned to her beloved Ibsen and presented *Hedda Gabler* in Vienna in March. D'Annunzio, a free agent as well, licensed *Francesca* to another company and began work on a new play, *La figlia di Iorio* (*Iorio's Daughter*), a tragic allegory about a simple peasant girl with spiritual gifts who is feared by ignorant villagers and burned at the stake as a witch. With uncanny synchronicity, d'Annunzio had flashed upon his idea at nearly the same moment that Sardou had conceived *The Sorceress* for Sarah.

Even a half century before Arthur Miller penned *The Crucible*, "witches" were a preoccupation of the time. The widespread practice of witch hunting and witch burning, which had claimed some thirty-five thousand women since it became formal church practice in 1481, had continued through the early nineteenth century, and the persecution was ongoing, at least in spirit.

Eleonora and Sarah were both spiritually gifted women, and it makes sense that their respective lover-writers might compose plays about witchcraft for them. The stories were allegories, in a sense, for their lives as celebrities—surrounded by the frenzied mob, the harsh critics, and fickle public.

Both d'Annunzio and Sardou would write their plays over the summer months of 1903. One witch would soar, the other would wither.

D'Annunzio, to his dismay, was feeling blocked again. Without his muse, the writing just wasn't coming. He had intended to model the protagonist of *Iorio's Daughter* on Eleonora as a young girl, but he wasn't feeling it anymore; he needed to be near her. So, in the summer of 1903, d'Annunzio proposed "an experiment in peace"—they would rent, once again, side-by-side luxury vacation homes, this time on the coast south of Rome, with bucolic views of the Tyrrhenian Sea.

Eleonora agreed. Though no longer lovers, Duse and d'Annunzio remained friends; and, while nonexclusive, they still maintained a professional commitment to each other. Duse clung, in fact, to the continued collaboration—the fantasy of creating "a *new form of art*" with d'Annunzio.

"I will never forget the sweet hours of hope—life and art and pain—that I lived next to you," Eleonora wrote d'Annunzio, while admitting her continued weakness "for your work, which still enchants me."

She wanted to be a part of this new play. But the other enchantment was over for her. "I am neither beautiful—nor young, nor happy—nor forgetful," she wrote. At forty-four, Duse was feeling old.

The sea breeze, briny and fresh, did wonders for Eleonora's lungs; she felt both healthy and happy. With d'Annunzio busy writing in the villa next door, Duse played host to the famed American starlet Alice Nielsen, a headliner of opera and Broadway. Barely thirty, Nielsen was already the biggest draw in America, touring over forty thousand miles a year—which outpaced even Sarah. But Nielsen felt that her fame had been getting in the way of her art; she was visiting Duse as a pupil.

Eleonora loved to mentor younger actresses she thought were sincere. She had never forgotten her own experience as an ingénue in Naples when she joined the company of established star Giacinta Pezzana, who had been surprisingly unthreatened and supportive of Eleonora's radical work. Pezzana's nod had given Duse just the boost she needed.

When two talented young sisters, Irma and Emma Gramatica, joined the then-rising Duse on a tour of South America, she did everything she could to support the girls and help them find their true voice as actors. That was the hope of Alice Nielsen for her summer with Eleonora. The American star was moved simply to be in the presence of Duse, who appeared saintlike to her, quite literally glowing: "A luminous unearthly sort of light emanated from her face and seemed to form a halo round her turbaned head."

"In her merry moods, Duse seemed to be joy incarnate," recalled the young American in her journal. But Eleonora was troubled, nonetheless, by things she rarely discussed. "Although she never mentioned it," Nielsen continued, "growing old was eating into the very marrow of her being. Often she would look searchingly into my face and sigh: 'Ah, you do not know how fortunate you are to be so young and fair.'"

It was an area where Eleonora may have envied Sarah, who, while fourteen years older, still appeared ageless on the stage with the help of makeup. Duse herself succumbed, finally, to makeup, both onstage and off. Yet for all her fretting, Duse was still handsome—photographs from this period show her striking face framing mournful, slightly drooping eyes. "Her face is unchanged," a critic would write of Duse later that year, "the face that blends the mystery of a tragic mask with the open, wide-eyed gaze of a child." Wrinkles or not, Duse's eyes remained forever young.

With d'Annunzio working long hours, the play came together like lightning—which tended to happen when d'Annunzio was within the vibrational sphere of his muse. As was his custom, d'Annunzio invited a few close friends to sit with Eleonora as he read the finished play to her.

The plot involves Aligi, a young shepherd, who gives shelter to Mila, a peasant girl suspected of witchery. But after Aligi protects her from superstitious villagers, he, too, is banished, and the two are forced into exile in the hills. One day his father catches Mila alone in the woods, accuses her of bewitching his son, and starts to rape her. Aligi stumbles upon the scene and savagely kills his father with his axe.

In the finale, Mila and Aligi have been caught by the townsfolk, who condemn the boy to death for patricide. But Mila intervenes and takes the blame. Offering herself up as a sacrificial lamb, she admits to bewitching Aligi—it was *she* who murdered his father, not Aligi, she says. Every villager is held rapt by her confession; none more so than Aligi, who knows the truth.

The girl drops her shawl and, knowing that the lamb must be slaughtered, quietly does it herself. Stepping onto the burning funeral pyre, the "witch" gazes back at the poor villagers, lost in their delusion. She smiles at Aligi and says "the flame is beautiful," before fire immolates her body.

Eleonora was in tears when d'Annunzio put down the manuscript. She called it a "divine work" that had touched her soul. She knew Mila; she *was* Mila—quite literally, the inspiration for the character. There was only one problem: Mila was a child of fifteen. Could she really be played by a woman in her midforties?

Duse sought answers in her mirrors. Certainly, she thought of her rival—this would have presented no impediment whatsoever for Sarah, who had played the teenaged Joan of Arc in her forties (she'd do so again in her sixties). But it was a real quandary for Eleonora, who felt torn between competing allegiances. On the one hand, *verismo* demanded an unequivocal commitment to "Truth" in all its details. Anything false on the stage would call attention to itself, making it harder for the audience to enter into the "make-believe" of the play. It was a different experience, in Duse's mind, from the *suspension of disbelief* required of audiences watching plays in the old style: "Look, there's Sarah Bernhardt, yes I know she's a grandmother, but isn't she glorious? Let's pretend (together) that Sarah is a teenage girl." That required far too much fussing.

In *verismo*, the actor and audience merge as one in the "Truth" of the play and its theme, one as transmitter, one as receiver. It was sacred—and fragile. Wouldn't it be jarring for Duse, who strove to avoid calling attention to her persona and personality onstage, to "pretend" to be three decades younger?

Yet here was Eleonora's dilemma. Naturalism was built on the idea of acting from the inside—from the level of the soul, which is ageless. There are no limits to the magic that can emanate from this realm. Duse believed she could pull it off, and she wanted to prove it to d'Annunzio.

But d'Annunzio had his own dilemma. While the role called for a younger actress, he still needed Duse's name on the marquee. D'Annunzio considered *Iorio* his finest play yet and had no intention of compromising on its casting. So he came up with a devilish plan. Among Italy's up-and-coming ingénues was a pair of sisters: Irma and Emma Gramatica, the same actresses Duse had mentored on her first visit to South America and continued to correspond with. His eyes set on Irma, d'Annunzio met secretly with Virgilio Talli, the director of her company, and proposed the following deal: Eleonora would temporarily join the company as a "visiting artist" and premiere in the role of Mila, before ceding it several shows later to her new protégée, Irma Gramatica.

Duse caught a bad cold that winter, deep in her lungs—the coughing became violent, day and night. It was the pattern for Eleonora after an emotional upheaval—like her debut in Paris, or the death of her father—where Duse had canceled a string of performances and taken to her bed. It transpired again in January of 1904, when d'Annunzio dropped the bombshell of finally telling Eleonora about the secret pact he'd made with Irma Gramatica and the Talli Company.

Eleonora was stupefied—*another* professional betrayal, even more awful than the last. Not that Irma was without talent—it was her age that was enraging. Gramatica was by now in her thirties, hardly the nubile teenager called for in the script. The message was unambiguous: at forty-five, Duse was over the hill. Yet,

astonishingly, Eleonora agreed to comply with d'Annunzio's humiliating plan—she would premiere the role, then step down.

Why? Sarah had just premiered her witch in Paris to gushing notices: "Madame Bernhardt is incomparable, prestigious, glamorous,"
enthused one. "Never has she been more beautiful," raved another.
"Never has her voice been fresher . . . never has her charm and tragic
appeal been more devastating." *La Sorcière*, indeed. The Divine
Sarah, at fifty-nine, was drinking from the fountain of youth.

Duse needed to prove to d'Annunzio that she, too, could still
play a teenager—even if only for a single performance. Yet even
this was not to be.

Her nagging cold deteriorated to the point where she lost her
voice, and Duse asked d'Annunzio to postpone the play. But he
balked: all the arrangements had been made. The production was
already in deficit by 100,000 lire, a sum covered by Eleonora's
banker friend, Robi Mendelssohn.

Eleonora's loyal friend Matilde Serao was with her on March 2,
when d'Annunzio's *La figlia di Iorio* opened with Irma Gramatica
at the Teatro Lirico in Milan. This time, Duse gave specific instructions that she preferred not to receive telegrams between acts. She
still acted out the part, however, line by line, as she had with *The
Dead City*—wistfully picturing herself onstage.

No one knew if the play could succeed without Duse. Ruggero
Ruggeri, the lead actor of *Iorio*, recalled the tense mood at the
theater:

> When the curtain rose, the immense crowd plunged into a deep
> silence from which it never emerged, not even for a moment,
> during the whole first act, which is quite long. . . . As the curtains
> closed, a sepulchral silence followed in the house. We looked
> at one another, all of us dumbfounded. Was it possible? What
> was happening? Was the work being received by a cold, hostile
> silence? But it was as if the audience, under the poetic spell of the
> work of art, had to make a collective effort to recover itself.

D'Annunzio's powerful ending—the "witch" choosing to immolate herself as a sacrificial offering upon the pyre—had been played to perfection by Irma Gramatica; her naturalistic performance had left the house speechless. It took a moment for the crowd to "emerge from the . . . fiction, and see again the theater, the actors, the performance behind the poetry." Then: "The ovation exploded in a formidable din."

D'Annunzio had scored the biggest success of his playwriting career. After years of struggling with artistic failures, with all the criticism, with the ridicule, he'd scored his only unbridled triumph—and Eleonora had had nothing to do with it. The hurt she felt was profound.

Duse began to picture a life without d'Annunzio. She was depressed, even suicidal, according to Matilde Serao. When her strength returned, Duse traveled back to Tuscany to collect some things from her villa. Underneath the pillows of the guest room, she found two golden hairpins belonging to another woman. The realization that her lover had had the callousness to host a mistress in Duse's home sent Eleonora into a rage. She was inconsolable as she charged outside, flaming torch in hand, running through the moonlit hedges of d'Annunzio's opulent villa next door. The dogs began to howl, horses snorted apprehensively in their stalls.

"You want the flame?" she yelled. "Take it! Take it!" sending embers in all directions as she slashed madly with the burning torch. She set fire to some drapes, an oriental screen. Servants scattered in search of water. "The flame! The flame!!" she cried. "It's necessary!"

She was twisting the final line of d'Annunzio's play: "The flame . . . it's beautiful!"

It was the end, finally, to one of the theater world's most complex romances—one that gave rise to some of its most grandiose productions and fanned one of its greatest rivalries. Duse's seven-year attachment to d'Annunzio's belabored plays may well have cost the actress her rightful place in history. Ultimately, the alliance served d'Annunzio better than it did his muse—and brought her far more pain than she could ever have imagined. As a young actress, pain was something Eleonora had thought she needed for her work. Now, she was done with it.

Just two weeks after the final break with d'Annunzio, Eleonora was back at the Teatro Lirico in Milan, the very theater where *Iorio* had premiered without her. She was presenting *La Dame aux camélias*—as far as she could get from d'Annunzio, who considered the fifty-year-old play to be dated and banal. Duse's choice of play and venue was certainly a swipe at d'Annunzio, but the decision had been largely a practical one.

D'Annunzio had left her with a head-spinning debt of 200,000 francs for a play she hadn't even acted in. It would have meant bankruptcy, if not for the intervention of Robi Mendelssohn, who covered the loss and assumed management of Duse's money and business affairs. Eleonora was forced to resort to Bernhardt's tactic of paying the bills by dusting off *La Dame aux camélias*—for which Eleonora was guaranteed 7,000 francs per show. And yet to do so, she needed d'Annunzio's permission, since the exclusivity clause in their contract was technically still in force. So Duse wrote dutifully to her former partner, asking for his authorization—but he never replied.

On opening night during intermission, Duse received the following telegram in her dressing room:

Is it true you have changed, you have renounced the mission?

Eleonora was outraged. The "mission" was their joint pact to elevate Italian theater and culture, which meant no more frivolous French plays. Coming from a man who had broken their exclusivity pact twice now, this was insolent.

That night, as she took the stage for the final act, Eleonora put her anguished feelings on display for all to see. She would later state: "I was Marguerite as I had never been before."

It was a different Marguerite, to be sure. In a binge of shopping therapy, Eleonora had commissioned new costumes from the House of Worth, her Paris designers, to spruce up her *Camille*. If she had to do a crowd-pleaser, what was the point of holding back? Though she'd be the last to admit it, it was a nod to Bernhardt. Given Duse's penchant for sartorial understatement, this change did not go unnoticed.

"This new incarnation of Marguerite moves, enfolded in white pepla, starred with rainbows of diamonds, like a figure of dreams and poetry," wrote a critic for *L'Illustrazione Italiana*. Yet the public yawned. As critic Ugo Ojetti wrote in the fall of 1904:

> Every time she returns to Italy, it seems that the public, the majority of the public, go to the theatre to judge her coldly, as if she were making her debut that evening, and her fame almost harmed her. Now, at the peak of her glory, she has in Italy neither a theatre nor an audience that is hers. Every time she performs she has to hire the theatre, win the public.

Contrast that with Bernhardt confidante and early biographer Madame Pierre Berton's description of a recent homecoming for Sarah:

> When she returned to France, warships fired salutes, the entire city of Havre was beflagged and illuminated, and some of the most distinguished persons in France were on the quay to greet her.

As Bernhardt was being embraced by her country, Duse was being dismissed by hers. Why? One could argue the French were more patriotic; the Italians, more cynical; that Sarah was more visible in the public eye, and so on. But it really comes down to something far simpler. France had been a nation for more than a century; Italy, at half that age, was still largely tribal. And Eleonora, the perennial nomad, didn't have a tribe—no one knew where she belonged.

— — —

Sarah could not believe what she was hearing: Duse had signed a contract to play the 1905 season *in Paris*. But not with a reputable troupe. No, she was joining a small, experimental theater company: the Théâtre de l'Œuvre, founded by radical actor-director Aurélien-Marie Lugné, whose matchbox theater was open only to subscription holders. While elitist, the director was also egalitarian—the monthly dues subsidized a hundred free tickets given away to the public.

Aurélien went by his stage name, Lugné-Poë, in honor of the hero of the French Symbolists: Edgar Allan Poe. Though disparaged by contemporary American writers like Emerson as "a jingle man," Poe was considered a genius in France for his work, which boldly rejected romanticism and yet was hardly an embrace of realism. Poe's stories were not in any sense "real," and yet they *were*—grotesquely so. This is the landscape where d'Annunzio thrived, along with other contrarians who felt there was something fundamentally pedestrian about realism. The biggest proponent of this thinking was a woman named Sarah Bernhardt. Oddly, this put her in the same camp as the iconoclastic Lugné-Poë. Though he'd later embrace Ibsen, Lugné-Poë had been an early rejecter of naturalism. It was he who had finally staged Oscar Wilde's *Salomé*, after the risqué play had been passed on by both Sarah and Eleonora.

As before, Bernhardt reached out to her rival. *"Ma petite, je suis désolée, désolée, désolée,"* she wrote, informing Duse that Lugné-Poë's theater would be far too small for her. She offered Eleonora, once again, the use of her own bigger space, the same tactic she'd used in 1897 when Duse came for her Paris debut. The results eight years ago had been mixed, so it's unclear what Sarah was hoping to accomplish.

But Duse refused the hospitality this time; she wanted nothing to do with Sarah. Duse was yearning to reconnect with the fearlessness of her youth—that's what had inspired the alliance with

Lugné-Poë, a fellow admirer of Henrik Ibsen. Duse had bonded with Lugné-Poë over their shared love for the Norwegian's plays.

While in Paris, Eleonora performed an intimate staging of Ibsen's *Hedda Gabler* at the Théâtre de l'Œuvre. On other nights, they ran *A Doll's House*, *The Master Builder*, and *The Enemy of the People*, all Ibsen plays, but Eleonora watched these productions from the audience. In a gesture of humility, Duse had agreed to share the season with Lugné-Poë's talented wife, Suzanne Desprès.

Eleonora quickly became enamored of them as a couple, perhaps even a little envious. "You two possess the *best* of happiness, working together, struggling together," she wrote. Duse signed the note—along with other letters to them—*Sociétaire de l'Œuvre*, meaning tenured-member or "lifer" in the company. She was proud to be associated with a group of vanguard actors doing exciting work and essentially donated her time to them.

"I asked her what her salary would be," wrote Lugné-Poë.

"What do you pay the boy who's so good as the lunatic?" she asked, naming a minor role from *Peer Gynt*.

"Ten francs," answered Lugné-Poë.

"Then pay me that," she said, according to Lugné-Poë's memoir, *Sous les étoiles.*

As Duse fell in love with *l'Œuvre* and the Lugné-Poës, she took Suzanne aside one evening to discuss something that had been gnawing at her, according to Lugné-Poë. He quoted Duse in his autobiography as saying to Suzanne: "If, once . . . your husband, if I possessed him . . . once . . . just once . . . you wouldn't bear me ill will, would you? It's the hinge of friendship."

Suzanne looked at her incredulously. Was she serious?

No—at least, not yet.

Some months later, Duse was back in Italy in bed with a fever. Feeling sorry for herself, she wrote to Lugné-Poë:

The only thing I know how to do in my life is to cry, to suffer and to die! Ah! Why have things gone this way? I feel so lost, so out of tune with life.

She was disenchanted with contemporary theater, which, while changing, was still rooted in the nineteenth century. Her actors chafed during the long rehearsals she demanded of them as she attempted to teach them about Ibsen. The text cannot simply be memorized, she would explain in exasperation—it must be studied . . . as a work of Art. You can't just deliver the lines, you must know the play's theme and understand your role in it. You must know your character's thoughts, for it's between lines that plays become interesting.

There was head scratching and blank stares. In Eleonora's frustration, she became hard on the other actors, even her costars, berating them in public and demanding to be addressed as "La Signora."

"Your acting is hopeless! Pitiful!" she told one actress. "Go on, cry, cry! It will do you some good."

Then Eleonora took a breath and softened: "Practice at home to put every word you speak deeper inside you, down in your body, not up in your head or in that little nose."

Other advice was harder to enact. When actors perform from the ego, she explained, there is nowhere to go. "We have an enemy within us," she would say. "We have to confront it and overcome it." But the idea of ego as enemy was still way ahead of its time.

As if making up for the years lost being faithful to d'Annunzio, Eleonora began an affair with Lugné-Poë. It wasn't the first time she had slept with a married man whose wife was a friend. Eleonora had already crossed that line with Robi Mendelssohn, the husband of her former traveling companion Giulietta, and now her financial adviser as well. It was in misguided retaliation, perhaps, for d'Annunzio's intense attraction to Giulietta, and for his obsession with her fictional counterpart, Donatella Arvale, in *The Flame*.

The misguided tryst with Lugné-Poë began during a 1905 to 1906 tour of Scandinavia. There were legitimate reasons for the two to be seen together, which created an ideal smoke screen. Lugné-Poë had become Eleonora's manager, and since she and his wife, Suzanne, were both leading ladies, they rarely crossed paths onstage.

The Scandinavia tour was calamitous. King Christian IX of Denmark died, which canceled their engagements in Copenhagen. On their way to Christiana (now Oslo), they received word that Ibsen was dying, too.

"Soon I shall go into the great darkness," Ibsen told his son, Sigurd, who had named his third child Eleonora in honor of the actress.

By the time Duse and Lugné-Poë arrived in Norway, Ibsen was too ill to receive them. Eleonora was devastated. After sending a note and a bouquet to Ibsen's wife, she dragged Lugné-Poë through the thick snow to wait beneath the master's window, lest he should appear and wave to well-wishers as he had been known to do. But Ibsen never rose from his deathbed.

That same winter, Eleonora wrote a letter to Suzanne Desprès, who remained oblivious to Duse's dalliance with her husband:

> I feel and I hope that "a tomorrow" of our work and our art
> lies in you—and this is why I speak to you and tell you—you
> alone—the sweet sorrow there is for me in this decision—
> now taken—to leave my work. . . . To my art I have given
> my love, my strength, my youth, my life: all—all—I have
> therefore decided that, this year, my work will be directed
> towards freedom.

Duse was, apparently, retiring from the stage.

CHAPTER SIXTEEN

In the months following Eleonora's letter to Suzanne Després, Bernhardt ventured into her rival's terrain. Whether she knew of Duse's intention to retire is unclear, but Paris is a small town where gossip abounds—especially in the theater world. Here's what we *do* know: Bernhardt tried her hand at Ibsen.

She gave one, and only one, performance of *The Lady from the Sea* in Geneva. She also talked about performing in *A Doll's House*, though that never materialized. Sarah quickly decided that Ibsen was not for her. But in November of 1906, Sarah played a part that may as well have been written for Duse: Saint Teresa of Ávila, a sixteenth-century mystic.

There were snickers, of course, when Sarah took the stage as a virgin saint. But the 1906 play, *La Vierge d'Avila*, by iconoclast Catulle Mendès, was actually quite racy in its suggestions about the taboos and fantasies of a cloistered life. The shocking play quickly became the must-see of the Paris season—Sarah's "most sublime creation," according to one influential critic.

Things changed when Bernhardt took *La Vierge d'Avila* on the road. In Spain, *La Vierge* was deemed a sacrilege. The archbishop of Ávila ordered his congregants to circle the town walls in prayer to exorcize the demons unleashed by the scandalous play, written by a Jew for a Jewess. Mendès was thrilled. But these grand productions were beginning to take their toll on Sarah, now over sixty. The constant need to top herself was exhausting.

Jean Cocteau described a curtain call he saw as a teenager by a thoroughly spent Sarah, leaning on the proscenium arch: "Like some Venetian palazzo, Sarah listed under the weight of her chokers and her fatigue, painted, gilded . . . and propped amid a columbarium of applause."

The play may have been risqué, but Sarah herself felt dated. Bernhardt at sixty had become at once glorious and grotesque, as Cocteau described her, "her body . . . like that of some splendid rag doll," her time on the stage "one long swoon broken by screams of rage."

But then Cocteau took the modern audience to task for mocking her. "We are so ridiculous," he wrote, "as to . . . take as an insult to ourselves the first unfamiliar sign of greatness." The old-school poses, once de rigueur, had become foreign to modern audiences.

So Bernhardt, to her credit, changed the way she performed. There was a new element to her splendid poses, one clearly influenced by Duse: Sarah now went still between each, creating a series of theatrical tableaus, frozen in time like a sequence of photographs—influenced perhaps by the advent of cinema and its early precursors such as flip-books. W. B. Yeats described the effect, after seeing her in London:

> For long periods the performers would merely stand and pose, and I once counted twenty-seven [beats] quite slowly before anybody on a fairly well-filled stage moved, as it seemed, so much as an eyelash. . . . Sara [*sic*] Bernhardt would keep her hands clasped over, let us say, her right breast for some time, then move them to the other side . . . and then, after another long stillness, she would unclasp them and hold one out, and so on, not lowering them till she had exhausted all the gestures of uplifted hands.

Was it ridiculous—or brilliant? While opinions differed, Bernhardt's ticket sales did not falter. In fact, she was more sought-after than ever.

— — —

The leg had been bothering her for years, decades really. Surgeons had told Sarah there was no choice: amputation was the only option. But it was hardly the first time she had heard *that*. Bernhardt had never stopped to let her leg properly heal after an injury playing Joan of Arc in 1891.

By 1902, P. T. Barnum, the American circus impresario, had asked for a meeting with Sarah in which he reportedly said: "I hear you're planning to cut off your leg" (or words to that effect), according to Madame Pierre Berton: "Barnum then proceeded to offer Bernhardt ten thousand dollars to use her severed limb 'for exhibition purposes.'"

He wanted the actress—part of her, at least—to be an attraction for his traveling circus, The Greatest Show on Earth. Sarah, astounded and appalled by the proposal, lifted her skirt and petticoat to show the audacious American her less-than-impressive leg, "which had shrunk a good deal owing to the injury," noted Berton. "'I am afraid that you would lose on your bargain,' said the actress to P. T. Barnum. 'Nobody would believe that *that*,' she wiggled it, 'was the leg of Sarah Bernhardt!'"

Despite her flippant response, the prospect of becoming a sideshow freak horrified Bernhardt—which is why she postponed dealing with her leg well past that point. But the swollen knee caused her so much pain that Sarah was unable to perform full-length plays in proper theaters when she embarked on her second "Farewell Tour" of America ten years later, in 1912. She was limited, instead, to half-hour shows on the Keith-Orpheum vaudeville circuit, where customers expected a quick, inexpensive laugh. Common people came in numbers to see the legendary Sarah Bernhardt. While on tour, she was propositioned by another pioneering showman from America: Adolph Zukor, who would one day control Paramount Pictures.

Once a furrier, Zukor had entered show business as an entrepreneur, establishing Famous Players, with the slogan "Famous Players in Famous Plays." His proposal for Sarah was simple: he wanted to turn her into a motion picture star.

For the tidy sum of $360 per day and 10 percent of the gross, Bernhardt appeared in *Elizabeth, Queen of England*, a rare four-reeler running nearly forty-five minutes. The film, about Elizabeth I and her ill-fated love affair with the Earl of Essex, was a big success. It earned $80,000 across America on an investment of $18,000 and was instrumental in pushing dime-show exhibitors to accept longer, "feature-length" productions. A full year before silent film legend Charlie Chaplin signed his first movie contract, Sarah Bernhardt became the original international movie star.

It was high time, grumbled Sarah, upon learning she was to receive France's highest accolade: being named a *Chevalier* of the Legion of Honor. Her artist friend Louise Abbéma had been accorded the honor years earlier. Bernhardt's knighting in early 1914 became the event of the season. "There is only one Sarah," affirmed the press:

> She has given her heart and soul to the French drama. She is endlessly active, conquering, Napoleonic. . . . In honoring Madame Sarah Bernhardt the State is honoring an Ambassadress of French poetry.

Once knighted, Bernhardt decided the time had come to give back to her profession. Using her theater as a school, one day per week, she began tutoring actresses of all ages, handpicked by audition— from beginners to more established players. Critic James Agate's sister, May, was one of Bernhardt's pupils in her early twenties and described the scene in her book *Madame Sarah*:

> We all sat around in a wide semi-circle. Madame Bernhardt was installed behind the producer's table down-stage . . . in her easy-chair, swathed in her famous chinchilla coat, rug over her knees, elbows on the table, and chin cupped in hand.

Getting the Bernhardt stare must have been intimidating, but "to the younger pupils [Bernhardt] was a veritable Mother Superior, and often the theater took on the aspect of a convent."

It was Bernhardt's attempt to fill the shoes of Reverend Mother Sainte-Sophie, who'd been so kind to her at the Couvent de Grand-Champs.

According to Agate's account, the Divine One regaled her new charges with mocking tales of her "old-school" instructors at the Conservatoire, who taught:

> Ridiculous exercises . . . they called *l'assiette* — that is to say, the way in which you sat down. There was the *assiette* which said "so pleased you have called," quite different from the one which said "I wish you hadn't!" The special gesture for "Sortez, Monsieur!" with its accompanying ferocious expression of face, and other absurdities of the old *régime* which she said she did her utmost to forget immediately.

Sarah was recasting herself as the rebel who had overturned the system — in other words, as Duse. She wanted to make sure that's how she was remembered, and it seemed to work, at least with students like May Agate, who wrote thirty years after the fact:

> My outstanding memory of her lessons is of one long outcry against the old school of acting. Their arm-waving and barnstorming must have been grotesque, but nobody saw it until Sarah came along and said it was meaningless.

Nobody but Duse, that is. But she was in retirement now. Bernhardt had outlasted her younger rival. She had the stage to herself again.

On August 3, 1914, Kaiser Wilhelm II declared war on France. As the massive German army marched on Paris, all of Sarah's friends fled to the provinces for refuge. But Bernhardt, now almost seventy years old, wouldn't budge. She had remained in the capital during the Franco-Prussian War, even helped with the wounded. Why should she leave now? Evidently, there was cause: friends had heard reports that Sarah's name was on a list of prominent hostages the Germans planned to take back to Berlin. Bernhardt laughed; even this would not sway her. Besides, she had her own reason for staying put. His name: Dr. Samuel Pozzi.

A close friend, handsome and worldly, Sarah called him Docteur Dieu (Dr. God), for he was the only surgeon she trusted. A gynecologist to the stars, Pozzi was also called "the love doctor" because of his many conquests, the actress Gabrielle Réjane and Sarah herself among them. John Singer Sargent captured Pozzi in a striking painting that hangs today in Los Angeles's Hammer Museum: Pozzi cuts an impressive figure, standing, very relaxed, a full-length maroon robe complementing his neatly trimmed beard.

But Sarah's interest in Pozzi in 1914 was strictly professional. She needed a doctor she could trust. Six months earlier, Bernhardt had written to him in desperation:

> My beloved Docteur Dieu: I beg you to take this letter
> seriously. On February seventh my leg will have been in a
> plaster cast for six months. I was suffering more than ever and
> asked the surgeon, Denucé, to remove it.

Dr. Denucé had not heeded Sarah's wishes, and now the situation had grown intolerable.

> Listen to me, my adored friend. I beg you, cut off my leg a
> little above the knee. Do not protest. I have perhaps ten or
> fifteen years left. Why condemn me to constant suffering? . . .
> With a well-constructed wooden leg I'll be able to give poetry
> readings and even make lecture tours.

Bernhardt, in a rare moment of weakness, was vastly underestimating herself.

On the day of the surgery, Sarah reported to the operating theater at ten sharp, and seemed very calm. She sent for her son, Maurice, who came to embrace her. "*Au revoir*, my beloved, my Maurice," she said, "*au revoir*."

Mademoiselle Coignt, the nurse anesthesiologist, couldn't believe her ears. "It was the same voice I had heard in *La Tosca, La Dame aux camélias, L'Aiglon,*" she marveled. "It was a great joy for me to be so close to the actress, who, one might say, has ruled the universe through her art."

Then the Divine One turned to Dr. Denucé, who had at last agreed to perform the operation, and said: "My darling, give me a kiss."

To the star-struck anesthesiologist, she said, "Mademoiselle, I'm in your hands. Promise you'll really put me to sleep. Let's go, quickly, quickly."

Mademoiselle Coignt fumbled nervously with the gas mask. Bernhardt had some trouble, at first, with the ether. She complained, then finally muttered: "Ah! That's good, It's working, working. I'm going, going, going. I'm gone."

Mademoiselle Coignt shook her head in wonder. "In all of this one could not help but see the tragedienne putting on an act. I felt I was at the theater."

One never knew with Sarah.

The twentysomething Béatrix Dussane was a rising star in Paris's fringe theater scene when she received word in 1916 that Sarah Bernhardt wished to speak with her. Béatrix was part of the counterculture; she detested Sarah Bernhardt and what she stood for. "Our generation reacted badly, perhaps unjustly, to her fame," she explained in her book, *Queens of the Theatre*. "It seemed monstrous somehow for anyone to have been idolized for so long a time. 'Why doesn't she retire?' we'd say."

Béatrix was part of the Théâtre des Armées, a ragtag group of actors who traveled to the front lines, putting on comedic skits in the muddy encampments so that bloody and exhausted men could remember how to smile. When she heard that the legendary Sarah Bernhardt wanted to volunteer, Béatrix had scoffed at first in derision. The idea of "The Divine One" joining the scrappy Théâtre des Armées was laughable. "The front was not pleasurable or brilliant, it was exhausting," explained Béatrix, even for young people. "Many of us, in fact, left a part of our young health behind."

It could never work with an amputee: "How could she be transported from barn to barn, from makeshift stages to army trucks?" It was impossible given "her bouquets, her furs, her sovereign luxury"—all the things she had never done without. "She would fall ill the first day, and that would be the end of the tour," Béatrix avowed. But her companions outvoted her; they saw some possibility in combining the old and the new.

Béatrix was dispatched to meet with Sarah. She recalled the meeting thus:

> I was ushered into her white boudoir. She was seated in the depths of a large armchair . . . with her thousand folds of satin and lace, her rumpled red hair . . . her wrinkles covered with every imaginable kind of makeup. It was upsetting, sad and upsetting. There she was, the great, the radiant Sarah, so small, so weak—a little pile of ashes.

But Bernhardt came to life as the actresses began to converse, rehearse, and order tea. Béatrix was in awe: "Like many before me, I witnessed a miracle . . . the little pile of ashes [began] throwing off sparks . . . [and] an inextinguishable sun burned under the painted, frilled decrepitude of the old actress."

Ever the patriot, Sarah felt it her duty to support the troops. The Great War had shaken the earth. France alone would lose a million men.

Bernhardt was accepted into the Théâtre des Armées, which valiantly set forth into the war zone. They would be playing a repertoire of patriotic scenes, along with some comedic ones—anything to lift the spirits of the shell-shocked infantrymen.

Sarah and Béatrix—the lone females—became roommates during the nights they slept near the front. "I helped her dress," recalled the younger actress. "She went from chair to table leaning on my arm, or hopping on her poor, seventy-two-year-old leg, saying with that infectious laugh of hers: 'Look, I'm just like a guineahen.' The way she ignored her handicap was beautiful—a victory of the spirit over the failing flesh."

On the day of their first performance, the troubadours entered an army camp near Commercy in northeastern France to bewildered stares. The sight must have been almost comical: Sarah in her floor-length tiger skin coat, carried by attendants like a Byzantine empress in a sedan chair. She disliked using a prosthetic.

"She smiles at every one who looks at her, so they don't dare pity her," Béatrix reminisced in admiration. Bernhardt had never liked playing the victim. And Sarah, like so many of the soldiers in these camps, was now an invalid—there were far too many of them, not enough beds in the hospitals back home. One might have thought she'd be a hero to these men. But when Sarah was deposited on the rickety stage, the reception was chilly:

> We waited for an ovation but it was long in coming, and even then there were only a few scattered bravos. . . . Illustrious names meant nothing to these sturdy farm boys. Sarah sensed this and shuddered. Then she began. Her every word was vibrant, delivered in a pounding rhythm that mounted like a charge into battle. . . . With her final cry "To Arms," the band attacked "La Marseillaise" and three thousand young Frenchmen rose to their feet to cheer.

Sarah had roused the entire camp.

— — —

From sparks that still smoldered within the ashes, the great fire returned. It was like a resurrection: Sarah, back on the boards performing the most famous plays in her repertoire, from *Camille* to *Hamlet*. No prosthetic, no crutches, not even a cane. Bernhardt, instead, arranged the onstage furniture so that there would always be places to sit or something to lean on—a chaise here, a settee there, and a few hops in between. Sarah was indefatigable.

The writer Colette remembered a morning that they had tea. "Don't I make coffee every bit as well as Catulle Mendès," asked Sarah, referring to their mutual friend, the iconoclastic writer of *La Vierge d'Avila*. As the Divine One stretched forth her hand to serve her young caller, Colette took note of Sarah's

> delicate faded hand offering a full cup; the cornflower blue of her eyes, so young, caught in a web of wrinkles; the laughing interrogative coquetry of the turn of her head. And that indomitable, endless desire to please, to please again, to please even unto the gates of death.

Who could resist her?

No sooner had she lost part of her leg than Bernhardt booked passage across the Atlantic for her third "Farewell Tour" of the United States. She adored the Americans. "I am sure the Americans must be great lovers," she had once said. "They are so strong, so primitive, and so childish in their ardor."

Bernhardt's motives were partly diplomatic. The Great War raged in Europe, yet America remained neutral. Sarah had decided to use her tour as a propaganda campaign to rally support for the war. A wave of patriotic fervor had been aroused in Bernhardt during the Franco-Prussian War of 1870; now nearly a half century later she was again using her celebrity in service to the French cause. But her motivation, in both cases, transcended nationalism—it was humanitarian.

Almost fifty years earlier, Sarah had witnessed the final breaths of soldiers in makeshift hospital beds at the Théâtre Odéon. This time she'd been to the front lines, seeing the glazed eyes up close, the bleeding amputees, too many to count. Sarah was determined to do her part to end the Great War, and that meant getting Americans to care about it. Woodrow Wilson had won the presidency in 1916 on the slogan of "He Kept Us Out of War." One year later, Bernhardt was running her own opposition campaign, giving speeches at every stop of her tour. It was unprecedented for a non-politician—let alone an actress. As *The Nation* put it:

> Her dedication to this cause (and her sheer endurance) forged what we still assume to be the dimensions of the celebrity's role in society. . . . The notion of the actor as our social conscience, above politics but on the side of the people, originated with Bernhardt.

Sarah's program at every stop of her American tour was always the same. She began with her most patriotic number, which she had written herself: *Aux champs d'honneur* (*To the Battlefield*). As the curtains rose, Sarah appeared seated, dressed as a wounded soldier in a torn and bloodied uniform. Her right leg was clearly amputated—a bandaged stump for all to see. The effect was chillingly realistic, and made for fantastic theater.

"Her makeup was dead white," remembered Margaret Mower, a bilingual actress who accompanied Bernhardt on the tour as an interpreter. "Her red mouth was wide and her eyes were deeply shadowed with blue kohl. She wore puttees and soldiers' shoes. The effect was miraculously youthful in a macabre, melodramatic way."

Bernhardt always triumphed in that patriotic opening monologue.

"I was bowled over," said Sir John Gielgud, who saw her at age thirteen at London's Coliseum, following Sarah's American tour. "She appeared lying on a tree trunk from which she pulled out as if by miracle the French tricolour, before declaiming a long patriotic poem in French."

You didn't need to know the language to be swept up by Sarah's performance. As a newspaper in Philadelphia wrote: "She is not in need of the consideration of having been the greatest actress of a former generation. She does not evoke admiration because of her many recent sufferings but purely and simply because she is the greatest living actress."

For act two of Bernhardt's American tour, the wounded soldier transformed into the splendid Marguerite Gautier, a courtesan of means. But Bernhardt had a severe limitation in the role. Because of her handicap, she performed the chosen scene on a bed, doing all of her acting with her arms and hands, making her antiquated style even more antiquated.

It was one thing to cheer an injured soldier, quite another to embrace an overacting, one-legged courtesan. Audiences snickered, as did her employees. "Sarah's actors were respectful only in her presence," reported Mower. "Behind her back they callously referred to her as the old madwoman, or simply as the old lady."

Reviewers, like *The American Spectator* founder George Jean Nathan, were vicious:

> To contend that Madame Sarah Bernhardt is still a great actress is to permit chivalry to obscure criticism. . . . The public goes to the theatre less to venerate Sarah Bernhardt the actress than to see Sarah Bernhardt the freak.

It is unknown whether Sarah read this particular review, but she would have likely laughed it off, at least externally. Another American critic had used the same verbiage to describe her 1900 portrayal of *Hamlet*, recommending the play "to the particular

attention of persons who are interested in the study of freaks."
Bernhardt had seen far worse. Vitriolic diatribes against Sarah had
been printed throughout her career, and she, unlike the obsessive
Duse, ignored them.

Sarah sailed back to France in the fall of 1918, just before Armistice Day. But while the fighting had stopped, there was another
danger—influenza. Sarah lost a dear friend that winter to the
highly contagious disease: playwright Edmond Rostand. The influenza pandemic would eventually take one hundred million lives, 5
percent of the world's population.

As Europe began to rebuild, great changes swept across the
continent. With Queen Victoria gone and Victorianism, too, it was
no longer taboo for Sarah, an illegitimate former courtesan, to be
hosted at Windsor Palace. In 1920, she gave a command performance for Queen Alexandra, wife of Edward VII, who was astonished at the septuagenarian's stamina and advised her to take more
rest. Sarah's reply: "Your Majesty, I shall die on the stage: 'tis my
battlefield."

CHAPTER SEVENTEEN

They lined the sidewalk, five rows deep, waiting below the balcony for the news. It came at eight on the evening of March 26, 1923. The shutters opened, a doctor leaned out and said gravely to the crowd: "Sarah Bernhardt is dead."

There was a gasp. Reporters rushed to their motorcars. Papers across the globe, for weeks now, had been running headlines on Bernhardt's deteriorating health, just as they had covered each paltry detail of a kidney operation Sarah had undergone in 1917.

Her son, Maurice, and his family were present with her at the time of her death, along with Sarah's lifelong friend, painter Louise Abbéma. Earlier in the day, the diva had noticed the crowd outside her window getting larger. "Are they journalists?" she had asked Maurice.

"Some of them are," he had replied.

"Then I'll keep them dangling," Sarah declared with a fiendish smile. "They tortured me all my life, now it's my turn." Those were the last words she spoke.

News of Sarah's death traveled quickly. That evening, all actors in the French capital paused their performances to observe two minutes of silence in her honor. Nearly a million people would line the streets for Bernhardt's funeral procession, which was filmed as a Pathé newsreel and distributed around the world. The *Los Angeles Times*, like papers everywhere, ran the story on page one:

There is but one sentence today on the lips of Paris—
"Bernhardt is dead." It has been uttered alike by concierges

and Cabinet ministers, midinettes and princesses. One hears it spoken softly in cafes and whispered in churches. . . .

Her body lay in state for public viewing for three days; twenty gendarmes were needed to keep the crowd flowing.

Sarah had been working until the end, having recently signed a contract with Hollywood for another film: *The Fortune Teller*. Since Bernhardt's health prevented travel, they had brought the production to her—turning Sarah's attic atelier into a motion picture studio, with cameras, scaffolding, and harsh lights that made Sarah blink so often she had required dark sunglasses between takes, along with eye drops.

Mary Marquet, a young actress who was part of the cast, remembered sadly: "There was nothing left to her." Wasted, with dull eyes, huddled in her chair, the seventy-eight-year-old Sarah clutched a small monkey, part of the scene. Marquet, a onetime student of Sarah's, watched nervously as the director leaned forward in his chair and called: "Camera!"

All at once, Marquet witnessed, like actress Béatrix Dussane and writer Colette, the miracle of Sarah igniting herself from within: "Her face lit up, her neck grew longer, her eyes shone . . . [and] her voice . . . was young and strong."

But Sarah's ability for resurrection had its limits. Bernhardt declined in the ensuing weeks; she wasn't able to finish the film. And then, suddenly, she was gone.

The obituaries were hagiographic, even revisionist in their exaltations. FACE OF GREAT ACTRESS SUBTLE EVEN IN DEATH, was the *Los Angeles Times* headline. Sarah had done many things in her seventy-eight years of exuberant life—"subtle" was not one of them.

Eleonora Duse read the news with great sadness.

In 1909, three years after the letter to Suzanne Desprès and desiring a simpler life without suitcases, Eleonora had indeed retired from the stage and settled into a modest house in the town of

Asolo, not far from her Venetian roots. Her abode, which stands to this day, formed part of the medieval city walls with spectacular vistas across the hills. When Eleonora opened the shutters of her bedroom window, she had a view of Mount Grappa. "I put two pots of flowers on the windowsill. Here's an altar," wrote Duse, who rarely traveled anymore, leading an almost cloistered life. But the news of Sarah's death reached everywhere, even Asolo. It came as a surprise to Eleonora. She had always wondered if Sarah, with her inexhaustible spirit, might have outlived her.

Despite their rivalry, despite their differences, Bernhardt had always been the vanguard for Duse, inspiring her until the last bow. Duse recalled the time their paths had first crossed all those years ago at the Teatro Carignano in Turin, when Eleonora was an impressionable ingénue and Bernhardt was already a legend. Eleonora was dazzled by Sarah at the time; she couldn't help but feel a deep admiration for this woman of profound inner strength, fully in control of her own destiny. And Duse's awe of that part of Sarah never diminished. Eleonora had recently been bowled over again when, just six months prior, Sarah had given her final stage performance at age seventy-seven, again in Turin.

The play had been Louis Verneuil's *Daniel*, about a sculptor addicted to morphine—in a few years, this role would become Sir John Gielgud's film debut.

"Now that the public is willing to accept me as I am," Bernhardt had told a critic, "I'm going to do new things." The comment hinted at a deeper truth perhaps: that Bernhardt wanted to be "seen" unvarnished on the stage, like Duse, and be loved for it. So Sarah donned trousers again, pinned up one leg, and took the stage as a jittery dope fiend—influenced no doubt by her late sister and husband, both of whom had died of morphine overdoses.

Eleonora was so impressed that she arranged to have two hundred roses delivered to Sarah's Turin dressing room. Bernhardt accepted them graciously—but was disappointed that her rival had not come herself.

Eleonora had wished to but felt her health wasn't up to it. Duse had even fantasized about how the encounter might have gone: "If we had met, she would have nonchalantly said, 'I lost a leg, and you, what have you lost? And I would have said, 'a lung.'" The divas actually missed each other.

But there had been times when Duse had wanted to throttle her rival. The low point surely had been a memoir that Sarah had published before the war, in which she had belittled Duse's talent, writing:

> Eleonora Duse is more of an actress than an artist. She walks in the tracks left by others.

"Others" meaning Sarah, of course. It was catty and mean-spirited— a low blow, even for Bernhardt.

> She does not imitate [others], to be sure, since she plants flowers where there were trees, and trees where there were flowers, but no personality emerges from her art that can be identified with her name.

Sarah's point was not without merit. Eleonora's art had been one of dissolving her "personality" and becoming invisible. It had maddened Sarah, who had taken great pains as the pioneer of celebrity culture to fashion an unforgettable persona in her professional as well as personal endeavors. The Divine Sarah was larger than life, a legend that would outlive its mortal frame by decades, if not centuries. Duse, on the other hand,

> puts on the gloves of others, but inside out. . . . She has not created a being, a vision, that will evoke her memory.

In 1915, the writer Colette was desperate to leave war-torn France. Though travel was difficult, she had managed to slip away from

Paris for a spring vacation in Italy—a country that had not yet entered the war. In a matter of months, Italy would send five million men into the trenches alongside the Allies. But none of this militarization was apparent on a humid day in mid-May on the streets of Rome, when Colette and a companion decided to duck into a cinema, where the friend noticed: "Behind us, that lady in the back is Eleonora Duse."

So it was. Colette gazed at the actress with respect. Though she had not seen Duse onstage for the better part of a decade, Colette later wrote:

> I recognized the luminous hair, combed back, flame-like, across her forehead, and held in check by a black hat, and the great, deep hollows that set off the brilliance of her eyes by enclosing them in shadow.

The film that night was mediocre, but Eleonora was caught up in it, nonetheless. That celebrated face, inclined first to one side and then to the other, was following the episode of a miserable film drama with an expression of great, tender, trusting naïveté.

Eleonora couldn't help herself. She wasn't going to the movies simply for enjoyment. Duse was there as a professional, studying this new medium that everyone seemed to think was the future. She had seen Sarah's success with *Elizabeth, Queen of England,* and now Duse was being courted out of retirement by her own Hollywood titan: D. W. Griffith, who had recently released his seminal and controversial twelve-reeler *The Birth of a Nation.* Griffith had heard of Duse's reputation and wanted to work with her.

The offer could not have come at a better time; Duse was nearly broke. She had recently been forced to pawn her rings in Florence for two thousand francs. She had even swallowed her pride and asked her own daughter—now married to a professor in England—for a loan, suggesting to Enrichetta that she sell a pearl necklace Eleonora had given her.

In this rare period where Duse was without romantic entangle-ments, Enrichetta had become the outlet for her hypergraphia. As she had done with d'Annunzio, Eleonora sent her multiple letters, sometimes on the same day. "The fever in my heart, ever since Griffith's offer, I have dreamed only of films," Duse wrote her daughter, explaining that the thought of pursuing cinema had come to her in meditation:

> I closed my eyes . . . sleepless. *I said: All right, calm down.*
> *Eleonora, you have always worked,* so retrace your steps . . . if
> your cough prevents you from *speaking,* then make films! *The*
> *art of silence*!

"I could still sell my soul a little, as I did in my youth," she joked, "before my *emphysema* worsens." But Duse had her doubts about making a pact with Hollywood: "So far I haven't signed . . . be-cause making a film is a *spiritual problem.*"

During the war, Duse had reconnected with her former lover Ar-rigo Boito, the erudite librettist of Giuseppe Verdi. "The Saint," she was fond of calling him, for what he had had to endure with her. She and Boito had taken up their perennial conversation about "Art," which got Eleonora wondering about the future of cinema. The medium was in its infancy; in the right hands, she believed it could offer the promise of greatness. But she abhorred the sensa-tional work of Cecil B. DeMille, who was already putting out ten films a year and making truckloads of money.

Night after night, Eleonora had gone to the cinema, hoping to catch a glimpse of a film that would feed her soul. She was always disappointed. Capturing The Grace on film seemed impossible to her, something more ephemeral than "a flash of lightning." For Duse, the magic happened in communion with a live audience, who acted as cocreators. As always, Duse wanted to use the new medium, but not as others had.

Following the success of *Elizabeth*, Bernhardt had made two more films: *La Tosca* and *La Dame aux camélias*. But all three had simply been filmed versions of plays—very static, and unimaginative. They never went outside in natural light or used creative angles, let alone motion. The only thing moving in the frame was Sarah, and because the early nonautomated cameras were often "under-cranked," Sarah jerked about the frame like a hyperactive puppet. Eleonora made a mental note to remember the power of stillness, if and when she were to star in a movie.

She wanted, above all, to work with Italians. The fledgling industry had innovators in Italy. Director Giovanni Pastrone had recently invented the dolly for his 1914 masterpiece *Cabiria*, featuring subtitles by Gabriele d'Annunzio. With its erupting volcanoes and impressive scenes of Hannibal crossing the Alps with an army of elephants, this pioneering Italian film influenced American directors like Cecil B. DeMille to create their own epics.

But these types of films did not appeal to Duse. "Trash—shame!" she lamented, "nothing that stimulates the soul—nothing that . . . frees the imagination!—Nothing of what is *not* seen and weaves life." Which is to say, The Grace.

But Duse had been in touch with a group of renegades in Rome who encouraged her to launch an enterprise called *contre-cinéma* as a way "to initiate something beautiful and worthy." She knew that good films must feature human drama, not simply sensationalism. A movie, like a play, required strong underlying material—a compelling situation with universal themes. Determined that her first film be based on an Italian story, Duse dove into her country's literature, reading exhaustively, searching for some book she could adapt. Finally, she came upon *Cenere* (*Ashes*) by Grazia Deledda, who would one day win the Nobel Prize for Literature. The story's themes were powerful and personal to Duse. "The Book," as she capitalized it in a letter to her daughter, "is based on the necessity (no matter why) of a *separation* of a mother from her son."

The story takes place in the rugged mountains of Sardinia, where Oli, an innocent fifteen-year-old daughter of a local shepherd, is frolicking on midsummer eve when she's seduced by a married man, Anania. When Oli becomes pregnant, she is disowned by her father and community, and she must raise her child in abject poverty.

Desiring a better life for her son, Oli gives the boy up, abandoning the infant on the doorstep of his father, who works for a wealthy agriculturalist. As the boy receives an education and becomes a man, he continues to wonder about the identity of his mother—whom he wishes to redeem from the errant and sinful life he has been told she lives.

Oli is desperately poor, very sick, and quite old when she finally finds her. The son, who is engaged to be married to a prominent young lady, suggests to his fiancée that they take in his mother—but the fiancée is confused and resistant. Oli can see that her son is torn by conflicting loyalties, so she takes her own life to give her son his freedom.

Eleonora was so taken with the story that she decided to write the adaptation herself. She would be collaborating on *Cenere* with actor-director Febo Mari, who would costar as her estranged son; Mari, like Duse, was dedicated to breaking new ground in this nascent medium.

Duse worked tirelessly on the script, her first, intent on getting it right. "I must learn the technical *things*," Eleonora wrote to her daughter. Her whole life she'd been searching in vain for a writer with the right voice for her. Now, finally, she was doing it herself— a prospect that both thrilled and daunted her. "I want the *execution* to be *modern*," she explained.

It was. They filmed outdoors, in natural settings, embracing both shadow and light. She pushed director Mari to "keep me in the shadows and don't, don't show my hands, because hands reveal the face." Duse hid her face often as she turned away in shame from her son.

When Grazia Deledda, the book's author, came to an early screening of the film, she was deeply moved. "You have made something beautiful and alive out of *Cenere*," she wrote to Eleonora.

> Now the work is yours, no longer mine, just as a flower
> belongs more to the sun that gives it warmth than to the earth
> that gives it roots.

Eleonora was proud of her work on the film, throughout which she never speaks. She had used the silent medium as it was meant to be used. In a dream sequence, the boy, now separated from his mother, imagines her reaching up to him from below his moonlit balcony. As Colette described it: "Those hands were such loving, beating wings, prolonged, extended by their shadows right up to the window sill." Duse knew instinctively in this medium of light and shadow that cinematography could be as important as acting; she contrived a way to manipulate the image with her arms. It was, according to Colette, who had recorded her impressions after seeing the film in Italy in 1916, Duse's "most beautiful scene."

At a time of war when Italian mothers were separated en masse from their soldiering sons, Duse embodied an archetype. "Women came into the dark room and voilà, the *mamans* understood," Eleonora wrote her daughter. Without speaking, Duse had conveyed the universal language of motherhood.

But *Cenere* was a flop commercially—the general public preferred lighter, more entertaining fare. They wanted spectacle.

Undaunted, Duse began planning her next movie, an adaptation of Ibsen's *The Lady from the Sea*, the last play she had performed prior to retiring from the stage in 1909. It was another narrative that lit up her soul. The longing of Ellida for her lost maritime lover reminded Eleonora of the feelings she had as a child, gazing out at the Adriatic.

But as she was preparing for production with the same company that had done *Cenere*, Eleonora had the scare of her life. She and two men from the production team had been scouting locations, taking a winding road along the Italian Riviera. The driver had swerved and collided with an oncoming vehicle. In a letter to her daughter, Duse chose to downplay the seriousness of the incident:

> Pupetta [her nickname for Enrichetta], I prefer to tell you this myself, because those stupid newspapers say all sorts of things. But the situation is this: (1) I am well, (2) nothing bad has happened to me, (3) it is stupid to tell these things, but I'm afraid of the newspapers, so I will tell you myself, (4) voilà: a little auto accident.

The collision had occurred on a cliff with a sheer drop to the sea. The windshield had shattered and showered Eleonora with glass splinters, causing nineteen minor wounds to her face. "I was thrown forward and banged up a bit, nothing serious," she assured Enrichetta. But it must have been a terrifying reminder of her mortality.

With lacerations on her face, she would not be acting on camera anytime soon. *The Lady from the Sea* was put on hold for good; *Cenere* was the one and only movie Duse would ever make.

Duse had entrusted all her savings to Robi Mendelssohn, who had invested everything in Germany. By 1921, because of the devalued deutsche mark, there was nothing left. In the hyperinflation of the Weimar Republic, a single loaf of bread cost two billion marks; Germans carried their currency in wheelbarrows to buy groceries.

Thus, at age sixty-three—after all that she had accomplished, all the accolades and all the pain—Eleonora Duse ended up exactly where she had started: as a pauper.

So in May 1921, twelve years after retiring, Duse made her

return to the stage, performing *The Lady from the Sea* in Rome, the same play that had marked her retirement in 1909, and that she had once hoped to bring to film. She had agreed to a short season with the company of a former manager from the d'Annunzio years; as usual, she took over all aspects of the production.

Eleonora took great comfort from the fact that Sarah had acted well into her seventies. But it was not easy. More than a decade had passed since she had faced an audience, and the rehearsals proved challenging. Duse was unaccustomed to speaking so continuously after the protracted years in relative silence in Asolo. Now she was back in the nation's capital, working long hours on her feet, and not particularly confident. Her fragile lungs went into coughing spasms at the dress rehearsal. But everything, as always, came together for opening night.

Renato Simoni described in *Corriere della Sera* that first performance: "From act to act, we saw her rising to greater heights, yet the greatness of her presentation was veiled by the stark simplicity of her speech . . . every word revealed a mystery to us."

The Grace had returned. Duse seemed to have a new aura around her—a fresh, mystical presence. In the week prior to the performance, Duse had spent a day in silence, meditating in Genoa and communing with the sea.

"I'm trying to forget myself. . . . That way, perhaps I won't be so afraid," is how she explained it to American actress Eva Le Gallienne, who would soon write a book about Duse.

Among those who saw her perform was future director Luchino Visconti, who would one day win the Palme d'Or at the Cannes Film Festival for his masterpiece *Death in Venice*. Even at fifteen he understood that Duse had "what the old actors called 'guts' and the romantics call 'heart.'"

Then there was American legend John Barrymore, who stumbled upon Duse in the lobby of the Hotel Danieli in Venice. "I was drunk, as usual," Barrymore recalled, "and broke, as usual."

"I saw a little old lady sitting alone in the corridor. She was dressed all in black—shabby black, I remember, and her gloves were black, too, and worn."

When Barrymore finally realized it was Duse, he was in awe; though he had not yet seen her perform, he knew of her legend.

"I would kiss your feet," he told Duse, "but I cannot do that in this public place. It would be my only way of telling you how great you are and what an ineffable inspiration you have been to artists all over the world." He had tears in his eyes. Duse regarded him for a moment.

"You are American?" she asked in her limited English.

"Yes, Madame," responded the Hollywood superstar.

"You are perhaps an actor?"

"Yes, Madame."

"A very good actor, I think." She smiled.

"A very bad one, I am afraid, Madame."

He would soon get a chance to see her onstage.

Duse's compromised health limited her performances to once or twice a week, even though the company was contracted to rent theaters on a weekly, not nightly, basis for their tour of Italy; a single performance was unlikely to offset that cost. So Duse was back at work, but losing money.

Eleonora added Ibsen's *Ghosts* to her repertoire, a scathing indictment of societal norms that ends with an aging mother debating whether or not she has it in her to inject her syphilitic and suffering son with a lethal dose of morphine. Eleonora's performance was chilling.

Another play she revived was d'Annunzio's *The Dead City*. During the war, d'Annunzio and Duse had reconciled. The compulsive hedonist had become a war hero after serving with amazing valor—first in the Italian cavalry, next as the captain of a torpedo boat, and finally as a pilot, where he had been wounded in action, losing an eye in a dogfight. Even after the armistice, he had refused to lay down his arms. In 1919, as a private citizen, d'Annunzio had led an army of mutineers in a campaign that made him a legend—taking over the disputed border town of Fiume (in modern-day Croatia) and installing himself as its artist-dictator for fifteen months.

Fiume became a model city-state, so politically innovative and culturally enlightened that it drew poets, socialists, anarchists, and refugees—the Haight-Ashbury of its day. D'Annunzio even received a pot of caviar from Vladimir Lenin, who called him the "only revolutionary in Europe."

Mussolini took note. Il Duce also asked for an introduction to Eleonora Duse, who, after repeated entreaties from d'Annunzio, consented to meet him. The encounter took place in her room at Rome's Hotel Royal on December 4, 1922. The dictator arrived at three sharp, not quite two months after he had seized control of the country. Mussolini was eager to meet—and possibly co-opt—this icon of Italian theater. The enthusiasm was not reciprocated. Duse was cordial, but when Mussolini later offered her a pension, she refused. It seemed like a bribe, a way of keeping her in the fold. Mussolini, like Lenin, believed that all art was political; for Duse, it was sacred. Given the direction in which the country was headed, she considered leaving Italy for good. The thought of moving to America had even crossed her mind. And why not?

Three months after Bernhardt's death made headlines world-wide in early 1923, Eleonora Duse made some news of her own, becoming the first woman to grace the cover of *Time* magazine. SHE HAS PLAYED THE GREATEST ROMANCES OF ART AND LIFE read the headline, which could have applied equally to either actress. In this case, *Time* was announcing Duse's comeback tour of the United States.

In the fall of 1923, Eleonora made her fifth landing in New York harbor. Her entourage this time included a clairvoyant mystic, Bathsheba Askowith, whom Duse called "La Russa." Before setting sail, Duse had made a statement to the press regarding her mission:

I should like to raise myself through my work—and for my work—to the level of the really great subjects—sacred subjects—to the very heart of the Mystery. The theater sprang from religion. It is my greatest wish that, somehow, through me—in some small way—they may be reunited.

Her tour, this time, was managed by Morris Gest, a visionary impresario who was also overseeing the concurrent tour of the Moscow Arts Theater, directed by Konstantin Stanislavski, who had been deeply influenced by Duse. Both Duse's and Stanislavski's 1923 tours would have lasting impacts on American acting.

Duse opened at the Met on Monday, October 29, playing Ibsen's *The Lady from the Sea.* The ticket line for the evening performance began forming at 8:00 a.m. and soon stretched across Thirty-Ninth Street and down Seventh Avenue, wrapping back on Thirty-Eighth to Broadway—around the block. The 3,867 tickets sold out in ten minutes. Morris Gest would later report total revenues of greater than thirty thousand dollars for that one show—obliterating the record (not quite $10,000) Sarah had set in Kansas City in 1906. Inflation aside, the difference was that ticket prices in the Midwest were as low as a dollar, whereas a ticket on Broadway cost ten times as much.

The audience at Duse's sellout show included Vanderbilts, Astors, Rockefellers, and Hollywood royalty: John Barrymore, finally getting his chance to see her, along with his sister Ethel, Rudolph Valentino, Gloria Swanson, and Lillian Gish, who insisted on a seat in the wings to be closer to Eleonora. The *New York Times* reported that "every seat and all the standing-room . . . was filled," with audience members filing in "three and four deep in the space at the rear of the orchestra seats. . . . More than one hundred and fifty extra seats in the musician's pit helped take care of the crowd." It was an audience to give even the world's greatest living actress stage fright.

"Duse came onstage," recalled Gish. "She swayed, as if she were about to faint. Then something mystical took place. There was thundering applause as the audience stood up and sent its strength to her. She absorbed it, seemed to grow taller, and went on to fill that huge theater with magic."

Later in the tour, Duse performed *Ghosts* at the Philharmonic Auditorium in Los Angeles, where D. W. Griffith's *Birth of a Nation* had had its world premiere. "A hush crept over the house as soon as the curtain rose," wrote *Los Angeles Daily Times* critic Edwin Schallert. "There was expressed an uncanny feeling that something mysterious and supernatural was about to happen . . . it was as if some legendary being had suddenly assumed form and substance." The following day's headline read: GENIUS EN-THRALLS THRONGS WITH HER 'SUPER-ART.'

One of the biggest stars in the world was there to see her that evening: Charlie Chaplin. Awestruck, he later wrote:

> Eleonora Duse is the greatest artiste I have ever seen. Her technique is so marvelously finished and complete that it ceases to be a technique. . . . Bernhardt was always studied and more or less artificial. Duse is direct and terrible. . . . [In] the climax . . . Duse sank in to a chair and curled up her body almost like a little child in pain. . . . She lay quietly and almost without moving. Only once through her body ran a sort of shudder of pain like a paroxysm. . . .
>
> I confess that it drew tears from me. . . . It was the finest thing I have seen on the stage.

The following month in Detroit, Chaplin's United Artists partners Mary Pickford and Douglas Fairbanks witnessed Duse's magic and were left speechless. It was like that everywhere.

On Monday, May 5, 1924, Benito Mussolini dictated the following dispatch to Prince Gelasio Caetani, his ambassador to the United States:

I request your Excellency to proceed to Pittsburgh in order to pay the homage of the Italian Government to the great actress just departed and to take steps to insure the transportation of the body to Italy.

Eleonora Duse had passed away in Pennsylvania, her death, like her birth, occurring in a hotel room.

After Detroit, Duse's tour had landed in Pittsburgh, where she checked into the stately William Penn Hotel on April 1. She soon changed her accommodations, however, after learning that the Hotel Schenley would be much closer to her theater, the Syria Mosque. Rumors had been circulating about Duse's faltering health; she kept oxygen tanks in her hotel and dressing rooms. Did she have the stamina to continue?

On a very rainy April 5, Eleonora and her assistant appeared at the Syria Mosque but were met with confusion; the stage door appeared to be locked. It was ironic, since Duse was there to perform a play called *La Porta Chiusa* (*The Closed Door*) by Marco Praga. As they waited for the door to be unlocked, the actress's clothes became drenched, exacerbating her already precarious lung condition. She managed to get through the show that evening, even impressing the local critics—but afterward she would be bedridden for weeks, forced to cancel her next stop in Cleveland.

She refused to be hospitalized, however; Eleonora had a lifelong fear of hospitals because her mother had died in one. So streams of medics came to her hotel room. "Ah! Asolo, Asolo," cried Duse between coughs, "how far away you are!" Despite public denials that anything was amiss, her condition worsened. On April 21, at the age of sixty-five, Eleonora Duse died of pneumonia.

After a small service in a local funeral home, Duse's body was moved to St. Patrick's Cathedral in New York, where hundreds of thousands paid their respects at the open casket. "She was my Madonna," said dancer Isadora Duncan, a lifelong friend, "my Beatrice the most beautiful of all."

Duncan had spent the summer of 1913 with Duse, after the tragic loss of both her children in an automobile accident. A bereaved Duncan later recounted that Duse "seemed to take my sorrow to her breast."

"I had not been able to bear the society of other people," Duncan continued, "because they all played the comedy of trying to cheer me with forgetfulness." Instead of shrinking from the tragedy, Duse encouraged Isadora to express her pain.

One night, she and Duse put a disc on the gramophone, and Isadora danced for the first time since her loss. Eleonora watched her, choked up with emotion. Afterward, when she went to embrace her, Duse said: "You must return to your art. It is your only salvation." Heeding the advice of her friend, Isadora went on to create dances in honor of her loss, entitled *Mother* and *Marche Funebre*.

Duncan was hardly the only artist in awe of Duse. Many had fallen under her spell, including poet Sara Teasdale, who composed a series of sonnets to the actress.

> *Oh beauty that is filled so full of tears,*
> *Where every passing anguish left its trace,*
> *The glory and the sadness of your face,*
> *Its longing unappeased through all the years.*

In Italy, Gabriele d'Annunzio was grief-stricken. Upon hearing of the death of the woman who had most deeply touched his soul, he wrote the following telegram to Il Duce, who had given him a generous stipend and the title Prince of Montenevoso:

> The tragic destiny of Duse could not have been fulfilled in a more tragic manner.
> Far from Italy, the most Italian of hearts has been stilled. I beg that the beloved remains be brought to Italy at the expense of the State. I am certain that my grief today is shared by all Italians.

Mussolini heeded the request of the national poet. He sent a wreath to St. Patrick's Cathedral with the inscription: TO ITALY'S FIRST DAUGHTER. Then the body was shipped to Naples on the *Duilio*, a luxury ocean liner. After an official state funeral in Rome, Eleonora's coffin was laid to rest in Asolo, where she had lived her final years. She was buried with a mystical glass prism, given to her by her spiritual mentor Arrigo Boito.

The day after Duse's death, the *New York Times* published the following editorial:

> The last to linger of the great histrionic group of the 1890s, Eleonora Duse has left the least legible character on the page of theatrical history, and the record that will soonest fade.

Bernhardt had said as much in her 1907 memoir. And she was prescient. Today, few but committed stage actors are aware of Duse, while Bernhardt remains, to some extent, a household name. The revision of history began, perhaps, with their flip-flopped epitaphs: Duse was posthumously labeled "histrionic," while Bernhardt, according to the *Los Angeles Times*, was "subtle even in death."

The media mix-up was probably not an accident. Sarah had worked the press her entire career, taking great pains to fashion herself as an icon, while Duse had shunned publicity and disappeared into her roles. "The actor vanishes without a trace," she had once said—which is not to suggest that she had no lasting impact. Both Duse and Bernhardt changed theater forever in very different ways.

According to the U.S. Census, the number of women who declared "actress" as their profession rose sixfold, from 780 to 4,652, in the decade of 1870 to 1880. By 1910 that number was 15,432, with 25 new women on the stage for every new man. This huge jump had much to do with the influence of Bernhardt and Duse, who had demonstrated how women could obtain wealth, mobility, and social power through their dominance in the theater. Bernhardt had been the vanguard here.

As early biographer Madame Berton attests: "It was Sarah Bernhardt, more than anyone else . . . who transformed, with her magic touch, the theatre in France from the superior, intellectual toy of the cultured few to the amusement and recreation of the many."

The "amusement and recreation" of the crowd was never a goal for Eleonora, who was obsessed with one thing more than anything else: the Truth, something that held only passing interest for her French rival. Indeed, when the Bibliotheque Nationale in Paris held a retrospective in honor of Sarah Bernhardt some seventy-five years after her death, they used the subtitle *The Divine Liar.*

As the *Guardian* reported in its recent review of the retrospective: "Bernhardt lied herself into being, and in so doing made herself captivating."

EPILOGUE

Future cornerstones of American acting, Stella Adler and Lee Strasberg watched in 1923 as Eleonora Duse took the New York stage. Both were twenty-two at the time. Though Strasberg, an immigrant from Eastern Europe, would one day be known as the Father of Method Acting, he had yet to act professionally. Stella, on the other hand, had begun acting at the age of four, pushed onto the boards prematurely, like Duse, by her father, Jacob Adler, who had fled Russia in 1883 after a ban on Yiddish theater. The Adlers eventually settled in Lower Manhattan, where they founded the Independent Yiddish Art Company.

Stella felt a kinship with Duse. She, too, had been robbed of her childhood, had wed impulsively and early, later leaving her husband to raise her only child, a girl. And she, too, desired to act with all her soul. But Adler had few female mentors: Seeing Duse that night was a revelation, an emancipation, similar to what Eleonora had experienced when she first saw Bernhardt in her Turin theater four decades before. It was a life-changer for the young ingénues — the experience of seeing these powerful icons of the stage.

They were in awe of these women. And watching them perform was like a sacrament. Night after night, Sarah Bernhardt would enact a passion play as the "martyr" for all humanity. To see Sarah die — it invariably sold the most tickets — was unforgettable. She met her demise onstage with seizures lasting for minutes at a time, writhing spasms, flails of anguish, and guttural moans. Always, the house would erupt in ovation; women dabbed their eyes, men stiffened their lips. It was catharsis. Sarah had died for all of us—and, as the curtain rose again for the calls, the diva was "reborn" in all her radiance.

Duse's liturgy was different. It began with the mysterious communion between the actress and her audience. "There was something that seemed like a ray that came from her and captured the house," recalled Eva Le Gallienne. Eleonora also "died" on the stage, but it was a quiet death: the dissolution of her ego.

Within a decade of seeing Duse in New York, Lee Strasberg and Stella Adler would team up with Elia Kazan, Clifford Odets, and an assortment of other theatrical renegades to form the Group Theater, which would become the most influential theater collective in American history. But Adler and Strasberg would have a falling-out, feuding—like Duse and Bernhardt—over a fundamental difference in technique.

The debate about what constitutes "true acting" continues to this day—a conflict going back to Quintilian, through Diderot and William Archer, between "actors" and "indicators." There is an apocryphal story of a conversation that took place on the set of *Marathon Man*, between Sir Laurence Olivier and Dustin Hoffman, who was in a state, apparently, about how to "feel" the torture scene. He didn't know how to be in the moment; Hoffman didn't have references from his own life that he could bring to bear, something that was essential for method acting. How was he going to pull it off? Sir Laurence gave the young American a quizzical look and simply said: "My dear boy, it's called acting." What a revelation. When you can't feel it, fake it. This was blasphemy to the purists.

Central to The Method—as taught by Lee Strasberg to students including Dustin Hoffman, Al Pacino, Steve McQueen, Gene Hackman, Robert Duvall, Jon Voight, Robert Redford, Paul Newman, Jack Nicholson, Anne Bancroft, and Faye Dunaway, among others—was the use of Affective Memory, a technique adapted from Konstantin Stanislavski in which actors recall emotionally charged moments from the past to summon the feelings they need onstage.

Stella had no quibble with an actor drawing from his past; this was a component of what she did in preparation for a part, along with detailed research on the time and place in which the play was set. Duse also thought about the connections between her own emotional life and that of the character. It was all part of their rehearsal process. What struck Adler as absurd was to bring that process onto the stage. It was "schizophrenic," she contended, to split your focus between autobiographical references and the thoughts and memories of your character.

Carting Affective Memory onto the stage was, for Adler, a clumsy overlay that took away from the magic of a spontaneous performance—precisely the reason Duse had rejected poses the century before. For Stella, as for Duse, performance was all about one thing—imagination.

Both actresses would prepare exhaustively for a role, marking up their scripts with notes on every page. They would use all their creative faculties to get inside the character's head—to know her thoughts, her history, her feelings—so that, come the actual performance, they could let go of their preparations and be entirely free. Though both Duse and Adler had strikingly similar processes in the way they approached their work, they had come upon their approaches independent of each other. But when Stella saw Eleonora's spontaneous freedom on the stage, she felt vindicated—and emboldened.

"You act with your soul," Adler would later tell her students. "That's why you all want to be actors, because your souls are not used up by life."

Adler devised all sorts of provocative exercises to stir her students' imaginations. As Broadway star Elaine Stritch recalled:

> One morning she said, "You are all chickens. And in your chicken coop there is a radio. Over the radio comes news of the bombing of Pearl Harbor. I want you all to react as chickens." All the bad actors began running around the auditorium going "bwak buk buk"—hollering chicken noises because Pearl Harbor had been attacked.

One fellow just sat in the corner and calmly laid an egg. Stella, intrigued, asked him why he had made that choice. His reply: "I'm a chicken, what do I know about bombs?" That was Marlon Brando, who instantly became her favorite student—and she, his guru.

"I no longer know how to read or to study or to think or to memorize without inviting Stella into my consciousness," Brando admitted in 1990. "She taught me everything."

After Brando's explosive debut in *A Streetcar Named Desire*, everyone wanted to be like him—raw, unpredictable, impulsive. As James Franco wrote in a 2014 op-ed for the *New York Times*: "Brando's performances revolutionized American acting precisely because he didn't seem to be 'performing,' in the sense that he wasn't putting something *on* as much as he was *being*." He could have been describing Eleonora Duse.

In seeking to imitate Brando, many, if not most, American actors in the decades that followed would assimilate the Duse-Adler lineage. Any actor who walks the stage today and creates, by ignoring the audience, the illusion of a Fourth Wall is part of the Duse legacy. But even film actors—*especially* film actors—must act from within. It's all in the eyes, as they say—particularly if those eyes take up a thirty-foot screen. When asked the secret to her screen acting (which resulted in ten Academy Award nominations), Bette Davis is quoted as having said: "Talk softly, think loudly." Duse could not have said it better.

Duse never codified her technique. She never taught, per se, except for a select few she mentored privately, like Eva Le Gallienne and Alice Nielsen. If Eleonora's legacy could be contained in a single maxim, it would be to be bold and take risks—something she had learned from Bernhardt.

Both actresses would have agreed with Stanislavski's greatest instructions: "Create your own method. Don't depend slavishly on mine. Make up something that will work for you! But keep breaking traditions, I beg you."

ACKNOWLEDGMENTS

I believe writers are conduits; and inspiration arrives from a realm that has many names. I like to think of it as the Source, and I am deeply grateful for its presence.

This story first came to my attention through Michelle Weissman, a writer, actress, and spiritualist who had studied with Stella Adler. We wrote it together in the form of a screenplay, initially. Subsequently, to deepen the narrative, I decided to explore the subject in book form. I am greatly indebted to Michelle for her blessing in this endeavor.

I owe special thanks to Daniel Manning, who studied theater at New York University; he did essential research for me on the historical feud between actors and "indicators." Thanks to Nina Luzzatto Gardner for leading me to Lavinia Pelosi, who did indispensable research for me in Italy.

Profound thanks to my agents, David Kuhn, Becky Sweren, and William LoTurco, for getting this into the hands of Priscilla Painton, a truly gifted editor, and her assistant, Megan Hogan, who were instrumental in shepherding this manuscript to publication. Thank you to my lawyer, Debby Klein, who read an early draft of this story in script form and has been a consistent supporter.

I feel deep gratitude toward my parents. Among the many gifts they bestowed was our childhood in Italy and, later, London. Thank you to my sister, Claudia, who was an ardent champion and early editor of this manuscript. Our connection to Italy runs deep, and it led me to my wife, Paola, the most profound of blessings. Paola has championed me through thick and thin. Thank you, Paola. And to our beautiful sons, Matteo and Luca—I love you.

NOTES

PROLOGUE

4 *"always swooned on the left"*: Michael Meyer, *Ibsen: A Biography* (Garden City, NY: Doubleday, 1971), 230.

4 *"By her extraordinary power of swooning"*: Jean Cocteau, quoted by Leigh Woods in *New Theatre Quarterly* 37, no. 10, vol. 10, part 1 (Cambridge: Cambridge University Press, 1994), 22.

4 *"too American"*: Henry James, quoted in Robert Gottlieb, *Sarah: The Life of Sarah Bernhardt* (New Haven, CT: Yale University Press, 2010), 81.

5 *"Sarah Bernhardt . . . is eminently a Russian princess"*: Jules Lemaître quoted by Robert Gottlieb, *Sarah*, 118–19.

8 *"the player must always divide his attention"*: Johann Wolfgang von Goethe, *Rules for Actors* (Frankfurt: 1803), 40.

9 *"It would be hard to imagine"*: Arthur Gold and Robert Fizdale, *The Divine Sarah* (New York: Alfred A. Knopf, 1991), 138.

10 *"If the actor were full, really full"*: Denis Diderot, *The Paradox of Acting*, trans. Walter Herries Pollock (London: Chatto & Windus, 1883), 38.

10 *"to speak and not declaim"*: Karl Mantzius (authorized translation by Louise von Cossel), *A History of Theatrical Art in Ancient and Modern Times, Volume V, Great Actors of the Eighteenth Century* (London: Duckworth & Co., 1909), 245.

10 *"Quintilian . . . is very explicit"*: William Archer, *Masks or Faces?: A Study in the Psychology of Acting* (London: Longmans, Green, and Co., 1888), 42–43.

CHAPTER ONE

18 *"She did not choose to be an actress"*: Eva Le Gallienne, *The Mystic in the Theatre: Eleonora Duse* (New York: Farrar, Straus & Giroux, 1966), 26.

19 *"Inanimate objects 'in their silence'"*: Helen Sheehy, *Eleonora Duse: A Biography* (New York: Alfred A. Knopf, 2003), 12.

19 *"She learned, early and without metaphor"*: William Weaver, *Duse: A Biography* (New York: Harcourt Brace Jovanovich, 1984), 17–18.

20 *"Disheveled, giggling and shouting"*: Duse, *Frammento autobiografico* (unpublished, unfinished memoir), printed in *Bibliotecca Teatrale*, July–September 1996, 121–56.

20 *"She was my first friend"*: Le Gallienne, *The Mystic in the Theatre*, 28.

20 *"a ticking petticoat"*: Duse, *Frammento autobiografico*.

22 *"The gossip of the Nurse"*: Gabriele d'Annunzio, *Il fuoco* (Milano: Fratelli Treves, 1900), 319.

22 *"my eyes would travel to the long grasses"*: Ibid., 448.

23 *"When I heard Romeo"*: Ibid., 447.

23 *"We crossed a bridge"*: Ibid., 451.

24 *"She had received her revelation"*: Le Gallienne, *The Mystic in the Theatre*, 16.

CHAPTER TWO

26 *"One does not know today"*: Maxime Du Camp quoted by Charles Bernheimer, *Figures of Ill Repute: Representing Prostitution in Nineteenth-Century France* (Durham, NC: Duke University Press, 1997), 92.

27 *"My mother was fond of traveling"*: Sarah Bernhardt, *My Double Life: Memoirs of Sarah Bernhardt* (London: William Heinemann, 1907), 1.

27 *"I was thrown, all smoking"*: Ibid., 2.

28 *"her golden hair and her eyes"*: Ibid.

29 *"One afternoon the janitor's wife returned"*: Madame Pierre Berton, as told to Basil Swoon, *Sarah Bernhardt as I Knew Her: The Memoirs of Madame Pierre Berton* (London: Hurst & Blackett, 1923), 37.

29 *"her single-minded will"*: Ibid.

29 *"One day I was playing"*: Bernhardt, *My Double Life*, 4.

30 *"I will pass over these two years"*: Ibid., 5.

31 *"gave herself airs"*: Ibid., 7.

32 *"these gentlemen were to make arrangements"*: Ibid.

32 *"I would thrill in every fiber"*: Ibid., 10.

33 *"My part involved some pretty realistic acting"*: Berton, *Sarah Bernhardt as I Knew Her*, 45.

33–34 *"head in the bedclothes, like an ostrich"*: Ibid., 48–49.

34 *"The idea that my wishes"*: Bernhardt, *My Double Life*, 11.

34 *"the most gentle and smiling face"*: Ibid., 17.

35 *"We certainly thought about you, dear"*: Ibid., 29.

37 *"it was now felt necessary to pamper and spoil me"*: Ibid., 56.

38 *"Well, you have completely failed"*: Ibid., 89.

39–40 *"most envied of actresses"*: Ibid., 57.

40 *"The very fat and very solemn"*: Ibid., 101.

CHAPTER THREE

42 *"My little work had already given me great pleasure"*: François Coppée, *Theatre Magazine*, vol. 8, 1908.

42 *"It's not that I prefer male roles"*: Sarah Bernhardt, quoted in Gottlieb, *Sarah*, 142.

42 *"the poetic talent of M'lle Bernhardt"*: Edgar Wakeman, "Wakeman's Wanderings," syndicated column, February 1869.

44 *"I raised my lantern to look at his face"*: Bernhardt, *My Double Life*, 184.

44 *"She seemed to me to be glory personified"*: Berton, *Sarah Bernhardt as I Knew Her*, 140.

45 *"I never thought I was coming to see you!"*: Bernhardt, *My Double Life*, 162.

45 *"Every seat had been taken"*: Berton, *Sarah Bernhardt as I Knew Her*, 154.

46 *"She often told me"*: Ibid.

46 *"melancholy queen"*: Gottlieb, *Sarah*, 61.

46 *"A sight I shall never forget"*: Bernhardt, *My Double Life*, 297.

47 *"she was not Mademoiselle Rachel, but Phèdre, herself"*: Théophile Gautier quoted in John Sayer, *Jean Racine: Life and Legend* (Bern: Peter Lang, 2006), 279.

47 *"Don't force your voice"*: Ibid., *Jean Racine*, 275.

47 *"not the kind that paralyzes"*: Gold and Fizdale, *The Divine Sarah*, 150.

47 *"The gods were with me"*: Ibid.

CHAPTER FOUR

49 *"still feeble when I forced it in big speeches"*: d'Annunzio, *Il fuoco*, 307–8.

52 *"Here was a young woman"*: Guido Noccioli, *Duse on Tour: Guido Noccioli's Diaries, 1906–07* (Manchester, UK: Manchester University Press, 1982), 3.

53 *"her way of acting is the truest and most natural"*: *L'arte drammatica*, May 27, 1878.

54 *"It was because I needed love!"*: Henry Russell, *The Passing Show* (Boston: Little, Brown, 1926), 93.

55 *"element of worship"*: Le Gallienne, *The Mystic in the Theatre*, 32.

56 *"Save me from the solitude of my silent room"*: Sheehy, *Eleonora Duse*, 34.

57 *"seeing her so alone"*: Weaver, *Duse*, 32–33.

57 *"What can humanly be done to make a woman happy"*: Ibid., 33.

58 *"How much whispered slander and open ridicule"*: Ibid., 56.

CHAPTER FIVE

59 *"Bernhardt prided herself on her ability"*: Berton, *Sarah Bernhardt as I Knew Her*, 245.

60 *"People spoke only of her in town"*: Jean Huret interview, May 24, 1887, quoted in Sheehy, *Eleonora Duse*, 46.

61 *"I went every night and cried"*: Weaver, *Duse*, 35.

61 *"a dark young girl"*: Camillo Antona-Traversi, *Eleonora Duse: sua vita, sua gloria, suo martirio* (Pisa: Nistri-Lischi, 1926), 35–36.

62 *"A woman had achieved all that!"*: Mario Fratti, *Eleonora Duse* (New York: Breakthrough Press, 1967), 25.

63 *"They did not interfere with me after that"*: Le Gallienne, *The Mystic in the Theatre*, 36.

63 *"I'd like a sea journey"*: Sheehy, *Eleonora Duse*, 69.

63 *"I use everything that I pick up in my memory"*: Ibid., 53.

64 *"You can well understand how her heart was beating"*: letter from Primoli to Dumas, Jan. 4, 1885, published in *Fortnightly Review*, June 1900.

66 *"with all her maladies of hysteria, anemia and neurosis"*: Claude Schumacher (editor), *Naturalism and Symbolism in European Theatre 1850–1918* (Cambridge, UK: Cambridge University Press, 1996), 442.

66 *"mysterious . . . sympathetic communication"*: *Corriere della Sera*, May 5, 1884.

66 *"I will make Art, always"*: Eleonora Duse letter to D'Arcais, May 15, 1884.

67 *"Il était beau"*: Le Gallienne, *The Mystic in the Theatre*, 39.

67 *"I felt small and helpless"*: Ibid., 38.

68 *"There before those footlights"*: Weaver, *Duse*, 53.

68 *"Dumas made Denise"*: Sheehy, *Eleonora Duse*, 71.

CHAPTER SIX

70 *"this ancient Greek god"*: See Dean Kalimniou, "Toy Boyz," *Diatribe*, October 27, 2008, http://diatribe-column.blogspot.com/2008/10/toy-boyz.html.

70 *"I am going to die"*: Bodeen DeWitt, *Ladies of the Footlights* (Pasadena, CA: Logan Printing & Binding, 1937), 80.

72 *"We ought to hate very rarely"*: *Pittsburgh Post-Gazette*, Nov. 22, 1877, 23.

73 *"enchantment smothered in artifice"*: Anton Chekhov, *The Undiscovered Chekhov: Thirty-Eight New Stories* (New York: Seven Stories Press, 2011), excerpted: http://www.nytimes.com/books/first/c/chekhov-undiscovered.html?mcubz=1.

74 *"to me more a symbol, an ideal"*: Nina Auerbach, *Ellen Terry, Player in Her Time* (Philadelphia: University of Pennsylvania Press, 1997), 280.

74 *"She conducts business"*: *La Chronique Parisienne*, Oct. 31, 1884.

76 *"attendants, guardians, eunuchs"*: *New York Times*, January 19, 1885.

76 *"the greatest achievement"*: Perrin is quoted by Félix Duquesnel in "A Propos de Théodora," *Le Théâtre*, February 1902, 3.

76 "Théodora *is the most beautiful"*: Ibid.

77 *"The press is unanimous"*: http://lafayette.org.uk/theodora_lit.html.

CHAPTER SEVEN

79 *"a sadness without a name"*: Eleonora Duse, letter to Cesare Rossi, Nov. 26, 1885.

80 *"Boito . . . sent to her by some higher power"*: Le Gallienne, *The Mystic in the Theatre*, 39–40.

81 *"The supreme power"*: Paul Radice, *Eleonora Duse–Arrigo Boito: Lettere d'Amore* (Milan: Il Saggiatore, 1979), 225.

83 *"It is said that Signora Duse"*: William Archer, review of *Cleopatra* in *Theatrical World*, June 28, 1893.

84 *"We only thought about one thing"*: Radice, *Eleonora Duse–Arrigo Boito*, 290.

85 *"A hateful country"*: Ibid., 624.

86 *"hacks"* and *"painted dolls"*: Ibid., 736.

88 *"There are no scenes written for effect"*: Weaver, *Duse*, 70.

88 *"Does he have a fungus on the brain?"*: Ibid., 387.

88 *"grand poseur"*: Catherine Schuler, *Women in Russian Theatre: The Actress in the Silver Age* (New York: Routledge, 1996), 13.

89 *"No, it is we who must bow to you"*: Gottlieb, *Sarah*, 111.

90 *"such a natural . . . and life-like manner"*: Laura Hansson, *Six Modern Women: Psychological Sketches* (Boston: Roberts Brothers, 1896), xv–xvi.

90 *"La Duse is a truly remarkable artist"*: Weaver, *Duse*, 88.

90–91 *"I have just seen the Italian actress"*: Ibid., 89.

91 *"Duse's emotionally lacerated heroines"*: Schuler, *Women in Russian Theatre*, 14.

91 *"Duse devotes herself to men"*: Ibid., 14.

CHAPTER EIGHT

93   *"To hear Mme. Bernhardt tell of her tour"*: New York Times, November 30, 1891.

95   *"By all means see Sarah Bernhardt"*: "La Dame de Challant and the Acting of Sarah Bernhardt," *New York Times*, Dec. 6, 1891.

95   *"This cherished blood of Israel"*: Gottlieb, *Sarah*, 120.

96   *"Ah, Sarah! Sarah!"*: Gold and Fizdale, *The Divine Sarah*, 232.

97   *"It is a miracle of impudence"*: quoted by Petra Dierkes-Thrun, *Salome's Modernity: Oscar Wilde and the Aesthetics of Transgression* (Ann Arbor: University of Michigan, 2012), 4.

98   *"Eleonora Duse is now reading* Salomé*"*: Quoted in John Stokes, Michael R. Booth, Susan Bassnett, *Bernhardt, Terry, Duse: The Actress in Her Time* (Cambridge, UK: Cambridge University Press, 1988), 248.

98   *"It is an arrangement in blood and ferocity"*: Guy Willoughby, *Art and Christhood: The Aesthetics of Oscar Wilde* (Teaneck NJ: Fairleigh Dickinson University Press, 1993), 151.

101 *"Her poses . . . had melted into a sort of radiance"*: Marcel Proust, quoted in Roberta Mock, *Jewish Women on Stage, Film, and Television* (New York: Palgrave Macmillan, 2007).

102 *"The idealized Phèdre"*: Stokes, Booth, Bassnett, *Bernhardt, Terry, Duse*, 52.

102 *"The moment I have put on the veils of* Phèdre*"*: Adolphe Brisson, *Phèdre et Mme Sarah Bernhardt* (Paris: Revue Illustrée, 1895), 36.

CHAPTER NINE

103 *"No theatricalities!"*: Paul Kuritz, *The Making of Theatre History* (Englewood Cliffs, NJ: Prentice Hall, 1988), 316.

104 *"It was held that the stranger the situation"*: Ibid., 328.

104 *"an old Norwegian pharmacist"*: Radice, *Eleonora Duse–Arrigo Boito*, 706.

105 *"She stands by the fireplace"*: Hansson, *Six Modern Women*, 108.

105 *"There was enough horror"*: Sheehy, *Eleonora Duse*, 207.

105 *"Ibsen very soon went out of fashion in Italy"*: Noccioli, *Duse on Tour*, 24.

106 *"she came out always pale"*: Weaver, *Duse*, 93.

107 *"She plays the gaiety that is not happiness"*: Hugo von Hofmannsthal, "Eleonora Duse, eine Wiener Theaterwoche," in *Werke. Prosa*, vol. I, (Frankfurt-am-Main: Fischer, 1936).

107 *"There are five kinds of actresses"*: Mark Twain, quoted by Pia Catton, "Why Bernhardt Was the Best of Her Generation," *New York Sun*, Dec. 13, 2005.

108 *"Jewess-Catholic-Protestant-Mohammedan-Buddhist-Atheist-Zoroaster-Theist-or-Deist"*: Bernhardt, *My Double Life*, 367.

108 *"When I set foot in America"*: Weaver, *Duse*, 97.

109 *"whether she is silent or talkative"*: Paul Schlenther, "Eleonora Duse," *The Looker-On*, March 1896.

109 *"I have always found it possible to succeed"*: Le Gallienne, *The Mystic in the Theatre*, 42.

109 *"the hermit of Murray Hill"*: Ibid., 43.

109 *"Sir, I do not know you"*: "Mme. Eleonora Duse Has Something to Say," *New York Dramatic Mirror*, January 28, 1893.

109 *"the muse of the newspaper"*: Gottlieb, *Sarah*, 81.

110 *"half empty house"*: Le Gallienne, *The Mystic in the Theatre*, 43.

111 *"mannered gesticulation"*: "A New Actress from Italy," *New York Times*, Jan. 24, 1893.

112 *"forgive Italy for the organ grinders"*: Sheehy, *Eleonora Duse*, 124.

112 *"It was set down in the agreement"*: Ron Grossman, "Hottest Ticket in Town? When Sarah Bernhardt Took Chicago by Storm," *Chicago Tribune*, September 23, 2016.

113 "SARAH BERNHARDT'S LATEST FREAK": *The Barrier Miner*, Dec. 28, 1892.

114 *"Like all French plays"*: *The San Francisco Call*, June 3, 1902.

115 *"only a part of the tremendous passion"*: *New York Herald*, Feb. 5, 1893.

115 *"passing out into the fresh air"*: William Archer, *Theatrical World*, 1893, 125–27.

116 *"You know that next year I am resting,"* Weaver, *Duse*, 106.

119 *"Giacosa—and others of your friends"*: Ibid., 125.

119 *"To describe her art"*: Ibid., 96.

119 *"The Parisians had little patience"*: Gold and Fizdale, *The Divine Sarah*, 255.

CHAPTER TEN

121 *"The contrast between the two Magdas"*: George Bernard Shaw, *Shaw's Dramatic Criticism (1895–98)*, ed. John F. Matthews (New York: Hill & Wang, 1959), 81.

124 *"large vehicles for expression of the absolute self"*: Max Beerbohm, *The Incomparable Max* (London: Heinemann, 1962), 113.

124 *"One suspects that the man who made love"*: Gold and Fizdale, *The Divine Sarah*, 258.

124 *"My prevailing impression"*: Jane Milling, Peter Thomson, Joseph Donohue, *The Cambridge History of British Theatre*, vol. 2 (Cambridge, UK: Cambridge University Press, 2004), 354.

124 *"Art is Bernhardt's dissipation"*: Willa Cather, *The Kingdom of Art: Willa*

Cather's First Principles and Critical Statements, 1893–1896 (Lincoln: University of Nebraska Press, 1967), 119.

125 *"The great French actress looks"*: *Rockland County Messenger,* Jan. 23, 1896.

126 *"I like all the characters that I play"*: *The Journal,* Jan. 13, 1896.

126 *"She is still the greatest of living actresses"*: *New York Times,* Jan. 21, 1896.

127 *"The role takes her to the extreme limit"*: *New York Times,* Feb. 18, 1894.

129 *"She is at times a tiger, a panther, a snake"*: Thomas A. Bogar, *American Presidents Attend the Theatre: The Playgoing Experience of Each Chief Executive* (Jefferson, NC: McFarland & Company, 2006), 176.

129 *"The moment the curtain descended"*: Ibid.

130 *"the sad and innocent look of a street-girl"*: Stokes, Booth, Bassnett, *Bernhardt, Terry, Duse,* 54.

131 *"She stood with heaving breast"*: Gold and Fizdale, *The Divine Sarah,* 264.

Chapter Eleven

133 *"As if she were preparing for a new role"*: Sheehy, *Eleonora Duse,* 137.

133 *"My soul is no longer impatient"*: Lucy Hughes-Hallett, *Gabriele d'Annunzio: Poet, Seducer, and Preacher of War* (New York: Alfred A. Knopf, 2013), 198.

134 *"That* diabolical*—divine* d'Annunzio?*"*: Sheehy, *Eleonora Duse,* 134.

135 *"the very personification of Italian decadence"*: Jonathan Galassi, "The Writer, Seducer, Aviator, Proto-Fascist, Megalomaniac Prince Who Shaped Modern Italy," *New Republic,* February 8, 2014.

135 *"He accepts . . . the whole physical basis of life"*: Arthur Symons, in his Introduction to *Gabriele d'Annunzio: The Child of Pleasure* (New York: Richmond & Son, 1898), vi.

136 *"I have felt your soul and discovered mine"*: d'Annunzio, *Il fuoco,* 184.

137 *"communion between his own soul"*: Ibid., 52.

138 *"I ask . . . that my soul not suffer"*: Weaver, *Duse,* 136, 138.

140 *"Madame, you are positively d'Annunzian"*: Gold and Fizdale, *The Divine Sarah,* 273.

140 *"retained all the sparkle and fire of youth"*: Berton, *Sarah Bernhardt as I Knew Her,* 342.

143 *"I still have hope for you"*: Eleonora Duse, Gabriele d'Annunzio, *Come il mare io ti parlo* (Collected Letters: 1894–1923) (Milan: Bompiani, 2014), April 23, 1897, 114.

144 *"When will you give me the dream?"*: Ibid.

CHAPTER TWELVE

145 *"It was more of a collision than a meeting"*: Gold and Fizdale, *The Divine Sarah*, 271–72.

148 *"We must see some material evidence"*: Jean-Philippe Worth, *A Century of Fashion* (Boston: Little, Brown, 1928), 215–16.

149 *"the all-powerful, magnanimous artist"*: Le Gallienne, *The Mystic in the Theatre*, 49.

150 *"her nervousness betrays her at every step"*: Victor Mapes, *Duse and the French* (New York: Dunlap Society, 1898), 19.

150 *"going into ecstasies"*: Le Gallienne, *The Mystic in the Theatre*, 50.

150 *"ruins her lovers by making them buy macaroni"*: Francisque Sarcey, quoted in William Weaver, *Duse*, 155.

151 *"A great fire burns in the fireplace"*: Jules Huret, *Le Figaro*, Ibid., 153.

153 *"rather have choked her than hugged her"*: *New York Times*, Feb. 1, 1925.

154 *"It is a matter of theatrical history"*: Ibid.

154 *underlined that direction three times*: Stokes, Booth, Bassnett, *Bernhardt, Terry, Duse*, 157.

155 *"What fly is biting her?"*: Francisque Sarcey, quoted in Frances Winwar, *Wingless Victory—A Biography of Gabriele D'Annunzio and Eleonora Duse* (Worcestershire, UK: Read Books Ltd, 2013), 201.

155 *"I was extremely courteous and polite"*: Gold and Fizdale, *The Divine Sarah*, 273–74.

156 *"La Duse then leaves victorious"*: Weaver, *Duse*, 160.

157 *"excitements of intrigue and cabal"*: *New York Times*, February 1, 1925.

157 *"La Duse . . . dressed in gray"*: Weaver, *Duse*, 202.

159 *"resembled little blobs of* merde*"*: "The Mysterious Sex Appeal of Gabriele d'Annunzio," March 26, 2013, http://www.roguesgalleryonline.com /the-mysterious-sex-appeal-of-gabriele-dannunzio/.

CHAPTER THIRTEEN

162 *"I have earned a few pennies"*: Hughes-Hallett, *Gabriele d'Annunzio*, 197.

163 *"poor deluded Duse"*: Sheehy, *Eleonora Duse*, 184.

163 *"THE DUSE'S OWN SAD TRAGEDY"*: *Boston Record*, Dec. 27, 1899.

165 *"a part of renunciation"*: *Public Opinion*, no. 33 (1902), 218.

165 *"One saw her see for the first time"*: Le Gallienne, *The Mystic in the Theatre*, 154.

166 *"The Dead City stands alone"*: William Sharp, *Some Dramas of Gabriele d'Annunzio*, http://sundown.pairsite.com/Sharp/WSVol_2/dannunzio.htm.

168 *"All of Italy talked of nothing else"*: *Giornale d'Italia*, Dec. 11, 1901.

168 *"unique in the annals of the theater"*: Tom Antongini, quoted in William Weaver, *Duse*, 236.

168 *"I believe I have never suffered so much"*: Luigi Pirandello, Ibid., 236–37.

169 *"mediocre provincial dramas written in barbarous jargon"*: Ibid., 238.

170 *"I know the book, and have authorized its publication"*: Ibid., 225.

170 *"the fury of Cassandra"*: d'Annunzio, *Il fuoco*, 151.

171 *"troubled by cruel dismay"*: Ibid., 160.

171 *"would cause great sorrow"*: William Weaver, *Duse*, 217.

171 *"the most swinish novel ever written"*: quoted by Professor Susan Bassnett, "A Very Venetian Affair," http://www2.warwick.ac.uk/news andevents/warwickbooks/venetian_miscellany/susan_bassnett/.

172 *"the Song-maiden reappeared on a background of shadow"*: d'Annunzio, *Il fuoco*, 128.

172 *"It's terrible"*: Weaver, *Duse*, 225.

172 *"filthy book"*: Sheehy, *Eleonora Duse*, 193.

173 *"If you loved, then, the beautiful creature"*: Eleonora Duse, Gabriele d'Annunzio, *Come il mare io ti parlo*, letter dated May 21, 1900.

174 *"gained the contempt of every woman in the land"*: George Tyler, quoted in William Drake, *Sara Teasdale, Woman & Poet* (Knoxville: University of Tennessee Press, 1989), 34.

176 *"every cliché and every technical error which a poem can have"*: S. Foster Damon, *Amy Lowell: A Chronicle with Extracts from Her Correspondence* (New York: Houghton Mifflin Company, 1935), 148.

176 *"If you could see how many roses"*: Eleonora Duse, Gabriele d'Annunzio, *Come il mare io ti parlo*, letter dated November 5, 1902.

177 *"very little moral danger to the spectators"*: Sheehy, *Eleonora Duse*, 207.

177 "A PLAY OF GREAT SUPERFICIAL BEAUTY BUT FUNDA-MENTALLY DECADENT": *New York Times*, November 8, 1902.

177 *"positively vile"*: *Sacred Heart Review*, no. 20, November 15, 1902.

177 *"effaced the boundary that separates nature from art"*: Arthur Symons, in the Introduction to Gabriele d'Annunzio, *The Dead City* (London: Heinemann, 1900).

179 *"Time and again"*: *New York Times*, January 8, 1903.

CHAPTER FOURTEEN

182 *"nothing of interest in that dreary hole"*: Wagram story told by Edmond Rostand, quoted in Gold and Fizdale, *The Divine Sarah*, 286.

185 *"Dear Grand Master"*: quoted in Caroline de Costa, *The Diva and Doctor God: Letters from Sarah Bernhardt to Samuel Pozzi* (Bloomington, IN: Xlibris, 2010), 214.

187 *"très grande dame"*: Gold and Fizdale, *The Divine Sarah*, 281.

187 *"Bernhardt's assumption of masculinity"*: Elizabeth Robins, "On Seeing Madame Bernhardt's Hamlet," *North American Review* 171 (December 1900), 908–19.

187 *"a marvel, a tiger, natural, easy, lifelike and princely"*: Maurice Baring, quoted in Benedict Nightingale, *Great Moments in the Theatre* (London: Oberon Books, 2012).

188 *"a sad German professor"*: Gold and Fizdale, *The Divine Sarah*, 282.

189 *"Everybody distinguished in the worlds of literature"*: "Rostand's New Play a Success," *New York Times*, March 16, 1900.

190 *"sharp pathos pierces the heart"*: Thomas Bailey Aldrich, "A Note on 'L'Aiglon,'" *The Century Illustrated*, no. 64, May 1902.

190 *"I understand. I am the expiation!"*: *The Outlook*, no. 7, 1901.

191 *"a woman is better suited"*: Sarah Bernhardt, *Boston Transcript*, April 1, 1901.

193 *"The Texans crowd into the tents and madly cheer and clap"*: Michael Barr, "Sarah Bernhardt's Texas Tent," http://www.texasescapes.com/Michael Barr/Sarah-Bernhardt-Texas-Tent.htm.

194 *"Sardou looked a little like Napoleon"*: Edmondo de Amicis quoted by Charles A. Weissert in the Introduction to his translation of *La Sorcière* (Boston: Gorham Press, 1917), 9.

195 *"Suddenly Sardou climbed up on a table"*: Marguerite Moreno, quoted in Gold and Fizdale, *The Divine Sarah*, 290.

Chapter Fifteen

197 *"I play them well . . because I am filled with sorrow"*: Olga Signorelli, *Eleonora Duse* (Rome: Gherardo Casini Editore, 1955), 258.

197 *"You are free towards me as towards life itself"*: Eleonora Duse, Gabriele d'Annunzio, *Come il mare io ti parlo*, letter dated March 31, 1903.

197 *"without a new form of life"*: Sheehy, *Eleonora Duse*, 205.

198 *"I am beyond right and left"*: Galassi, "The Writer, Seducer, Aviator."

199 *"I will never forget the sweet hours of hope"*: Eleonora Duse, Gabriele d'Annunzio, *Come il mare io ti parlo*, letter dated July 15, 1903.

200 *"A luminous unearthly sort of light"*: Alice Nielsen, "Duse Returns to the Stage," *Theatre*, January 1921.

200 *"Her face is unchanged"*: "Duse Plays in London," *New York Times*, October 6, 1903.

203 *"Never has she been more beautiful"*: Gold and Fizdale, *The Divine Sarah*, 291.

203 *"When the curtain rose"*: Weaver, *Duse*, 256.

205 *"renounced the mission"*: Ibid, 266.

206 *"new incarnation of Marguerite"*: Ibid.

206 *"Every time she returns to Italy"*: Ibid., 267.

206 *"When she returned to France"*: Berton, *Sarah Bernhardt as I Knew Her*, 241.

208 *"If, once . . . your husband"*: Aurélien-François-Marie Lugné-Poë, *Sous les étoile: Souvenirs de theater, 1902–1912* (Paris: Artheme Fayard, 1932), 83.

209 *"Your acting is hopeless! Pitiful!"*: Noccioli, *Duse on Tour*, 53–54.

210 *"Soon I shall go into the great darkness"*: Henrik Ibsen, quoted in Michael Leverson Meyer, *Henrik Ibsen: The Top of a Cold Mountain, 1883–1906* (London: Hart-Davis, 1967), 330.

210 *"I feel and I hope that 'a tomorrow'"*: Weaver, *Duse*, 271–72.

CHAPTER SIXTEEN

212 *"Sarah listed under the weight"*: Gold and Fizdale, *The Divine Sarah*, 302.

212 *"the performers would merely stand and pose"*: Stokes, Booth, Bassnett, *Bernhardt, Terry, Duse*, 59.

213 *"ten thousand dollars to use her severed limb"*: Berton, *Sarah Bernhardt as I Knew Her*, 294.

214 *"She has given her heart and soul to the French drama"*: Gold and Fizdale, *The Divine Sarah*, 312.

214 *"We all sat around in a wide semi-circle"*: May Agate, *Madame Sarah* (London: Home & Van Thal Ltd., 1946), 21.

216 *"My beloved Docteur Dieu"*: Gold and Fizdale, *The Divine Sarah*, 315.

217 *"the same voice I had heard in* La Tosca*"*: Ibid., 316–17.

217 *"Our generation reacted badly"*: Ibid., 318.

220 *"Don't I make coffee every bit as well as Catulle Mendès"*: Gottlieb, *Sarah*, 207.

221 *"Her dedication to this cause"*: Jana Prikryl, "The Dirty Halo: On Sarah Bernhardt," *The Nation*, November 23, 2010.

221 *"Her makeup was dead white"*: Margaret Mower, quoted in Gold and Fizdale, *The Divine Sarah*, 323.

222 *"I was bowled over"*: Sir John Gielgud, quoted in *The Guardian*, October 24, 2000.

222 *"she is the greatest living actress"*: Gold and Fizdale, *The Divine Sarah*, 322.

222 *"Sarah's actors were respectful only in her presence"*: Margaret Mower, quoted in Ibid., 323.

222 *"To contend that Madame Sarah Bernhardt is still a great actress"*: Ibid., 322.

223 *"persons who are interested in the study of freaks"*: Ron Grossman,

"Hottest Ticket in Town? When Sarah Bernhardt Took Chicago by Storm," *Chigaco Tribune*, September 23, 2016.

223 *"Your Majesty, I shall die on the stage"*: Sarah Bernhardt, quoted in Gold and Fizdale, *The Divine Sarah*, 327.

CHAPTER SEVENTEEN

225 *"Are they journalists?"*: Sarah Bernhardt, quoted in Gold and Fizdale, *The Divine Sarah*, 330.

225 *"There is but one sentence today on the lips of Paris"*: "Face of Great Actress Subtle Even in Death," *Los Angeles Times*, March 28, 1923.

226 *"There was nothing left to her"*: Mary Marquet, quoted in Susan Griffin, *The Book of the Courtesans: A Catalogue of Their Virtues* (New York: Crown Archetype, 2002), 266.

227 *"Now that the public is willing to accept me"*: Gold and Fizdale, *The Divine Sarah*, 326.

228 *"I lost a leg, and you"*: Sheehy, *Eleonora Duse*, 306.

228 *"Eleonora Duse is more of an actress than an artist"*: Bernhardt, *My Double Life*.

229 *"I recognized the luminous hair"*: Colette, quoted in William Weaver, *Duse*, 302.

230 *"The fever in my heart, ever since Griffith's offer"*: Sheehy, *Eleonora Duse*, 275.

232 *"keep me in the shadows"*: Ibid., 278.

233 *"Now the work is yours"*: Margherita Heyer-Caput, *Grazia Deledda's Dance of Modernity* (Toronto: University of Toronto Press, 2008), 96.

233 *"Those hands were such loving, beating wings"*: Colette, *Earthly Paradise* (New York: Farrar, Straus & Giroux, 1966), 289.

233 *"Women came into the dark room and voilà"*: Weaver, *Duse*, 312.

234 *"I prefer to tell you this myself"*: Ibid., 313.

235 *"From act to act, we saw her rising to greater heights"*: Le Gallienne, *The Mystic in the Theatre*, 61.

235 *"I'm trying to forget myself"*: Ibid, 166–67.

235 *"what the old actors called 'guts'"*: Sheehy, *Eleonora Duse*, 298.

235 *"I was drunk, as usual"*: John Barrymore, transcript of an unpublished interview, courtesy of Barrymore biographer Michael A. Morrison, author of *John Barrymore, Shakespearian Actor*.

238 *"I should like to raise myself through my work"*: Le Gallienne, *The Mystic in the Theatre*, 183–84.

238 *"She swayed, as if she were about to faint"*: Lillian Gish, with Ann Pichot, *The Movies, Mr. Griffith and Me* (Englewood Cliffs, NJ: Prentice-Hall, 1969), 257.

239 *"A hush crept over the house"*: Sheehy, *Eleonora Duse*, 317.

239 *"Eleonora Duse is the greatest artiste I have ever seen"*: Charles Spencer Chaplin, "Duse Seen as Soul Art," *Los Angeles Daily News*, February 20, 1924.

241 *"seemed to take my sorrow to her breast"*: Isadora Duncan, *My Life* (London: Victor Gollancz, 1928), 310.

242 *"The last to linger of the great histrionic group"*: *New York Times*, April 22, 1923.

242 *"The actor vanishes without a trace"*: Wendy Smith, "The Mother of Modern Theater," *Los Angeles Times*, August 24, 2003.

243 *"transformed, with her magic touch, the theatre"*: Berton, *Sarah Bernhardt as I Knew Her*, 242.

243 *"Bernhardt lied herself into being"*: Stuart Jeffries, "Desperately Seeking Sarah," *The Guardian*, October 24, 2000.

Epilogue

247 *"You act with your soul"*: Stella Adler, "Awake and Dream!," *American Masters*, July 17, 1989, http://www.pbs.org/wnet/americanmasters/stella-adler-about-stella-adler/526/.

247 *"One morning she said, 'You are all chickens'"*: Pope Brock, "Stella Adler," http://people.com/archive/stella-adler-vol-32-no-3/.

248 *"She taught me everything"*: Marlon Brando, quoted in James Grissom, "Brando on Stella Adler: Believing in Majesty," http://jamesgrissom.blogspot.com/2012/08/brando-on-stella-adler-believing-in.html.

248 *"Brando's performances revolutionized American acting"*: James Franco, "Why Actors Act Out," *New York Times*, February 19, 2014.

248 *"Create your own method"*: Konstantin Stanislavski, quoted in Elizabeth Hess, *Acting and Being: Explorations in Embodied Performance* (London: Palgrave Macmillan, 2017), 5.

Index

About the Author

Peter Rader, who resides in Los Angeles with his wife and two sons, began his writing career as a screenwriter. His first script, *Waterworld*, was released by Universal in 1995, starring Kevin Costner. Rader went on to develop projects with industry leaders such as Steven Spielberg, John Davis, and Dino De Laurentiis.

His first book, *Mike Wallace: A Life*, was published by St. Martin's Press in 2012.